What's Left Unsaid

What's Left Unsaid

My Life at the Center of Power, Politics & Crisis

Melissa DeRosa

UNION
SQUARE
& CO.

NEW YORK

UNION
SQUARE
& CO.

NEW YORK

ISBN 978-1-4549-5233-6
ISBN 978-1-4549-5234-3 (e-book)

For information about custom editions, special sales, and premium
purchases, please contact specialsales@unionsquareandco.com.

Printed in the United States of America

2 4 6 8 10 9 7 5 3 1

unionsquareandco.com

Cover design by Melissa Farris
Interior design by Rich Hazelton

We stand on the shoulders of those who came before us.
In loving memory of my nonna, Corradina "Dina" DeRosa.

Contents

Dramatis Personae

Adler, Norman: Melissa DeRosa's mentor and her father's longtime business partner

Apple, Craig: Albany County sheriff (2011–present)

Azzopardi, Rich: Director of communications and senior adviser to Gov. Cuomo (2012–21)

Bennett, Charlotte: Briefer in the executive chamber (2019–20)

Benton, Stephanie: Director of governor's offices (2011–21)

Biaggi, Alessandra: New York State senator (2019–22)

Bloomberg, Michael: Mayor of New York City (2002–13); CEO of Bloomberg LP (2014–present)

Boylan, Lindsey: Chief of staff to Howard Zemsky, president and CEO of Empire State Development (2015–18); deputy secretary for New York State Economic Development (2018)

Caitlin: Press secretary to Gov. Cuomo (2018–21)

Chartock, Alan: North Country Public Radio host

Ciccone, LouAnn: Secretary to Speaker of the New York State Assembly, Carl Heastie (2020–22)

Cindy: Executive assistant to Melissa DeRosa, based in New York City

Clark, Anne: Plaintiff's attorney appointed by Letitia James to lead investigation into sexual harassment allegations against Gov. Cuomo

Cohen, Steven "Steve": Secretary to Gov. Cuomo (2011–12)

Commisso, Brittany: Executive assistant to Melissa DeRosa and Gov. Cuomo (2020–21)

Confessore, Nicholas "Nick": *New York Times* political and investigative reporter (2004–present)

Cotton, Rick: Executive director of the Port Authority of New York and New Jersey (2017–present)

Cummings, Kelly: Deputy chief of staff turned New York State director of operations (2016–21)

Cuomo, Chris: Andrew Cuomo's younger brother and host of *Cuomo Prime Time* on CNN (2018–21)

Cuomo, Matt: Gov. Cuomo's cousin

Davos, Jessica: Melissa DeRosa's older sister

Davos, Jim: Melissa DeRosa's brother-in-law

de Blasio, Bill: Mayor of New York City (2014–21)

DeRosa, Corradina "Dina": Melissa DeRosa's grandmother, "Nonna"

DeRosa, Gaetano: Melissa DeRosa's grandfather, "Nonno"

DeRosa, Giorgio: Melissa DeRosa's father

DeRosa, Joey: Melissa DeRosa's younger brother

DeRosa, Kathleen: Melissa DeRosa's sister-in-law

DeRosa, Maureen: Giorgio DeRosa's wife

DeRosa, Melody: Melissa DeRosa's mother

DesRosiers, Jill: Chief of staff and longtime aide to Gov. Cuomo (2012–21)

Farrah: Executive assistant to Melissa DeRosa and Gov. Cuomo, based in Albany

Fauci, Anthony: Director of the National Institute of Allergy and Infectious Diseases (1984–2022) and member of the White House Coronavirus Task Force (2020)

Fine, Liz: General counsel for Empire State Development Corporation (2014–22); counsel to Gov. Hochul (2021–present)

Garvey, Elizabeth "Beth": Special counsel and acting counsel to Gov. Cuomo (2019–21)

Glaser, Howard: New York State director of operations (2011–14)

Glavin, Rita: Private counsel representing Gov. Cuomo (2021–present)

Gollust, Allison: Communications director to Gov. Cuomo (2012–13); executive vice president and chief marketing officer at CNN (2013–22)

Heastie, Carl: Speaker of the New York State Assembly (2015–present)

Hinton, Karen: Wife of Howard Glaser; press secretary to Mayor Bill de Blasio (2015–16); press secretary to former HUD secretary Andrew Cuomo (1990s)

Hochul, Kathy: Lt. Gov. of New York State (2015–21), Gov. of New York State (2021–present)

Hogan, Bernadette: New York Post reporter (2019–present)

James, Letitia "Tish": New York State attorney general (2019–present)

Kaitlin: Executive assistant to Gov. Cuomo in New York City office (2017)

Kaplan, Roberta "Robbie": Chairperson of Time's Up (2018–21)

Kennedy-Cuomo, Cara: Gov. Cuomo's daughter

Kennedy-Cuomo, Mariah: Gov. Cuomo's daughter

Kennedy-Cuomo, Michaela: Gov. Cuomo's daughter

Khan, Ibrahim: Chief of staff to Attorney General Letitia James (2019–22)

Kim, Joon: Lawyer appointed by Letitia James to lead investigation into sexual harassment allegations

Kim, Ron: New York State assemblyman from Queens (2013–present)

Kopy, Mike: New York State director of Emergency Management (2019–21)

Kushner, Jared: Donald Trump's son-in-law and senior adviser (2017–21)

Lacewell, Linda: Chief of staff and counselor to Gov. Cuomo (2017–19); superintendent of New York State Department of Financial Services (2019–21)

Lamont, Ned: Governor of Connecticut (2019–present)

Lever, Dani: Communications director to Gov. Cuomo (2018–20)

Limmiatis, Virginia: Woman who took photo with Gov. Cuomo at a public event

Liss, Ana: Executive assistant to New York State director of operations Howard Glaser (2013–15)

Malatras, James "Jim": Longtime adviser and senior aide to Andrew Cuomo (2007–17); New York State College president and SUNY chancellor (2017–22)

McGrath, Alyssa: Brittany Commisso's lifelong best friend and executive assistant to Melissa DeRosa and Gov. Cuomo (2020–21)

McKinley, Jesse: New York Times Albany bureau chief (2017–21)

Mogul, Judy: Special counsel to Gov. Cuomo (2019–21)

Mujica, Robert "Rob": Director of the New York State Budget (2016–22)

Mulrow, William "Bill": Secretary to Gov. Cuomo (2015–17)

Murphy, Phil: Governor of New Jersey (2018–present)

Reisner, Mimi: Senior adviser for communications to Gov. Cuomo (2016–20)

Ricchetti, Steve: Counselor to President Joe Biden (2021–present)

Rosen, Hilary: Board member of Time's Up (2019–21)

Ryan, Caroyln: New York Times managing editor (2020–present)

Schneiderman, Eric: New York State attorney general (2011–18)

Schwartz, Larry: Secretary to Gov. Cuomo (2011–15)

Shea, Dermot: Police commissioner of New York City (2019–21)

Smith, Shontell: Chief of staff to New York State Senate Majority Leader Andrea Stewart-Cousins (2019–22)

Soares, David: Albany County district attorney (2005–present)

Stefanik, Elise: Childhood friend of Melissa DeRosa; US Congress representative (R-NY) (2015–present)

Stewart-Cousins, Andrea: New York State Senate Majority Leader (2019–present)

Straface, Vincent "Vinnie": Head of New York State Police security detail for Gov. Cuomo (c. 2017–21)

Tchen, Tina: CEO of Time's Up (2019–21)

Tracey, Michael: Substack journalist (2019–present)

Tracy: Executive assistant to Gov. Cuomo and Melissa DeRosa, based in Albany

Traister, Rebecca: writer-at-large for *New York* magazine

Walsh, Annabel: Director of scheduling for Gov. Cuomo (2013–20)

Wemple, Erik: *Washington Post* media reporter (2011–present)

Wing, Matt: Melissa DeRosa's husband (2016–22)

Wolfe, Emma: Deputy mayor for administration and chief of staff to New York City mayor Bill de Blasio (2020–21)

Zemsky, Howard: President and CEO of Empire State Development (2015–19)

Zucker, Howard: Commissioner of New York State Department of Health (2015–21)

Zucker, Jeff: President of CNN Worldwide (2013–22)

What Just Happened?

August 12, 2021

"ARE YOU OKAY?" MY SISTER, JESSICA, CAME INTO MY DARK BEDROOM. It was shortly after 6:00 a.m., I noted in the moment, even though time had become insignificant to me, a profound irony given that it used to define my life.

"Uh-huh." I kept my voice to a whisper, desperate to numb my pain.

"Can I get you something?" she asked, rubbing my back. "Water, coffee, an egg sandwich?" She was deeply concerned about me. Rightfully so.

"I love you—I just need a few minutes." I responded without moving. The handful of words alone required more energy than I had to spare, but I didn't want her to worry. Older by two years, Jessica had always been more than my big sister—she was my best friend.

"Okay, Missy Monster," Jessica said, "I'm here, whatever you need . . ." She trailed off, running her fingers through my unwashed hair. She wanted so badly to help me, but she couldn't.

No one could.

I'd been whisked to Jessica's in-laws' house in West Yarmouth on Cape Cod the day before. With photographers stationed at my Brooklyn Heights town house, my father's Albany and lake houses, my mother's house in Hudson, New York, and my younger brother Joey's house upstate, there was nowhere else I could think of to go. In what felt like some bizarre 1990s thriller handoff, Joey had taken custody of me in a dark parking garage at Dad's office near the capitol in Albany, where we'd successfully evaded the paparazzi. The memory was a blur, like watching a movie about a protagonist who was not me. Now an unfamiliar guest room 228 miles away had become my cocoon. I burrowed beneath the white bedspread. The house felt hushed, as if it, too, were holding its breath waiting for this to end.

Just months earlier, everything in my life had possessed purpose and meaning. At age thirty-eight, I was the most senior member of New York governor Andrew Cuomo's team leading the nation through a once-in-a-century pandemic, making life-or-death decisions, projecting our administration's competence to an admiring world. But now I had been transformed into a caricature I didn't recognize—a person I never was and didn't want to be. It had all unfolded too quickly to slow or stop, like falling onto the tracks of an oncoming train. The words *What just happened?* wouldn't stop reverberating through my entire body. None of it made sense.

At the thought of this, I began to sob, for what felt like the zillionth time in the last twenty-four hours.

I was in so much pain.

I just wanted it all to end.

CHAPTER 1

What Defines an Emergency?

"WHAT DO WE THINK ABOUT PUTTING SURROGACY AT THE TOP?" I asked, leaning back in the brown leather chair that had been a fixture in the office for years, ankles crossed on top of my desk. It was January 3, 2020, and two floors below, the streets of Albany were desolate, as was usual at that time of year with everyone home for the Christmas holiday.

Everyone, that is, except us.

My longtime colleague, Jim Malatras—the professor, as we called him—stood across the room at the whiteboard we were using to track policy ideas for the year. Many of us had nicknames, a playful gesture that sometimes eased the seriousness and stress of our work. We were mere days away from the start of the legislative session, and we were still debating which issues our boss, Governor Andrew Cuomo, would want prioritized.

"Sure, Melissa. I'll put it next to 'high-speed rail' and maybe, just maybe it'll get done by the time Max is in college," Jim teased. Max, Jim's seven-year-old son, sat nearby, playing on his iPad. Max had grown up in the halls of the capitol, shadowing Jim's every move when his dad had served as Cuomo's director of state operations. Jim had since moved on to become president of Empire State College, but, devoted to the core, he remained always on call for us in times of crisis, and the task at hand met that criteria.

"Ha ha, you're so funny," I said. "This is our year. It's getting done, with or without you!"

Although legal in forty-six states, surrogacy was against the law in New York—a policy hangover from the 1980s, when feminists led the charge to ban the practice for fear it would lead to the exploitation of the wombs of impoverished women by the rich and powerful who wanted children, but not enough to go through the physical act of pregnancy. Norms change, and while those earlier efforts were well intentioned at the time, feminists of today viewed the practice more through a lens of compassion than commerce, as a way for infertile women and gay couples to fulfill their dreams of parenthood. Overturning the ban was staunchly opposed by the majority of women in the Democratic-led assembly—many of whom were over sixty and still firmly rooted in their Gloria Steinem–led beliefs from decades earlier. The speaker of the assembly would defer to them, and, for the last few years, attempting to get the measure through became something of a fool's errand. But that wouldn't stop us. Much like marriage equality or the $15 minimum wage, advocates—in this case, infertile women and same-sex couples hoping to create families—came to us to get it done, because our team made the impossible possible. And this year, we wouldn't let them down.

"You've got it, MDR. Then it goes on the whiteboard," Jim responded, scribbling the words "surrogacy/bullet train—MDR" at the top of the already incoherent whiteboard in front of us. To the extent that I had an office nickname, MDR was mine.

Tracy, the longest-serving of my assistants, popped her head into the doorway. "Melissa, you told me to tell you when it is three o'clock," she said, her tone almost apologetic, even though she was simply following my instructions. "It's three o'clock."

I glanced down at my iPhone and confirmed it for myself: it was, in fact, three o'clock. And I needed to get on the road. I had actually needed to get on the road an hour earlier, although that was never realistic, not given the fact that the governor's annual State of the State address was days away and we were still nowhere. I could feel my pulse begin to race while the excuses for my inevitable tardiness churned.

Matt, my husband of three years, would be annoyed and passive-aggressive; I would be defensive, never acknowledging an inch of possible wrongdoing.

That was the way.

Our way.

No matter how well-intentioned, my husband had an expectation that I would disappoint, and I lived up to it. Every. Single. Time.

"Petro is on the ramp," Tracy said, referring to my driver that afternoon, John Petrosino. Petro, as everyone referred to him, was essentially a Hells Angel frozen in time. He wore a black leather vest with acid-washed jeans. He couldn't do enough to be helpful. He filled up your gas tank without asking. He put your water of choice (Saratoga Sparkling, for me) in the cupholder. He kept your favorite snack (milk-chocolate Cadbury eggs) in the glove compartment, just in case.

Jim looked at me in disbelief. "Hey, DeRosa," he said, "what are you, keeping bankers' hours? The speech is in a few days. Does the boss know you're sneaking out?"

"Matt is going to California in the morning," I said, my right arm finding its way through the tear in the silk lining of my long, fitted black peacoat. "I'll be back first thing tomorrow, and, yes, *he* knows and is okay with it."

I kicked off my stilettos and slid into the ballet flats tucked under my desk for the ride home, grabbing the worn, overstuffed canvas duffel bag beside me. "Seriously, I'll be back in the morning—and I'll be on my phone every five seconds. Please, please help carry this ball over the finish line?" I batted my blue eyes playfully at Jim, knowing he was the only person who could possibly help the governor get the speech—and more important, the 500-page policy book full of proposals—done in time.

"You're lucky I love you, MDR," he said. His smile let me off the hook.

"I am," I replied as I scurried out, glancing up at Tracy, Farrah, and Katie, the three executive assistants the governor and I both relied upon to get through the day. "Please put any calls through to my cell, and have a good night—thanks, guys!" I said as the door closed behind me.

I waved goodbye to the trooper standing guard in the hall and hurried down the stairs. I flicked my pass at the electronic door opener and walked into an arctic blast, the frigid air practically knocking me sideways. Snow flurries were flying, but the door of a black GMC Jimmy was open, waiting for me. Of course it was; Petro was happy to freeze for my convenience.

I climbed in and slammed the door shut. I looked at the clock: 3:38. Fuck.

It wasn't enough that our senior staff was still struggling to put the year's policy proposals to bed. Or that my girlfriends were pissed that I had missed our annual post-Christmas Cornell get-together to see everyone's children and husbands. No: I would soon be confronted by Matt with the fact that I was a failure. A failure as a wife. A failure as a partner. A failure as a friend. And, as much as I wanted to, as much as I struggled to, I couldn't make him happy. Or myself, for that matter.

I had, in short order, become a crushing New York cliché: that woman who to the outside world seemingly accomplishes everything—marriage, career, family, friends—while privately feeling like I was succeeding at absolutely nothing.

Brrrrrring. Like a Swiss watch. Matt instinctively knew I was going to be late. And he was going to make sure I knew he knew.

"Hello?" I answered, dreading the conversation that was coming.

"Oh, hello. Is this the one and only Ms. Melissa DeRosa?" Matt asked coyly.

"Who's calling?" I played along, hoping I could flirt my way out of the inevitable.

"I think she may be expecting me. It's her husband. Matthew Lawrence Wing. The guy who is leaving in the morning. I'm pretty sure she's running late for dinner—can you check with her?"

"Hey, I'll have you know," I protested, breaking character, "I'm already on the road!"

"Oh, *really?* What time did you leave?" Matt taunted.

"Forty-five minutes ago. And I'll be on time, and ready for adult conversation, appropriately dressed, and not at all preoccupied with work."

"So," Matt shot back, "you left five minutes ago. You'll be thirty minutes late for dinner, and you'd like me to call you an Uber to get to dinner? Got it. See you soon."

Click.

While his tone was sarcastic, everything Matt said struck at the core of where we were and how we got there. A communications exec for Uber, he was relocating to company headquarters in San Francisco and would live in a corporate apartment. *For three months.* On advice of our couple's therapist. Our third couple's therapist. This one had lasted longer than the others, but that may have been because we both gave up fighting. Fighting each other and for one another. It was easier to go along to get along. And this time, three and a half short years into our marriage, the recommendation was separation. And cutting off communication. Tonight was a final goodbye before we went dark for ninety days to decide whether we missed each other or could live without one another.

Of course I would be late. Brooklyn is a two-and-a-half-hour commute from Albany, assuming traffic and the weather both cooperated. But none of that mattered, anyway, because as far as Matt was concerned, the only reason I was ever late was because I was putting work first. That condemnation upset me more than any other; after all, we had met while working together in the governor's office, when I was communications director and Matt was press secretary. He knew the landscape of my professional life better than anyone else. It was part of the intimate connection we shared, fluency in the same second language.

I didn't wait for Petro to bring the car to a complete stop before thanking him for the ride and opening the door to jump out. I sprinted up the narrow stairs of our town house and went straight to my closet, rifling to find a pair of patent-leather Mary Janes and the black, strappy La Ligne dress Matt had bought me for Christmas.

The Uber driver Matt sent was set to give me a less-than-five-star rating after my stress manifested into me being short with him for no good reason as he drove down the steep hill to the River Café. It was incredible that the two of us had fallen in love with this particular restaurant. It required a jacket and played jazz and was far too stuffy for Matt's pretentious-less preference. And it was in Brooklyn proper, not Soho or the West Village, where I preferred to dine. Not unlike our unlikely marriage, our favorite spot perfectly suited us in ways neither of us preferred to acknowledge.

The reservation was for 6:15. I arrived at 6:43.

"I ordered the caviar, and you're getting the branzino," Matt greeted me. "You were late, and I was worried we'd lose the table, so, like it or not, that's your menu for the evening, and we'll all just have to learn to deal with it." He glanced up at me with a half smirk, knowing how happy I'd be with the order.

"I'm sorry, I . . ."

"Yes, I know. And how is the State of the State going?"

"It's nowhere. We're nowhere. But . . . ," I trailed off. "That's not what we should be focused on tonight. How is this going to work? I know things haven't been easy, but you're . . . you're my best friend." I knew this day was coming but couldn't, until this moment, acknowledge what it would mean.

"Melissa, we're stuck," he responded, closing his menu. "We've been stuck for a long time. Either we move forward or we move back. This isn't fair to either of us. I love you, but I'm not sure that's enough anymore. And we're too young to compromise our lives." He sounded resigned to this fate; I would have preferred to ignore it altogether. But defeat trumped denial.

"What if I need you?" I wondered aloud. While our relationship was strained, he was my other half, and I knew how much I would miss

him. He was the one I trusted and turned to for advice and compan-
ionship. My *person.*

"We have rules," Matt gently reminded me. "We discussed it in
therapy. We cannot do the thing where we call or text or ask how each
other's families are doing. That's part of this. That's the whole point."

"So we just don't speak for ninety days?"

"No," he said. "Unless . . ."

"Unless what?" I asked, hopeful, though I knew better.

"Unless it's an emergency. An honest-to-God emergency," he said,
wiping a tear off my cheek. Everything else was to be dealt with via
email, devoid of emotion.

"Okay," I said, swallowing back hard. "But what defines an
emergency?"

"You know, I don't know," he paused. "But we'll know it if it
happens."

CHAPTER 2

It's the Flu

As I stared up at the ceiling, my body stretched atop a gurney at the NYU Langone Fertility Center in Manhattan, all I could think about was why I'd waited so long to do this. How could I have let it get to this point without a plan? I'd never been a procrastinator.

A precocious child who asked questions incessantly, I was hungry to understand things big and small about how the world worked. *Who plows after a snowstorm? Who says you can't drive more than 65 mph? Who decides how many days we have to go to school?* Who were all these wizards behind all these curtains? All answers led to government in some form or fashion. And the more questions I asked, the more I learned about the impact that politics and government had on our own family. Making the complex machinery of daily life run reliably didn't rely on magic after all; it took people who were capable and trustworthy. And politics, from my earliest perspective, was never remote or lofty. In fact, I couldn't imagine any job that was more deeply personal. It was part of my DNA.

The daughter of a successful restaurateur, my mother, Melody, was raised in West Irondequoit, an affluent suburb of Rochester, New York, where she was captain of the cheerleading squad at the high-performing public school she attended. The son of Italian immigrants, my father was raised in a working-class neighborhood consisting primarily of Blacks, Puerto Ricans, and Italians in the city of Rochester, where he was captain of the varsity soccer team at the all-boys Catholic school he attended. They met at a YMCA tennis camp at age sixteen, quickly fell in love, and married after high school graduation (a marriage that would last twenty-eight years). It was an act of defiance that severed my mother's relationship with her own parents, who disapproved of their new son-in-law's blue-collar background.

Intent on making it work, Mom and Dad attended college at night while juggling odd jobs, from waiting tables to construction and retail by day, to afford the rent on their one-bedroom apartment. Then, when they were twenty, my sister came along, followed by me two years later and my brother eleven months after that. Kids themselves, my parents suddenly had three children under four at home, increasing the pressure to make ends meet.

Eventually, Dad got a job at the General Motors assembly plant where his father worked. That was a big deal. GM plants were unionized, and unions were a source of strength and fairness for the employees. There was nothing academic or intellectual about it. It was real, and it was practical. Unions provided health care, worker protections, retirement benefits, and negotiating strength. Unions meant a better life for our family. And the union movement was synonymous with the Democratic Party. As a child, I saw them as one and the same. My father became active in the powerful United Auto Workers union and was selected to participate in a summer course at the Cornell University School of Industrial and Labor Relations—an Ivy League accomplishment unfathomable to a young working-class, inner-city man. Afterward, in 1986, the UAW selected my father to be dispatched to a local campaign as the union's representative.

The campaign was for New York's thirtieth congressional district in Rochester, and the candidate was Louise Slaughter. A tough-talking, no-nonsense Kentucky native with a southern drawl, Louise was running against an entrenched incumbent in an overwhelmingly Republican district. Her opponent believed in a smaller government; she fought for social services. He was a staunch conservative; she was a working-class centrist. A Democrat hadn't won the seat since 1963, and she wasn't supposed to—a fact my father told me over and over to manage my four-year-old expectations as we went door-to-door together to rally the vote.

But against all odds, Slaughter did win, by just one point. And in that moment, feeling the special high reserved for winning campaigns and innocent preschoolers, I thought, "I can do that, too."

Afterward, Slaughter asked my father to join her staff as her district director, opening a new chapter in our family's life and giving me a front-row seat to government. I all but considered us partners by then, father and daughter bound by the fascination we shared with the heady world of public service Dad now inhabited.

As I got older, the more information I consumed, the more I recognized that government was a unique vehicle for massive change. Government could pass laws to give people civil rights, build literal bridges, and deploy the military to defend our democracy. And, I marveled at the thought of one day playing a role in it. Admittedly, shouldering that lifelong ambition did not foster a normal childhood. My father was a scrappy, driven, working-class guy with something to prove; I inherited my drive from him. My mother was beautiful, poised, and self-assured; I derived my confidence from her.

Throughout grade school, I marched in parades and knocked on doors for Dad's preferred candidates, wearing T-shirts bearing campaign logos and handing out literature. By fourteen, I was reading multiple newspapers each day. I never missed a Sunday episode of *Meet the Press* and spearheaded policy negotiations on "the Hill" in my head.

At sixteen, I called in my first political favor and asked my dad to help me get an internship with a colleague of his: the political director of the New York State AFL-CIO, the largest federation of unions in the country. I thought it would provide both invaluable practical experience and an important credential as I applied to college. Like my father before me, I had my sights set on Cornell University's School of Industrial and Labor Relations. But Dad wasn't as gung ho about my request as I'd assumed he would be.

"Melissa," he said, sitting down across from me with a solemn expression on his face—the kind I generally only encountered when in trouble—"if I help you with this opportunity, there will be people in this town who will never forget it. They'll always wonder if you deserve what you have." He exhaled deeply, put his hand on my shoulder, and leaned in close. "You're my daughter, so I will prop this door open, but you have to walk through it yourself. After that, you're on your own, which is in your best interest . . . actually, it's your *only* interest. And Melissa," Dad continued, "don't kid yourself. You're a young woman who wants to make it in a male-dominated business. It's not fair, but the reality is you'll be judged differently. You're going to need to lace up your sneakers, run faster, and jump higher," he paused. "And never, ever let them see you sweat."

Challenge extended and accepted. I was ready to dig in.

It was 1999, and the AFL-CIO was preparing to endorse then First Lady Hillary Clinton for Daniel Patrick Moynihan's recently vacant US Senate seat. Her opponent was New York City Mayor Rudolph Giuliani, but health and marital problems prompted him to withdraw, putting Rick Lazio on the Republican ballot instead. It was more than a marquee contest; it was history in the making.

The opportunity was a twofer: I was able to gain important experience while working to support a campaign for someone I looked up to.

Hillary Clinton was my role model. Educated at Wellesley and Yale, she radiated strength, intellect, and effectiveness. Not only did she not shy away from a fight, she picked plenty of them on behalf of causes she believed in. She championed women and the working class. And she was as tough as they come, stronger than any male politician I'd ever seen. No matter how many times the Far Right or the media attempted to tear her down, she always seemed to come back stronger and more resolved than ever.

The union was all in for Clinton, headquarters abuzz with everyone working around the clock, gaming out what the campaign was going to look like, and what tactics they would deploy to ensure her success. My role was administrative: stuff envelopes, get coffee, and answer phones. I showed up early, stayed late, and tried to learn by osmosis, sitting in on meetings when invited and eavesdropping on high-level conversations that were in earshot. Always eager, never complaining, I felt lucky to be *near* the room where it happened. But as I was doing the envelope-stuffing and answering the phones, I liked to picture myself sitting in the war room someday, driving those conversations and mapping out strategy in a meaningful way, making a difference.

In what would end up as the most-expensive and highest-profile Senate race in the country's history, Clinton won, becoming the only former first lady to ever serve in the United States Senate and the first woman elected to the Senate from New York. Meanwhile, I had won my first campaign, too, and was officially a member of Cornell's class of 2004.

After graduation, though, diploma in hand, I did the unthinkable: I took a job as a fashion publicist for a clothing company—an unexpected offer that presented itself over beer pong during senior week. A friend's older sister had been working at a designer fashion company, Theory, as director of public relations and was looking for a press assistant. We hit it off, and, in a moment of extreme impulse, I accepted. At the time, my parents had an apartment on the Upper East Side of Manhattan that my sister, Jessica, was living in—a situation that allowed me to move to one of the most expensive cities in the world on a salary of $27,000 a year. A multi-billion-dollar cutthroat industry, fashion was demanding, hard charging, and glamorous. I received my first BlackBerry, along with instructions that I was to respond to emails within fifteen minutes of receiving them; was taught how to pitch editors at *Vogue*; and brushed shoulders with Leonardo DiCaprio. I became fluent in the language spoken only by those devoted to the *New York Post*'s Page Six. And I loved every minute of it. My parents played along with it—for a time. But after a year, they were done, a message that was delivered over dinner with my father.

"Melissa, are we finished with this little experiment yet?" he asked, his patience clearly worn. "Your mother and I always said we wanted to give you enough to do *something*, but not enough to do *nothing*. And this feels like nothing."

If I wanted to keep doing what I was doing, I would be on my own financially. In the end, it wasn't a fight. While my stint in fashion had been fun and like nothing I'd ever been exposed to, I knew it was just that—a stint. It was time to return to my original love. And so I did, diving headfirst back into the political waters, hopscotching from campaign to campaign to the halls of Congress before returning to Cornell for graduate school.

A long, dues-paying decade later, I was working as acting chief of staff for New York State Attorney General Eric Schneiderman when I got a phone call from an old Cornell classmate. Josh Vlasto was working as chief of staff to Governor Cuomo. He swore me to secrecy before telling me that their communications director would be departing soon.

That was puzzling, I thought. I knew Allison Gollust had only been on the job a few months. Cuomo had put himself on the national radar with some big moves, and he was being talked about as a possible candidate for president. Why leave now?

"Her old boss just landed a big gig running a network and offered her the chance to go with him," Josh explained. The old boss was Jeff Zucker, and the network was CNN. "Anyway, we've been talking about it over here, and we think you'd be perfect for the job."

I was truly conflicted. Once a sleepy position, the office of the New York Attorney General had gained national prominence in recent years as a result of two larger-than-life figures: Eliot Spitzer and Andrew Cuomo. At age thirty, I had been promoted to acting chief of staff just two weeks earlier—a position given to me by my close friend and boss, Neal Kwatra, one of New York's most highly regarded strategists, who had taken me under his wing and trained me after bringing me into the office two years earlier. Complicating matters, Schneiderman viewed Cuomo as a political adversary he believed was constantly working to undercut him, making my possible abandonment a much more personal betrayal.

I told Josh I'd consider the offer. But there was no way I could say no. While we had been doing great things in the AG's office—taking on mortgage-backed securities fraud, holding the opioid industry accountable, and toppling Trump "University"—it was nothing compared to what Andrew Cuomo was doing.

People use the word *Machiavellian* to describe Cuomo, but what they really mean is effective. A car mechanic who fundamentally likes to fix things, Cuomo is a micromanager who obsessively and single-mindedly focuses on the problem in front of him until it's resolved. He played hard with the legislature, pushed the bureaucracy, and needled the press. But the people it benefited didn't care about his tactics. He was the one who delivered same-sex marriage for the LGBTQ+ community, got the nation's strongest gun-violence-prevention laws passed, and raised the minimum wage to $15 an hour. Yes, he threatened state contractors with debarment, but the result was the Second Avenue Subway finally opening after a century of pols talking about it. And travelers passing through LaGuardia and JFK or driving over the Mario Cuomo Bridge didn't care whose arms he'd twisted to rebuild them. Cuomo and his team were making government work for people like my grandparents, who had relied on it for a shot to get ahead. And I watched jealously from the sidelines, wanting to be a part of it. A few weeks later, I would replace Allison Gollust as communications director for the governor, putting me on the path to, in April 2017, finally shattering the glass ceiling I'd been reaching for since I was a child.

The Cuomo administration had a reputation for being aggressive and demanding. Cuomo worked around the clock, and the team he surrounded himself with matched his drive and commitment. He responded to eye contact, confidence, proven preparedness and effectiveness, and lack thereof. It was the type of environment I thrived in. The stakes and the pressure were high, but so was the payoff. I loved the pace and the adrenaline that came along with going to battle for something I believed in and getting it done. I'd been working my way up the ladder for four years in the administration when Cuomo's right-hand man dropped by my desk at the governor's Manhattan satellite offices at 633 Third Avenue. "Melissa, do you have a minute?" Bill Mulrow wanted to know.

An Irish guy from the Bronx and self-made son of blue-collar union workers, Bill had been lured away from his job as senior managing partner at Blackstone, one of the world's most successful private equity firms, to serve as secretary to the governor, the state's highest-appointed position. He was the whole package: educated at Yale and Harvard, successful, savvy, generous, and kind. In a business where no one really likes anyone, people loved Bill. I was first introduced to him fresh out of college by my dad's business partner and my mentor, Norman Adler. At the time, I was preparing to apply for graduate school, and Norman believed Bill would be a good sounding board for advice. We had been friends ever since.

Now I set my BlackBerry down to give Bill my undivided attention.

"As you know, when I agreed to take the job as secretary, I told the gov I would do it for two years—transition into the second term, make sure the ship was strong and steady, and then go back to my family and real life," Bill began, shutting my office door behind him. "It's now been two years and four months."

"Okay, have you spoken to the boss about this?" I asked, anticipating the answer I got.

"Not yet. I wanted to talk to you first," he responded.

"Well, you know you'll always have my support. Do you want me to think through a press strategy on how to deal with the exit?" I asked, wondering how I fit into the equation.

"No, Melissa. I want to talk to you about my replacement," he continued.

"Eesh, that's going to be tough, Bill," I answered. "It's an impossible position to fill. It has to be someone who understands how to manage the government, who has the right personality, is willing to work the long hours, knows the players, understands the politics,"

I continued. "They have to be willing to do the Albany thing, and gain the team's trust."

"Exactly. There's one person for this job, and only one person," he answered. "You."

Politics and government aren't something that can be taught—you learn by experience, and, like Andrew Cuomo (although on a much lesser scale), I had been given a first-rate education by osmosis since I was a child. Having been brought up in and around power my entire life, I was neither impressed by it nor cowed by it. I saw the entire field and never shied away from speaking up. I was unflappable and unflinching, my political instincts and negotiating skills well honed. I knew how to use the press and the political levers to move the pieces on the chessboard. And blessed with incredible recall, I had the ability to recite arcane facts and statutory language like other people rattle off a grocery list. The *Daily News* referred to me as "hard charging" in a piece they wrote . . . about my wedding. The *New York Times* called me "steely" and "steady" with an "adamantine core." By the time Bill appeared in my doorway that day, I had interned for Hillary Clinton at nineteen, worked as a press secretary in Congress at twenty-five, as state director for President Obama's political operation at twenty-six, and as deputy chief of staff to the attorney general at twenty-eight—and, in four years in the Cuomo administration, I had risen from communications director to chief of staff.

It was the moment I had been working for and yearning for, yet as the words fell out of Bill's mouth, I hesitated. Every time that I had moved up the ladder professionally, there was an outsized focus on my lobbyist father, straining our relationship and creating an optics problem for the governor in the press. I wasn't sure I wanted to go through that again, or on this scale. I waffled for several weeks, with the governor and Bill lobbying and coaching me, before I finally accepted the role. On April 17, 2017, I was formally named secretary to the governor, New York's equivalent to White House chief of staff. I was one of the youngest ever to hold the position, and the first female. While the title itself may have sounded insignificant—"secretary" couldn't help but conjure images of steno pads and typing pools—it carried along with it the weight of the world. Or more specifically, all of New York, with its 19.5 million citizens and nearly 55,000 square miles of industry, agriculture, transportation, education, and everything else that constituted daily life.

The day after the announcement was made, the adrenaline and pride I felt—the culmination of everything I had worked so hard for— came crashing down when I picked up the hardcopy of the *New York Times* and read "Cuomo's Chief of Staff, Daughter of a Powerful Lobbyist, Is Promoted to Secretary." In a single headline, the *Times* took fifteen years of my professional life away from me, defining me not in the context of my accomplishments or my experience or my capacity, but through what they viewed as my most defining attribute: my father. Reading the headline filled me with a wave of emotion, blood rushing to my face, tears welling up in my eyes, my hands beginning to shake. Then I got angry. I crumpled up the paper and threw it in the recycling bin where it belonged, and picked up the phone to call the then metro editor, Wendell Jamison. To his credit, Wendell—who had been on vacation the day before and had not been a part of the decision to print the headline—acknowledged it was wrong and apologized. When I hung up the phone, I closed my office door, leaned back in my chair, and looked up at the ceiling thinking, *Is this how people see me? How many things do I need to achieve and how many years do I have to work and how many titles do I have to hold before I will be judged by my own accomplishments?* I didn't know the answer, but in that moment I told myself I would work as hard as necessary to find out.

Within days, I was contemplating freezing my eggs.

Acknowledging to myself that childbearing would pose a tremendous challenge on top of my all-consuming job, I made an appointment to meet with one of the city's most-qualified fertility specialists.

I wanted a backup plan, a safety net. I knew, or maybe hoped, that there would come a time when I could devote myself more completely to being a mom. And I wanted to reserve a table well in advance.

"So, how old did you say you are?" Dr. H asked. I couldn't help but notice that she was strikingly attractive and, if I had to guess, no more than a few years older than me. She probably had a whole brood of perfect kids at home.

"I'm thirty-four," I imagined the number emblazoned on my chest like a scarlet letter.

"I'm going to be direct with you, Melissa," the doctor said. "Your age isn't going to make this any easier." I winced. We hadn't even gotten started, and already I was an impediment to myself.

"I know. I probably should have done this sooner, but everything I've read says that thirty-four is still young enough to pursue egg freezing." *How had proactive planning flipped so suddenly into plea-bargaining?*

"True, for most women, but . . ."

But? Did I not fall under the umbrella of *most women*? I braced myself for Dr. H to finish her sentence.

"This may seem scary. Just know that we can still try and see how it goes."

Try?

"I don't understand. Is there an issue?" I didn't even know if I wanted kids, but suddenly the thought of not having the option was too much to bear.

"There's no simple way to say this, but your AMH [Anti-Müllerian hormone] level is very off," she said with a grimace. "Normal for a woman your age should be between 1.5 and 4.0. Low-normal is 1.0 to 1.5. And Low is 0.5 to 1.0."

My brain was trying to wrap itself around this bizarre new language.

"Okay, so you're saying I'm below normal?" Of course, I knew that infertility impacted millions of women, but I was literally dumbfounded to hear I was now one of them. The possibility had just never entered my mind.

"You're below Low. Your number is 0.2, which means you essentially have the AMH level of a fifty-five-year-old postmenopausal woman. You're not a great candidate for egg freezing."

I felt my chest tighten as questions raced through my mind. *How is this possible? I don't smoke. I don't drink excessively. I run every morning, and I've never skipped my annual gynecologist appointment. My mother used to joke that she and Dad just had to look at each other and she would get pregnant. How did this happen to me?*

Suddenly, lying there in my white paper gown, with my legs secured in stirrups, I was the definition of inadequate. Without warning, a deep sadness overwhelmed me, and I strained to fight back tears as images of my nieces flashed in my head—my gorgeous, blond, blue-eyed, sassy, sweet nieces—like children I might never be able to have.

At that moment, my phone rang.

"I'm sorry, Doctor, would you mind grabbing my purse for me?" I pointed to the chair where I'd placed it earlier, when I'd thought that becoming a mother was more than a pipe dream. "I just need to see who it is." I knew it wasn't the right time to be taking a call, but I couldn't help myself. I needed the interruption.

"It can't wait?" the doctor asked, confirming my suspicion about the protocol here.

"Usually no, it can't," I insisted, implicitly acknowledging the very reason why I was freezing my eggs.

Reluctantly, the doctor handed me my bag, and I fumbled through the oversized leather tote to fish out both my iPhone and BlackBerry. It was Dani Lever, Governor Cuomo's director of communications, which indicated that there was likely a problem with the press.

"Is everything okay?" I answered breathlessly, even though I was completely immobile.

"Meliss? I'm so sorry to bother you, but it's the *New York Times*." Dani spoke to the *Times* multiple times a day. If she was calling me about it, it couldn't be good.

"I'll be at the office in fifteen minutes," I replied without further discussion and then looked up at Dr. H sheepishly. "I'm so sorry, but I really have to get going." Given that my personal life had just been upended, I needed to tackle something I could actually fix, and that meant hightailing it across town and back to my professional life as quickly as possible.

"Melissa, I know what I just said is jarring," the doctor appealed to me as I pulled on my blouse. She was probably used to patients who wanted more of her time, not less. "The research is fuzzy on why certain women have low AMH levels at your age."

"I understand." Desperately wanting the conversation to end, I began scrolling through the dozens of emails I'd missed in the twenty minutes I'd neglected my BlackBerry.

"One train of thought does indicate that a possible predictor of egg viability is stress," she added, stressing the word *stress*.

"I see." I swallowed a lump in my throat. Her suggestion felt like blame. And that blame triggered guilt.

"It has a tremendous impact on how our bodies function and . . ."

"I understand." I cut her off. I didn't want to hear anymore. It was too much to take.

And the message was already loud and clear.

My purported sterility was my fault. It wasn't enough that I was working eighteen hours a day, managing the government for the state of New York. I was supposed to be doing that without any pressure at all in order for my thirty-four-year-old body to be able to create eggs, so I could fulfill my expectation of motherhood, someday, maybe.

"Should I have the office be in touch to schedule a follow-up? If you want to do this, you really shouldn't wait any longer," she went on.

"You know what, I'll reach out later this week. Thanks so much for your time!" I forced a smile as I ran out the door, desperate to return to a locus of control.

I never made the appointment. And, just like that, three years went by.

So here I was on a gurney again. It was 7:00 a.m., and I had the coveted first appointment of the day for egg retrieval, a slot I'd secured the morning prior by casually mentioning to the doctor on duty that I was working on NY's COVID response and needed the anesthesia to wear off in time for me to be lucid enough to work. This being my sixth round of egg freezing, I knew how to game the system, including how to sneak my iPhone and BlackBerry into the operating room and surreptitiously tuck them underneath my thigh where the nurses wouldn't see them (or at least could plausibly ignore them in good conscience). I didn't believe there was any other way to do my job.

They say that most people are in pain and loopy for at least twelve hours after surgery. But for whatever reason, the anesthesia had almost no effect on me. If not for NYU's strict policy that patients weren't allowed to leave without the accompaniment of a responsible adult, I would have sailed out the door, hopped into a car, and driven myself over the Brooklyn Bridge home.

The five times I'd had the procedure before, my husband had been sitting dutifully in the waiting room to pick me up, using his forearm as support to guide me through the bright white hallways, down the elevator, and then into the Uber he would have had ready to take us home. Only, on this day, with our marriage on life support, Matt was three thousand miles away, a decision we agreed to keep secret from even those closest to us. So I was on my own—and making up ever-evolving excuses to explain Matt's absence—which came with its own set of complicated emotions. Rather than confront those, I would throw myself deeper into work.

"Would you like any juice or crackers?" the nurse in the recovery room asked.

"No, really, I'm fine. Is my friend here to take me home? I really need to get moving."

"The doctor insists you need a few more minutes of observation before we can let you go, but yes, your friend checked in and is down the hall."

I slid my iPhone out from under the blanket to do a quick check. It was already 8:03 a.m. Our health commissioner was conducting a senior staff call at 9:00 a.m., and I had to be in front of a computer for that. If I left immediately, with morning traffic factored in, I'd make it home by the skin of my teeth.

"I appreciate your concern," I said to the nurse, who was attempting to politely hold me hostage. "But I really have to get going." I stood up and took two woozy steps toward the dressing area before gaining my balance and making a beeline for the door.

Within minutes, I was in the back seat of my oldest friend Rachel's SUV, sitting next to her nine-month-old son, Jack, with her husband, Marc, at the wheel.

"How'd it go?" Marc asked innocently.

"Marc, she just got out. Can you give her a minute?" Rachel craned her head around her seat to look at me and whispered, "Did it go okay, Missy?" To the rest of the world I was Melissa, but to my oldest friends, I would always be Missy.

"Yes, all fine. It wasn't exactly a banner morning in the egg-retrieval business for me, but what else is new? I'll take what I can get." I shrugged, as if it wasn't a critical part of my life we were talking about.

Egg freezing is notoriously expensive, ranging upward of $30,000 per round, but thanks to the generous health-insurance plan provided by Matt's employer, up to five were covered. And thank God for that, because while most women are able to produce between ten and twenty eggs per retrieval, I averaged four. Just nature's way of telling me: you're fundamentally and irreversibly broken. And that was indescribably soul crushing. So much so that every time the doctor delivered the news of how few eggs were harvested, despite trying to convince myself that I had made peace with the situation, I still burst into tears.

"Not to change the subject, but can we talk about COVID?" Marc asked, meeting my eyes in the rearview mirror.

"Marc, Missy is not your personal news aggregator," Rachel interjected. "Let's leave her alone."

"No, no, it's fine. I'm happy to change the subject." It was the truth. Rachel rolled her eyes.

"So, what's the story?" Marc pressed. "Do we think COVID is in New York already?"

"Not yet," I replied, uncertainly. "But we are not sure. The CDC is controlling all the testing, and they claim they have the airports very closely monitored. We don't have any proof that what they're saying is unreliable," I added, checking my watch.

As we pulled up to my town house, I thanked Rachel and Marc for the ride, kissed baby Jack on the forehead, and hurried up the stairs, where I threw back three ibuprofen with a red Gatorade and cracked open my laptop. It was 8:58 a.m. on the nose—just in time.

There were three dozen people on the call, all in search of answers from Dr. Howard Zucker, the sixteenth commissioner of the New York State Department of Health. Former assistant director general of the World Health Organization and deputy assistant secretary at the Department of Health and Human Services, Zucker was the consummate professional. We had been engaged in a series of conversations throughout the month as we monitored the developing situation around COVID.

"Let's get started," I said, attempting to take immediate command of the situation. It felt good, considering the morning I'd had. "Dr. Zucker, what's the latest information on COVID?" With a handful of confirmed cases in California and Washington State, it felt like it was only a matter of time before it would reach New York.

On January 21, roughly a month earlier, the United States confirmed its first case of COVID-19: a Washington State resident in his thirties who had just returned from China. Days later, on January 26, Anthony Fauci, director of the National Institute of Allergies and Infectious Diseases, appeared on WABC, a New York radio station, when host John Catsimatidis had asked, "What can you tell the American people about what's been going on? Should they be scared?"

"I don't think so," Dr. Fauci said. "The American people should not be worried or frightened by this. It's a very, very low risk to the United States, but it's something we, as public-health officials, need to take very seriously."

At that point, COVID, a "mysterious" respiratory virus that had originated in Wuhan, China, had killed six people and caused hundreds more to become sick in Asia. In the time since, the virus had migrated to Europe before making its way to Iran. While the World Health Organization had declared a global state of emergency, it didn't *feel* like an emergency—at least not in the United States. The Trump administration suspended travel to and from China, but otherwise the virus didn't impact daily life.

No one understood what the virus was or how it was spreading— and the American press wasn't focused on it, their coverage dominated by the ongoing Democratic presidential nomination fight. Plus, after years of false alarms sounded on everything from Ebola to the avian and swine flus—global pandemics whose effects were not felt in the United States—the country had developed a studied indifference to WHO's dire warnings. We had tried to get information from federal agencies and the WHO itself, but either they didn't know what was happening, or they weren't saying.

Dr. Zucker explained that, traditionally, in a public-health emergency, the state's job was to guide local health departments and help facilitate information and resources from the federal government, but not to *direct* them per se. With COVID, the federal government had made it clear they were taking the lead, controlling testing, data, access to information, and resources.

"Dr. Zucker, you've met the governor, right?" I asked rhetorically. "Do you really think I can go to him with 'there's a possible pandemic on the horizon, but the state's job is to defer to the locals and the feds, and oh by the way, that means Trump and de Blasio are in charge' and still have a job by the end of the day?"

"I hear your point, Melissa, but the CDC won't allow states to test—resources are very limited." At first, the CDC's protocols dictated that access to testing would be reserved only for those people with symptoms who had traveled to China; later, they would amend their rules to include other international hot spots. The process was a bureaucratic maze. Those being tested were labeled PUIs, "people under investigation." Samples would be taken in each of the fifty states and mailed to the CDC's primary lab in Atlanta. Days would go by before they were processed. The feds would then send daily emails to health departments around the country with an update on the PUIs in their state. Every day, the email I received was the same: New York has no confirmed cases of COVID-19 at this time.

"Are there labs in New York that we believe *can* do the testing?" Beth Garvey, the governor's counsel, chimed in. Savvy, politically astute, and intellectually brilliant, Beth knew the law inside out and, after nearly two decades in government, had seen almost everything. She knew Cuomo wouldn't take "no testing" for an answer.

"Yes—Wadsworth—and we're pursuing that, but it requires the feds to sign off, and they haven't given us permission yet." The Wadsworth Center, located a stone's throw from the capitol in Albany, is New York State's primary research laboratory and one of the most sophisticated in the country.

"Dr. Zucker, who's *they*?" Beth pressed, anticipating the governor's next line of questioning.

"The federal government, the CDC, the coronavirus task force."

"Who is the most senior person Andrew Cuomo can appeal to?" I asked.

"That would be Vice President Pence. He's the head of Trump's COVID task force."

"Okay—Steph, did you hear that?" I checked. Stephanie Benton, director of the governor's offices, had worked for Cuomo since his first year as attorney general and was the only one of us who had both the institutional knowledge and the instincts to keep up with him. Our relationship had been a little frosty when I'd first started working in the administration—in a climate of alpha males, she was the only person on the floor who truly intimidated me—but over time we'd become inseparable.

"Yep, I'm on it," Steph responded.

"Okay, now we need to start communicating to the public. Dani, what are your thoughts?" I asked, turning it over to our communications director.

"Well, we need the public to understand what this is, and what we're doing to protect them. It would be helpful if the people on this call, including myself, understood it, too," she responded sheepishly.

A senior health official jumped in. "Guys, I agree this is likely very serious—how serious, we don't know yet—but at the same time, I think it's important that, internally and externally, we all understand that, according to top medical professionals at the CDC and WHO, by all accounts, say this virus acts like, well, the flu," he said.

"The flu?" I asked, honestly confused.

"Yes, the flu; that's what the federal government is saying."

"Okay, accepting that premise, can I ask you a stupid question?" I went on.

"Of course."

"Isn't the major difference between this and the flu is that the flu has a vaccine?"

The silence on the line was deafening. No one—not the feds, not the press, not the health officials in Washington—knew what we were dealing with.

"Okay, I think that's enough for today!" I couldn't end the call quickly enough. "Thank you, everybody."

CHAPTER 3

Lighting Up the Bat Signal

I COLLAPSED ON THE LIVING ROOM SOFA, COVERED MY FACE WITH my hands, and let out a deep sigh. We didn't know what this was and how bad it could be—no one did—and that feeling overwhelmed me. It was time to call the governor.

"Helloooo, hellooooo, Melissa De-Ros-a, hellooooooo!" he answered in the baritone voice he used when he was in a particularly good mood.

"Hi, Governor." I responded, attempting to sound upbeat back.

"How are you feeling?"

"Well, not great."

"Are you okay?" It dawned on me that the boss was asking about my doctor's appointment, not COVID.

"Oh, that. That was what it was. But we don't have time to talk about that now," I quickly answered.

"What's going on?" His tone shifted to all business.

"I just did a call with the health department . . . "

I filled him in on needing to contact Vice President Pence about testing.

"Okay, what else?" he wanted to know.

"Rick Cotton called about issues at the airports," I launched in. Rick was the executive director at the Port Authority. Established in 1921 as a joint venture between New York and New Jersey, the Port Authority oversees much of the regional transportation infrastructure: all major bridges, tunnels, seaports, and airports—including three of the nation's busiest: LaGuardia, JFK, and Newark International. A consummate professional and all-star lawyer with incredible management skills and a full head of white hair, Rick had the ability to move massive bureaucracies; he never picked up the phone with a problem unless he had run out of possible solutions.

"With this virus jumping from country to country, Rick's concerned about logistics around tracking passengers coming in through the airports," I continued. "He said the federal government's protocols are a mess; it doesn't seem like any of this could possibly work."

"Yes, I've been speaking with Rick," Cuomo interjected, seemingly unfazed. "What else?" He had an uncanny sense for things being left unsaid.

"I just . . . I don't know," I paused. "I don't think the federal government is really in control of this."

"Oh, come on, Melissa," Cuomo chided. "You've been doing this long enough to know that control is an illusory concept. I'll call Zucker and Pence and Cotton." He paused.

"What are you thinking?" I asked, hoping he'd deliver a quick, confident answer.

"We're not going to rely on the feds," the governor declared. "And we're going to call the legislature: if we're going to properly manage this, we're going to need the authority and resources to do it. Get Beth and begin to engage the leaders." He was adamant that if he was going to be in charge of the state's pandemic response, he needed the legal authority to do it. In this case, that meant the legal power to institute mass quarantines, order businesses to close, suspend laws, and issue sweeping directives.

"I'll call Shontell and LouAnn," I offered. Shontell Smith and LouAnn Ciccone were my counterparts in the senate and assembly, respectively. Despite our competing interests, the three of us had become good friends and trusted one another; we fought for our principles, and while sometimes it was ugly, we did so honestly and generally went out for drinks after. It was time to bring them in and come up with a plan.

"In the meantime, don't let that obsessive brain of yours make you crazy." Cuomo often teased me about being Type A. "Takes one to know one" was my usual wry response.

In a crisis, Andrew Cuomo always played it consummately cool, no matter how hot the water was. While I played through every possible worst-case scenario and spun myself up, he organized, strategized, and pre-deployed. He was known by the Albany press corps as "Governor Windbreaker" (a nod to his emergency-management attire): blizzards, floods, and hurricanes were his forte. He had been secretary of Housing and Urban Development in the administration of Bill Clinton and had handled crises across the country decades before. Over the years, Cuomo would push me to convert nervous energy into productivity. We had no idea what was about to unfold, but we had run out of time to wait around for someone else to figure it out.

Ready or not, it was time to take matters into our own hands.

The first day in March 2020 was like any other typical Sunday. I woke up while it was still dark and went for a run. I spent the morning responding to emails and doing back-to-back conference calls on the state budget and the emergency-powers legislation. I had brunch with a few girlfriends and checked in with my parents. And by 5:00 p.m., I was in sweatpants, watching MSNBC, and ordering takeout. Former mayor of South Bend, Indiana, Pete Buttigieg had just announced he was dropping out of the Democratic presidential primary, and pundits were abuzz about who of the remaining candidates would benefit from his departure. A footnote to the day's political news appeared on the chyron scrolling along the bottom of the screen: twenty-four hours earlier, the United States had reported its first COVID death in Seattle, Washington.

And then my phone rang. And the world turned upside down.

"Dr. Zucker," I said, warily. "How are you?"

"Melissa, I just received word from Wadsworth," he said by way of answer. "New York has our first confirmed case of COVID." It had barely been twenty-four hours since Cuomo had successfully lobbied Vice President Pence for the ability to conduct COVID testing in New York, and already we had our first confirmed case. While being granted access to do our own in-state testing was a significant development, Wadsworth only had the capacity to run about 400 tests a day. New York had 19.5 million people. How many more were there that we didn't know about?

"Are we sure?" I asked, as questions suddenly flooded my brain. While we had begun preparing for this moment, what COVID was and the extent of its possible damage were still largely unknown.

"We're sure."

I hastily conferenced the governor into the call. He was in Albany at the time. Zucker quickly briefed us. The patient was a thirty-nine-year-old female health-care worker who had been working in Iran and had just flown back to New York. She had come down with a fever, which is what prompted her to be tested, but was otherwise healthy. Masked the entire time, she had taken an Uber from the airport and was currently isolated in her Midtown Manhattan apartment.

"But if she was on a plane and took an Uber, doesn't that mean . . . ?" I interjected. In a heartbeat, the abstract concept of "tracing" everyone an infected person had come in contact with became a reality. My head started to spin—the possible connections were exponential.

"We're going to have to make sure the Uber driver is tested and work with the federal government to identify everyone that was on the plane, figure out if any of them got onto other planes, and make sure they are made aware and isolated," Zucker was explaining.

"Oh, they'll be made aware, all right. The entire world is about to be made aware," Cuomo said, unironically. "What else do we know, Doctor?"

"That's it for the moment, Governor."

"Okay, Melissa, we're going to need to tell the public," Cuomo said. "People need the facts, or pandemonium could ensue."

I cut in. "Yes, Governor, I've been working on a draft statement while we've been on the phone. I'll send it over for your review."

"And call Emma to notify de Blasio," he added. "We'll need to do a press conference together in the morning. We'll need to present a unified front." Emma Wolfe was chief of staff to New York City Mayor Bill de Blasio.

The relationship between the governor of New York and the mayor of New York City is historically fraught, but ours was particularly toxic and stood in stark contrast to the one we had had with de Blasio's predecessor. Mike Bloomberg, an executive from the private sector known for his competence, was a self-made billionaire many times over. He was in the office by 8:00 a.m. and the last person in City Hall to turn the lights out at night. He surrounded himself with the best and the brightest. Similarly, our team was known for being highly professional, competent, and effective. When Bloomberg was mayor, our administrations coexisted in a mostly peaceful manner based on mutual admiration. Game respect game.

The dynamic between us and de Blasio was the opposite. The press referred to the two as "frenemies." It was much more complicated than that. The governor and de Blasio had known each other for twenty-five years and considered each other real friends. As HUD secretary, Cuomo had given de Blasio his first serious political job as his New York regional representative. Both Mario and Andrew Cuomo endorsed de Blasio for his first City Council race, while every other political heavyweight, including the Clintons, sat on the sidelines, despite the fact that de Blasio had just worked as Hillary's campaign manager for her US Senate seat. During de Blasio's mayoral campaign, he moved to the Far Left, believing that's where the future of the party was going. As the son of Mario Cuomo, who was known as the Liberal Lion, Andrew Cuomo considered himself an "aggressive progressive" but rejected the extreme Left, which he believed was long on rhetoric and short on results. Cuomo's mantra was "you can't be a progressive without progress," whereas de Blasio was happy to champion pie-in-the-sky policies with no practical plan to accomplish them. It set up the two on a collision course.

After being sworn in as mayor, de Blasio, who had never been in an executive position, appeared visibly bored by the job and was always looking for the next best thing. His delusions of grandeur even prompted de Blasio to engage in an embarrassing campaign for president, dropping out four months later, never polling above 0 percent. But as dysfunctional as the relationship between the mayor and governor could be, Emma and I had managed—for the most part—to maintain a friendly, productive relationship; we respected each other and the jobs we had to do.

"Check in with Beth to see where things stand with the legislature on the emergency-powers bill. We need it finalized and introduced immediately," he continued.

"Got it," I said, jotting down notes.

"Let Annabel know we'll fly back to Albany after the press conference. I'd like to pull the cabinet together for a meeting." Annabel Walsh was our director of scheduling. At twenty-six, she was whip-smart, hardworking, and sassy. I looked at her as a little sister.

We hung up and started executing. New York City was briefed, and our team was in gear. The mayor would join the governor for the press conference. Beth reported back that the emergency-powers legislation was still being negotiated but would likely be ready to introduce the next morning. My leisurely Sunday was over. I hastily threw together a garment bag with two weeks' worth of clothing, toiletries, and my laptop for my Monday-morning flight to Albany.

I wouldn't see the inside of my home again for five months.

While we live in a global economy, Americans operate with a very nationalist mentality: If something isn't happening here or impacting us directly, it may as well not be happening at all. That goes double for New Yorkers. While COVID had been rapidly making its way around the globe, it didn't truly become real until it reached New York City.

Before the press conference, Cuomo, Dr. Zucker, and I huddled around the governor's conference room table to get on the same page with five of the city's top health professionals. The federal government and the medical community, from Dr. Fauci on down, were all telling us the same thing: Remain calm. Take the subway. Go about your life. Whatever you do, do not panic. They were still comparing it to the flu. That was the message, and we wouldn't deviate.

As we stood up to walk the one flight down to the thirty-eighth floor to begin the press conference, Annabel pulled me aside.

"We had planned to save a seat for you in the front row, but the room is packed. Do you mind watching from up here?"

"Sure," I said, taken aback. "How many people are down there?"

"More than have ever fit in that room before." Annabel responded, her eyes wide.

The press conference attracted nearly three dozen television cameras, requiring an overflow space be set up for reporters who hadn't arrived early enough to secure a seat. The jam-packed room underscored how little we understood about the virus.

Flanked by Mayor de Blasio and an onslaught of medical professionals, the governor dutifully conveyed the confidence of a father assuring his children everything was going to be alright.

"My daughter called me and said, don't tell me to relax—tell me why I should be relaxed," he proclaimed, the entire country's eyes on him. "So I want to make sure I tell the people of New York what I told my daughter. In this situation, the facts defeat fear, because the reality is reassuring."

Outwardly, he conveyed confidence; privately, I sensed he was deeply concerned. By the next afternoon, another COVID patient was identified: this time a lawyer in his fifties from New Rochelle, a small town twenty miles north of New York City. Patient Zero, as he would come to be known, had been hospitalized and put into a medically induced coma. Unlike the doctor diagnosed two days before, this man had no recent travel history; the only possible way he could have contracted the virus was by moving around in the course of his daily life. A new phrase was introduced: community spread. But how? Where had it come from? And who else had he unknowingly infected? Suddenly, the nightmare scenario was undeniable reality. The feds were wrong. COVID had been silently spreading in New York for who knew how long.

There had been strong opposition in the legislature, but COVID was officially in New York, and that was enough to push them over the finish line. A few hours later, they convened to pass the governor's emergency-powers legislation, along with a $40 million appropriation to address unforeseen health costs. (Ironically, a number of legislators contracted COVID while in the capitol debating the emergency-powers bill.)

The questions were piling up, but answers were in short supply. When did COVID get to New York? How many people have it? How fast could the virus spread? How lethal was it? What was our hospital capacity? After meeting with our cabinet and then separately with top officials from the state's Department of Health, the governor's mood shifted, and I could sense something was wrong.

"Do you have a second?" I asked. The governor was sitting in his conference room at the head of the long wooden table, making a to-do list. "Is everything okay?"

Cuomo looked up, took his glasses off, brow furrowed, "A state government has never done this before," he said.

"What do you mean?" I asked. "Done what?"

"Melissa, this is going to be a massive operational undertaking on tasks never performed before. We are going to need to set up testing sites, get labs to do the testing, put together a real contact-tracing program, secure thousands of pieces of personal protective equipment (PPE)—and that's only the things we know we're going to have to do, not to mention everything we're not aware of yet."

"Okay," I responded, "and we'll get it done, just like we always do."

"Melissa, you were in that meeting. Do you honestly think that we have the manpower for this?" Cuomo leaned back in his chair, looked up at the ceiling, and let out a long exhale. I took that as my cue to leave him alone.

I turned around, walked into my office, and closed the door. He was right. We couldn't do this alone. We needed extra hands. I picked up a legal pad and started to jot down names.

Steve Cohen and Bill Mulrow. Steve and Bill had both served as secretary to the governor earlier on in the administration and had Cuomo's full confidence. Smart, steady, and wise to their core, they were the consummate counselors. Check.

Larry Schwartz. Larry was an operational genius and a bulldog. He had the patience to vet every single action and relentlessly push a task over the finish line. He had been secretary to two governors and deputy county executive to two of the state's largest counties. Larry had been working in the private sector for the last few years; he was one of those rare people who felt compelled by a sense of duty. If we called, there was no way he would say no. Check.

Linda Lacewell. Linda was superintendent for the department of financial services. One of the nation's most well-regarded lawyers, she was savvy, intelligent, relentless, and effective, and she worked twenty-four hours a day. She was also a close friend of mine whose devotion to the administration was unmatched. We needed her. Check.

Jim Malatras. Jim had worked for the governor since he was attorney general, first as head of policy and then later as director of state operations. He was a genius. He was universally respected, understood New York State law inside out, and knew how to move the unwieldy bureaucracy. He was serving as president of Empire State College. Check.

Mimi Reisner. Mimi had worked for the State Department under Hillary Clinton before working for us years later managing overall messaging. Communicating to the public was almost as important as hardening our operational capacity, and Mimi's brain moved a thousand miles a minute, always generating new ideas and seeing problems before they materialized. Mimi was between projects. There's no way she would say no. Check.

I walked back into the governor's conference room, catching him between phone calls.

"I have an idea," I said.

"What do you got?" he asked, without looking up from his to-do list.

"I heard what you said before," I began. "And I don't necessarily disagree."

"So?"

"So let's bring back the old team."

"What do you mean?" He responded, looking up.

"I mean Steve, Bill, Larry, Linda, Jim, Mimi. It's just a start, and we'll need more, but let's get this group and build out from there. They'll do it. I know they will."

"Okay," he responded, unconvinced. "Give it a shot. Let me know what they say."

Danger, darkness, the unknown all loomed; it was time to send up the Bat Signal. In an industry known for people coming and going (loyalty optional), many on our team had worked together for decades, dating back to Mario Cuomo's administration in the 1980s. And whereas many political teams are notorious for internecine battles, people who leaked to the press, and internal factions, none of that existed in our operation. The people who thrived were top-level professionals, and they knew it. Performance mattered, and everyone was expected to carry their own weight. The pace and stress level were grueling on a good day and not for the faint of heart. But born from that intensity was a family. We trusted each other and had one another's backs.

One by one, they said yes. Linda would immediately fly back from a conference she was attending in London. Larry would move into the governor's mansion and camp out until the storm had passed. Jim would temporarily relocate his office to the capitol. And Mimi would start to hire as much talent as she could. I leaned back in my chair. Help was on the way. Whatever this was, we would figure it out together.

It was clear that no one could yet fathom the depth of what was happening around us, but now that we had mustered our forces, we needed to start making decisions. Big ones.

CHAPTER 4

State of Emergency

IN THE SPAN OF A WEEK, ONE CASE BECAME 117. THE GOVERNOR WAS continuing to urge the public to stay calm, while officially declaring a state of emergency.

Patient Zero had attended more mass gatherings in the days before falling ill than some people do in a year: a wedding, a funeral, and a bar mitzvah all centered around his synagogue in New Rochelle. Young Israel had more than 1,000 congregants, and almost all had attended some iteration of the events. Most of them had then gone to work or school, many traveling by mass transit and coming into contact with an untold number of additional people. The impact of the potential multiplier effect was dizzying. And all of them needed to be quarantined. It was a cluster, literally, the nation's first COVID hot spot. Not only was the federal government not telling us what to do or how to handle it, Trump continued to confuse the public, repeating over and over again that COVID would just "disappear."

"We need to contain this," the governor said to Dr. Zucker and me, huddled around his conference room table in Albany.

"How?" I asked, my question matching the other blank faces seated in front of him.

"Steph, please grab a map," he said, calling out to Steph at her desk. His wheels were turning.

Stephanie appeared a few minutes later with a 2 × 3-foot printout of Westchester County. Now what? I wondered as we peered down at it.

"Steph, can you please grab us a protractor?" the Governor asked.

"A protractor?" she asked, somewhat confused.

"A protractor," he responded, without looking up.

"What are you thinking?" Dr. Zucker asked.

"We're going to implement a containment zone," he responded. "We'll close the schools and houses of worship, and cancel gatherings within the zone."

"What should we make the center?" I asked.

"Well, nearly two-thirds of the state's cases are associated with events that occurred at the temple," Dr. Zucker responded.

"The temple it is," said the governor.

The governor put a pin in the spot on the map where the temple was located, and we played with different iterations of how big the zone should be, ultimately agreeing to a zone with a one-mile radius from the temple. The National Guard would be mobilized to assist with sanitizing the interior of locations known to have had COVID spread and delivering food for those under quarantine.

The announcement of the first designated "containment zone" in the United States was international news, conjuring up images from the movie *Contagion* and setting off a wave of panic throughout the community. Residents feared they wouldn't be permitted to leave the "zone," mistakenly under the impression that the National Guard were being sent to police it. Several clarifying statements later, in a quiet moment, the governor and I discussed the communications mishap. In a crisis, every single word mattered. The only way we were going to get through whatever this was would require the public to subscribe to what we were saying. "No more mistakes," he said, a message he was underscoring for himself as much as for me.

Shortly after the day's press conference ended, I broke our sixty-eight-day silence. I was as estranged from normalcy as I was from my husband. Conveying confidence and focusing on the seemingly endless operational and communications tasks in front of us had become our new routine, but in the moments when adrenaline wore off and the noise would fade, I was afraid. And I needed to talk to him.

I dialed, not knowing if he would answer, but he did, on the third ring.

"Melissa?" he asked.

"Matt?" I responded, tentatively. He knew that if I was calling, it was serious.

"What's wrong?"

"Remember when you said we shouldn't talk unless it was an emergency? Well . . . it's an emergency."

I let it all tumble out in a rush, how I thought the federal government was on the verge of grounding all planes . . . that he needed to come home now or potentially end up stranded in California for God knows how long . . . that even though we didn't know the risks for sure, I didn't want his parents on the subway. I told him that the information we were getting from the medical community was shifting hourly and that it didn't feel like anyone knew what they were talking about—or if they did, they weren't telling us. He heard me loud and clear; he would fly back to the city. He would talk to his mom and dad.

From there, things only got worse. To the best of our knowledge, we had yet to have a single COVID death, but the extent to which the virus had metastasized became more evident in the daily testing numbers. At the same time, all eyes were on northern Italy, where images of COVID patients dying on gurneys in hallways served as a dire warning of what could come.

The federal government has sole authority over the country's airports and airspace. While Trump had enacted a China travel ban on January 31, he would not suspend travel to and from Europe until March 13—the same day the federal government declared COVID a national emergency. Little did we know that the rampant spread of COVID that had brought Italy's hospital system to the brink of collapse had been silently infiltrating the United States from the East Coast, primarily through JFK and Newark International airports.

"We cannot, we will not be Italy," the governor said to a group of senior staff and Department of Health officials.

Dr. Zucker advised that more sweeping action was necessary. Every day was a flurry of activity. While we understood very little about the virus, the medical community was certain it was especially dangerous for the immunocompromised and the elderly, a situation we saw playing out in Seattle, Washington, where nursing homes were being enveloped by COVID spread. And so the governor took the devastating step of banning visitation in nursing homes, while requiring health screenings for all nursing home workers each day upon entering a facility and requiring all staff to wear surgical masks to guard against any potential asymptomatic spread. He canceled the famous St. Patrick's Day Parade in New York City and banned gatherings of over 500 people. We closed public colleges while urging private universities to follow suit. Discussions were underway with the teacher's union about closing all public schools in the downstate area. And no one was happy.

When we closed schools in New Rochelle, the local parent-teachers association was furious and dispatched their assemblywoman to protest. When we floated the prospect of closing restaurants, business owners decried what they said was tyrannical government overreach. When we announced that we would use empty college dorms to quarantine American kids returning from semesters abroad cut short, school administrators were outraged.

After a press conference on March 14, one of the directives we announced that morning struck a nerve with someone a little closer to home.

"Meliss?" Dani was standing in my doorway.

"Hey, Dani. What's happening?" I asked, without looking up from my keyboard.

"I just got this text message."

I temporarily paused my attempted multitasking and gave her my full attention.

"Okay, from whom?"

"Lindsey Boylan."

"Lindsey Boylan? What does she want?" Lindsey Boylan had worked for our economic development agency before joining our senior team. Her employment ended when she quit two years earlier after a slew of complaints were made stating that she had bullied three agency employees and was responsible for fostering a toxic work environment. When confronted with the complaints, she abruptly resigned, only to call a few days later, asking for her job back. In consultation with counsel, we declined. I hadn't spoken to her since.

"It's really bizarre, Meliss," Dani said. "It's about the executive order we announced today on petitioning."

"Petitioning?" I couldn't imagine what that had to do with Lindsey Boylan.

"She's running for Congress, and it seems like she's very upset by the executive order changing the petitioning period," Dani explained. "It's like she thinks we made the change because of her."

"What? That doesn't make any sense. Let me see." Dani handed me her iPhone. Lindsey had copied and pasted a tweet we had issued from the governor's official Twitter account:

NEWS: The safety of NYers is our top priority.

I'm signing an executive order to reduce the # of petition signatures to 30 percent of the statutory threshold; Petition period will end at 5:00 p.m., Tues. 3/17.

This will ensure our electoral process goes on while safeguarding public health.

"So what?" I asked as I handed Dani back her phone.

"Meliss—scroll down," Dani said, pushing it back across the desk in my direction.

Then I saw the series of text messages Lindsey had sent to Dani below the tweet:

Absolutely not helpful specific response to a
tragedy but please relay that while we are okay,
I see what the point is here, and I will find ways
to respond to the message. The future is coming
after assholes.

The texts were accompanied by a selfie of Lindsey and her young daughter wearing paint on their faces. *What. The. Actual. Fuck.* Did she seriously think we enacted a statewide policy related to collecting petitions in the middle of a pandemic to somehow hurt her? Was she delusional?

"When did she send this?" I wondered aloud.

"Just now," Dani replied. "Not to be dramatic, but it feels oddly threatening."

I shared Dani's unease. "Look, you know my opinion about Lindsey," I told her. "If I were you, I would send her back a text clearly telling her that you don't want her to contact you anymore."

Dani shook her head. "I don't want to start a thing with her. I'll just ignore it for now."

"Okay, Dani, but, seriously, if she does it again, you should tell her to knock it off."

"I hear you," she promised.

As Dani left my office, I turned back to my computer to refocus.

"Hey, lady—do you have a minute?" Steph asked from my door. "He's asking for you." I nodded. We were in the middle of developing contingency plans with counties in preparation for school closings, including how to provide meals to food-insecure children and ensure families had adequate access to childcare—that's where my head needed to be.

"Steph, can you please get Governors Lamont and Murphy on the phone?" Cuomo asked as I reached his conference room door to find Rob Mujica, our budget director, already seated at the table. Rob was as indispensable as they come. He had worked for the Senate Republicans for years, negotiating the budget on their behalf. He was the best the governor had ever gone up against, and so we made it our mission to take him off the field, eventually succeeding when he agreed to join our administration at the end of 2015. Inscrutable, unflappable, and politically brilliant, Rob had become one of my closest confidants during our time working together.

"What's going on in New Jersey and Connecticut?" I asked, wondering what was next.

"Ned, Phil, and I have been speaking this morning and agree. If we're going to move to announce major closures, we have to do it in lockstep. Otherwise, we're risking the potential of venue shopping across the tri-state area and will only ensure the virus continues to spread," he answered. The New York City region is unique in how interconnected it is with its neighbors. While the tri-state area may comprise three separate and distinct states, its residents flow freely from one state to the next to work, shop, and dine. Nonresidents account for roughly 15 percent of New York's income taxes. If one of us made a move, we would all have to or damn one another to fail. In the absence of any federal guidance, we agreed to act in the best interests of the region and move as a block. The three governors decided to start by closing restaurants, bars, casinos, movie theaters, and gyms and banning all gatherings of over fifty people. They would also lock arms and urge all nonessential businesses to keep their workforce home. "We will make the announcement first thing Monday morning," he continued. "Rob and Melissa, I need you to start making calls to brief business leaders; they shouldn't hear about this for the first time in the press."

Rob and I nodded dutifully, standing up to head to my office.

"Sorry, Governor—quick, potentially very stupid question," I paused.

"Go ahead," he responded.

"Which businesses are nonessential? It will be the first question we get from the press, and we need to be very clear," I continued.

"That's actually a very good question, Melissa. Why don't you and Rob get Dr. Zucker and the senior team together and come back with a recommendation," he answered.

"Wait—there's no list?" I asked, stunned.

The governor turned to Rob. "Rob, down in the budget office, is there a secret list of nonessential businesses in case of a once-in-a-century pandemic that I'm not aware of?"

Rob smirked, "Not that I know of, Governor, no."

"If Rob doesn't know of one, and you don't know of one, and I don't know of one, I think it's safe to assume one doesn't exist," he responded, turning his attention back to his upcoming call on hardening the state's hospital system.

Rob and I headed back to my office and closed the door.

"Is this an actual joke?" I asked, incredulously. "The feds can't even provide us with this?"

"Melissa, it's fine," Rob said, reassuringly. He could tell I was about to spiral. "I'll talk to my office and get a list of businesses by category, and we'll figure it out together."

We huddled at the small, round wooden table in the corner of my office, making decisions on which businesses were essential. Some, like grocery stores and pharmacies, were obvious, while others were not.

"Dry cleaners, Rob? Seriously?" I asked. "We're supposed to be figuring out the bare minimum here."

The consequence of the decisions we were making could not be overstated. Those deemed essential would still require employees to show up every day and interact with customers, potentially exposing them to COVID and grave illness, or worse. Those deemed not essential could potentially be doomed to bankruptcy, closed forever.

"Melissa, police officers and firefighters have uniforms, and those uniforms have to be cleaned. I know it sounds ridiculous, but think about it."

"Okay, but you can be the one to defend that recommendation when we sit with the governor," I responded.

While we were attempting to be consistent and clear in our public-facing messaging, presenting numbers and facts about the quickly evolving situation and rationales for the decisions we made, de Blasio was flailing. At that point, it was clear that the New York City schools needed to close. Jim Malatras and I had started the conversation in earnest the weekend before, on March 8, with senior staff from City Hall and the head of the New York City Teachers Union, in a conference call that started off friendly but quickly grew heated. The mayor's office and teachers union were unified in their position: they were adamantly opposed to closing schools in the City, no ifs, ands, or buts about it. By the middle of the week, though, the union, inundated by the very real fears of its members, had changed its tune. But every time I checked in with de Blasio's office, the answer from Emma was the same: "He's [de Blasio] still not there." Up until that point, we were still leaving decisions on schools up to the locality, but by Friday knew we couldn't wait any longer.

The governor, Jim, Rob, and I spent the weekend negotiating with SEIU 1199, the nation's largest health-care workers' union, and the executives of New York City's neighboring counties. If schools would close, hospital workers could be forced to stay home in order to provide childcare, inadvertently creating staffing shortages. We agreed on a plan that would ensure day care for essential workers and meal deliveries for food-insecure families. That Sunday, we held a conference call with Long Island and Westchester's county executives, announcing that the schools in the state's three most populous counties bordering New York City would close the following day, boxing in de Blasio to do the same.

After the press call, though, de Blasio was still waffling, and the governor was done waiting. Parents needed to know what their children were doing the next day. Cuomo decided to exercise the authority granted by the legislature, calling into local TV station NY1 to make the announcement that New York City's public schools would be closed. At almost the exact same time, de Blasio hastily called a press conference to make the same announcement we had just made.

This dynamic with the mayor continued to play out unabated. As we prepared to close restaurants and bars, de Blasio was urging the public to keep patronizing local businesses. The morning we announced the closure of gyms, he was at the gym doing his beloved personal work-out. We were stuck between Trump, who kept insisting COVID would just—poof!—disappear, and de Blasio, whose words and actions confused an overly anxious public. And messaging mattered.

Over the next two days, confirmed COVID cases skyrocketed exponentially. Contact tracing proved to be a laughable exercise as it became clear that the virus had invisibly been running rampant for months before we identified our first case. We aggressively and emotionally appealed to the public to stay home, every day closing more and more businesses. We needed people to buy into what we were saying, because government by decree alone was impotent. If we ordered everything closed and the public refused to abide by the closures, what was the option? Put people in jail? Have police stand guard? It was a ridiculous concept that we didn't have the manpower to enforce anyway.

It was a time of crisis unlike any of us had ever faced. People were traumatized, and the governor believed it was vital to give them a sense of stability in an otherwise out-of-control world. And so the daily briefing was born. The importance of the daily press conferences was their effectiveness. People heard us, and they responded. The governor spoke not as a politician, but as a government leader, presenting the public with the facts and gaining their trust. Cuomo believed that if the people understood what was going on, they would choose to do what we asked them to do. Almost instantly, our daily news briefings became must-see TV, not just in New York and across the country, but around the globe.

The governor likened our actions to "adjusting a valve"—turning it tighter and tighter as we neared total closure. By Wednesday, it was time to stop voluntarily urging workers in nonessential businesses to stay home; we would start closing the valve: first by 50 percent, then by 75 percent on Thursday.

I was answering emails and jumping between back-to-back calls as Cuomo prepared for the inevitable when Dani came into my office, looking flustered again.

"You know how you told me to have the entire press team come to Albany this week?"

"Yes, Dani?"

"So, Caitlin is here. She got here Monday afternoon. And she has been feeling a little off. Which I wasn't really worried about, but this afternoon, she . . ."

"She what?"

"She said she was heating up. She really didn't feel well. So I sent her home. I know you'll think I was being dramatic, but with COVID, I . . ."

"Okay, Dlev, got it. Caitlin didn't feel well, and you freaked out and sent her to the hotel."

"Meliss, I was in that little suite of offices with her for the last three days. The entire press team was. And I just . . . What if . . . ?"

"Dani, my love, while I generally appreciate your flair for the dramatic, we really don't have time for this," I said, attempting to coax her out of it. "I'm sure she's fine, and you're fine, and the entire press team is fine. Let's get back to work, please? We need to figure out what Trump is saying tonight, and what we should be saying tomorrow. That's where our focus needs to be, okay?

On the morning of March 20, the governor would close the valve altogether, putting New York "on PAUSE." We would shut down all remaining nonessential businesses and, in doing so, bring the economic center of the world to a screeching halt.

CHAPTER 5

What Goes Up

IT WAS 3:34 A.M. WHEN MY PHONE RANG THAT MORNING, JOLTING ME awake. I know the precise time because I confirmed it on my BlackBerry as I stumbled around in search of my glasses so I could find my iPhone, still ringing incessantly. While my mother and brother have perfect 20/20 vision, my sister and I inherited our father's eyes, which meant we were essentially legally blind without contacts or glasses. Regretting the glass of wine I'd had before bed a few hours earlier, I groggily played Marco Polo with the taunting iPhone, feeling around walls, patting countertops, until I made my way to the kitchen and used the dim neon glow of the microwave's digital clock—yep, 3:34 a.m.—to find a light switch. By the time I found the phone—wedged between a leg of the bed and the nightstand, covered by the dust ruffle—the ringing had stopped. Caller ID told me it had been Jill DesRosiers.

Jill was our chief of staff. She did a little bit of everything and was a political and operational genius, the silent MVP of the team who asked for zero public-facing credit in return. And she was one of my closest friends. Why would she be calling? I dialed back.

"Jill?"

"Hey, sorry to call so late," she immediately apologized, "or early, I guess? It's Caitlin."

"Caitlin?" I asked, totally confused. Caitlin was our press secretary. She had just relocated from her New York City base to Albany earlier in the week as part of our all-hands-on-deck COVID response.

"Yesterday afternoon, Dani told me Caitlin said she wasn't feeling well, and . . ." Jill began.

FUCKKKKKKKKKK!

Panic instantly overrode my confusion.

What if Caitlin actually had COVID? What if the governor had COVID? What if I had COVID and unknowingly had brought it home to my brother and his fiancée last night when I came to stay with them at their loft?

"Jill, I'm getting dressed and going to the office," I interrupted. "I'll call you back!"

When I came to Albany for work, I generally bounced around to stay with various family members. Rotating between my father, sister, and brother served the dual purpose of allowing me to spend time with each of them while also not asking them to put up with a house guest for too long in any given period of time. I was grateful for their hospitality and open-door policy, but at that moment, I couldn't get out of my brother's home fast enough.

I started furiously packing my things, grabbing fistfuls of clothes and putting them into my overnight bag. I didn't know where I was going to sleep that night or any night after that, but it was clear I couldn't stay with family anymore. It was too dangerous. *I* was too dangerous. We still didn't understand how deadly the virus was, and if I ever got any of them sick, I would never forgive myself.

It was 4:00 a.m., still dark and freezing cold, as I walked the four blocks up State Street from my brother's apartment to the office. Shortly after I arrived, Linda Lacewell got busy putting new protocols into place: The assistants who normally sat outside my office were moved across the hall. Doorknobs and surfaces throughout the suite were to be disinfected daily. Only Stephanie and I would have free access to the governor; no one else would be allowed past the trooper outside Cuomo's door without express permission. It felt as if we were in an alternate universe, but if COVID had already found its way down the hall to our press office, there was no precaution too great. We couldn't risk the governor getting sick.

I moved into the Renaissance Hotel catty-corner from the capitol. When I arrived, there were plastic partitions around the host stand, where guests would traditionally be greeted. Check-in had been replaced by automated machines near the elevator. The lobby was only partially lit, the attached restaurant roped off and closed. The entire thing was eerie; it was as though I was moving into an abandoned hotel from a Stanley Kubrick movie.

Shortly after I finished unpacking, my phone rang. Jill again.

"We have confirmation," she said. "Caitlin has COVID, and a pretty terrible fever."

My heart sank. "We should have Dr. Zucker call and check on her," I suggested.

"Already done." Of course, Jill was on top of it.

"What does this mean for the others?" I asked. The whole communications team—including Dani, whose concerns I had so glibly deflected just a day earlier—had been jammed like sardines into two small, connected offices after arriving in Albany ten days earlier.

No one had symptoms, Jill assured me, but they would all have to quarantine for the next two weeks; so would the operations staff, which had been in close proximity.

"We have to manage this thing without our press and operations staff?" I was incredulous. Did we just go from all-hands-on-deck to half-staffed in a nanosecond?

"It appears so, yes," Jill confirmed.

Jesus Christ.

"Any other good news?" I asked wryly.

Jill knew better than to feed my sarcasm. "Nope, that's it for the moment," she signed off. "I'll check in with you later."

Overwhelmed, I plopped down on the hotel bed, looking out the window at the capitol, and instinctively reached for my phone to text Matt. But before giving into the impulse, I set it down again. The seal had been broken on our silence pact, but that didn't mean I was supposed to abuse it. I lay back and closed my eyes.

My entire life, I had faith in medicine and science, my belief unwavering that the people in charge knew what they were doing. Now, in the course of one month, I had discovered that they didn't. COVID didn't arrive in New York on March 1 with that health-care worker from Iran. The deadly virus had been here silently and invisibly spreading for months. How did no one know that? If we needed to shut down businesses, why hadn't the Centers for Disease Control or the World Health Organization or Dr. Fauci recommended that three weeks earlier? If the federal government knew COVID was killing people in Italy, why didn't Trump ground planes from Europe? Why hadn't his advisers advised it? And when we made the decision to close the economy, why were Rob Mujica and I the ones recommending which businesses should be considered essential and stay open? What expertise did we have?

I was always a workaholic, but those first early weeks of COVID pushed me to my absolute limit. I would work every minute my eyes were open, waking up between 3:45 and 4:30 a.m.—I didn't need an alarm, my brain was too full—often arriving at the office by 6:00 a.m. and not leaving until after 11:00 p.m. Our days were now filled with having the government do things that had never been done before. Mornings were spent analyzing hospitalizations, the ever-growing rate of positive cases, and death projections. *Death projections.* Afterward, we'd hold what felt like never-ending press briefings to update the public.

Afternoons were divide and conquer. While Cuomo manhandled the logistical and operational nightmare of manufacturing hand sanitizer, setting up testing sites, ensuring the hospital system wouldn't collapse, and managing PPE shortages, I spent hours troubleshooting agency emergencies like the Department of Labor's unemployment system, which had crumbled under the sheer volume of incoming, and on tedious calls with the counsel's office, preparing to advise the governor on a range of endless decisions—big and small—about which laws to suspend, rules to enact, and regulations to change, a dizzying exercise with far-reaching consequences. Some things were obvious, others seemingly trivial but necessary. Most people couldn't work and, by extension, couldn't pay their rent, so we had to put an eviction moratorium in place. Permission was granted to allow for notaries to witness signings on Zoom instead of in person. Courts were closed, so statutes of limitations had to be extended. Gatherings were banned, so we allowed couples to be married online. We postponed the presidential primary and the state's tax filing. In total, we issued 113 executive orders, each with up to a dozen subsections, unilaterally writing or rewriting entire sections of state law.

On top of that, we were in the midst of tense negotiations with the legislature over the state's $177 billion budget, which was due on April 1. The governor turned to Rob, Beth, and me.

"Guys, I am going to be too busy dealing with COVID to focus on the budget," he said. "I need you to carry the ball over the finish line. If there are any big decisions you need me on, I'm here, but otherwise I trust your judgment. Kelly will work with me on the operational tasks, so to the extent you can, try to leave her alone." Kelly Cummings was our state operations director; her innate attention to detail, combined with seemingly endless energy and drive, made her the perfect choice to manage the state agencies—all of them, from the Bridge Authority to the Department of Tax and Finance. During COVID, her operational fortitude was on full display.

The budget is the most important task the legislature deals with every year, doling out billions of dollars for education, health care, and local governments. It's also a negotiation process that gives the governor the upper hand. The legislature is allowed to make amendments to it, but as chief executive, the governor controls it. If the budget isn't enacted by April 1, the state government shuts down, sending tens of thousands of government employees home and freezing services like the DMV, the tax department, and other agencies heavily relied on by everyday New Yorkers. But this year, the stakes in our annual chess match were much, much higher: If the legislature failed to enact the budget on time, the State Health Department would shut down, jeopardizing our COVID response.

While past governors allowed the legislature to blow through the deadline year after year, passing a budget extender to keep state government operating, Andrew Cuomo refused, instead using April 1 to hold everyone's feet to the fire. We leveraged the full weight of the dynamic to strong-arm contentious policy priorities through the legislature, and did it successfully. What resulted was the enactment of major progressive victories like a $15-per-hour minimum wage and the nation's strongest paid-family-leave plan, passed through a divided legislature. By refusing to give on the budget deadline, we were able to ban ghost guns, raise the age of criminal responsibility, and strengthen the statute of limitations on rape. And the legislature resented us for it. They preferred to pass legislation their own way, on their own time. Members were each individually elected and didn't like feeling as though they were being pushed around. Understandable, but we placed a higher premium on getting stuff done for the people and accepted hostility from the legislature in exchange.

"Melissa, I really think the legislative leaders need a call with the governor to discuss some of these big-ticket items," Shontell, my counterpart in the state senate, said on a hastily orchestrated conference call that afternoon.

"He doesn't have time," I responded, matter of fact. "Rob, Beth, and I have his proxy; anything the majority leader or speaker needs, we can answer."

Rob took the lead on the financials, Beth on the policy. I drove the political decisions on what we would ultimately fight to include or allow to drop out.

"We have a lot of work to do and only a few days to do it, so let's get our staff going," I said.

"Melissa, some of this policy stuff does not need to be done in the budget. We're stretched thin. Can't we all just agree to make a good-faith agreement to negotiate *after* we get through this?" LouAnn Ciccone, the assembly speaker's right-hand person, piped in.

"The governor is confident we can walk and chew gum," I answered, not giving an inch. "And guys," I paused, thinking back to two months earlier with Jim and the whiteboard, "that includes surrogacy."

Shontell called me back a few minutes later. "You really think we can get this done like this?" she asked, genuinely.

"We don't have a choice," I replied.

"LouAnn called after we hung up."

"Uh-huh?" I wasn't at all surprised to hear the two had had a side conference.

"She asked, 'Is the governor really going to make us do surrogacy?'"

I laughed. "Oh, yeah? What did you say?"

"I told her, 'No, the governor's busy with COVID, he's not going to make us . . . but Melissa is.'" The senate was with us on the issue, and Shontell was happy to let me ride roughshod on this one.

"You're damn right," I said, my resolve hardened.

Three days later, the budget passed. It included paid sick leave, a first-of-its-kind domestic-terrorism law, a ban on flavored e-cigarettes, and—after three decades of failed attempts—legalized surrogacy.

In the grand scheme of things, with the feeling that the world could be on the brink of collapse, it was a small, fleeting moment. But knowing that, because of us, same-sex couples and reproductively challenged women would have the opportunity to have children of their own, I felt a rush of genuine pride and a sense of accomplishment. It was the kind of moment that made everything else worth it. Many legislators were livid; they felt we used the situation to force their hand, and they were right. On top of that, the legislature had no role in the state's COVID response, and many members were resentful about the positive attention the governor was getting for his leadership.

As New York quickly became the global epicenter of COVID, all eyes turned to Governor Cuomo. He became de facto commander in chief. The entire nation looked to him for facts and honesty, including acknowledging when there were things he didn't know. Within days, he brought the full weight of our team to bear, constructing field hospitals and drive-through testing sites, and hardening the state's disparate hospital system. He stood up to Republican President Donald Trump *and* Democratic leadership in Congress.

And for the first time in his forty years of public service, Andrew Cuomo let down his guard and invited the public into his private life. He introduced them to his children, bringing them to press conferences and disclosing private conversations between them. He shared the fears he had about his mother and how he missed his father. He was vulnerable and strong at the same time. Commentators from MSNBC to Fox News gushed about him, comparing his leadership to that of Winston Churchill and FDR during World War II. The term *Cuomosexual* became part of the vernacular. And our daily press briefings and PowerPoints became must-see TV, not only in New York, but nationwide and around the globe. He had been the same governor for ten years, but all of a sudden, with the world in crisis, he was a hero . . . and a bona fide celebrity. Our mailroom flooded with fan mail from women wanting to date him. *Rolling Stone* put him on the cover (a mantle generally reserved for actual rockstars), *People* magazine published articles on his "famous family," and *GQ* dissected his wardrobe.

Cuomo's star power didn't go unnoticed by network brass, either. He was *the* top get in terms of guests for everyone from talk-show hosts like Ellen DeGeneres and Trevor Noah to network and cable news broadcasters. And while he went on with almost all of them, even Fox News' own Sean Hannity, no one brought more attention and fanfare than when CNN suspended its internal protocols to allow Chris Cuomo to interview his own brother.

The dynamic between our office and CNN was always complicated. Allison Gollust, their director of communications, had been Cuomo's director of communications first and was my immediate predecessor. The first time I had met her in person was in 2014, roughly a year and a half into her tenure at CNN, when she attended a State of the State strategy meeting on the thirty-eighth floor of our Third Avenue office. The governor had wanted to include members of our "kitchen cabinet," which was mainly made up of former senior staff and campaign advisers. The meeting she attended included a number of his former press staff, including my then-boyfriend and future husband, Matt. Anytime Allison raised a point in the meeting, the governor would defer to her judgment. She had a direct line to him in a way that no other media flack in the nation did, and when she spoke, he listened. The two had maintained a strong relationship in the years since, meeting occasionally for a meal and texting or talking on the phone about politics and current affairs and their other common interest: the governor's younger brother, Chris.

She and I did not have a relationship. Allison didn't need to go through me to get to my boss the way that other networks producers or bookers did. When she wanted him on a show, she would text him directly, and I would hear about it on the back end. If our press office or I wanted to pitch something to CNN and reached out to her, our overtures were often met with silence. It was a one-way street, and I resented it.

Complicating matters was Allison's boss, Jeff Zucker—also Chris's boss. Jeff and Allison had worked together for decades, were incredibly close, and were known as an unstoppable team. I only met Jeff a handful of times. Cuomo did not like to leave the state, a trait he inherited from his father, who believed the job of governing was done from New York, not gallivanting around the world like other ambitious politicians. As a result, the rare occasions when we did travel would be confined to a twenty-four-hour window—the diplomatic equivalent of speed dating. On one of those whirlwind jaunts, we traveled to Israel, spending less than sixteen hours on the ground. Upon arriving at the King David Hotel, our home base for the day, we bumped into Allison in the lobby. She and Jeff were there for CNN. The four of us had dinner that night in full view of the Albany reporters who had traveled there to cover our trip.

Jeff Zucker was known as a media mastermind. He had an uncanny ability to understand what the American people wanted to see, and where Zucker went, ratings usually followed. He was known as the wunderkind of the *Today Show* and was blamed for Donald Trump's rise, having masterminded NBC's reality show *The Apprentice* in 2004, making Trump a household name. After Trump's presidential campaign launch, Zucker was accused by other candidates of giving Trump an outsized platform on CNN at the expense of equal time and impartiality. But, in 2015, Zucker saw in Trump what he had seen eleven years earlier: blockbuster ratings.

A rising star in the world of TV news, Chris Cuomo joined CNN in 2013 and quickly rose from field correspondent to host of the network's prime-time morning show, *New Day*. That December, the nation's eyes turned to New York. A Metro-North train traveling from Poughkeepsie to Grand Central Station derailed in the Bronx, tragically killing four people and injuring sixty-one others. The train, traveling more than three times the posted speed limit, jumped the track as it entered a curve, causing a number of cars to flip over. It was a gruesome scene of twisted metal and carnage, the deadliest train accident in New York City in over twenty years, happening just days after Thanksgiving. It was the type of incident that a New York City mayor would have been the face of, but Mayor Bloomberg was away at his weekend home in Bermuda when the accident occurred.

As was his instinct, Governor Cuomo dispatched to the scene immediately and camped out there with the head of the Metropolitan Transportation Authority for days to oversee the response and brief the public. That Monday morning, as requests poured in from national and local media, Allison reached out to the governor with two questions: Could he appear on *New Day* for an interview with Chris, and could he do it *before* he went on MSNBC's *Morning Joe*. *Morning Joe* was *New Day*'s competitor in terms of their time slot, but not in terms of ratings. *New Day* was just starting out, while *Morning Joe* and its hosts, Mika Brzezinski and Joe Scarborough, were well established and had a loyal following; their viewership trounced CNN on a daily basis. There was no other scenario in which our press-savvy office would have ever contemplated such a move, but that morning we did. In response to our attempted bait and switch, MSNBC canceled our interview. Within hours of the first-ever Cuomo-on-Cuomo appearance, media critics pounced; *New York* magazine bluntly summed up the debacle with the headline: NO, CHRIS CUOMO SHOULD NOT HAVE INTERVIEWED HIS BROTHER, THE GOVERNOR. It was an annoying and unnecessary side-show for our office, but the fault didn't lie with us. Journalists laid blame at the feet of CNN and, more specifically, Chris Cuomo, who was put in the uncomfortable position of publicly defending the decision to do the interview and tap-dancing around what would be ethical or not.

The fallout led to CNN establishing a strict protocol to avoid future distractions: Chris would not interview the governor of New York, aka his big brother, a policy that remained strictly intact. That is, until March 11, 2020. That's when CNN changed its position, suspending the brother ban. In the three weeks that would follow, Chris's ratings grew 118 percent—a jump that would presumably be felt in ad revenue. While the official line cited the extraordinary circumstance of the pandemic, Jeff Zucker was chasing more than news: Andrew Cuomo was one of the most-watched and sought-after politicians in the world, and CNN wanted the ratings that came along with his celebrity. And they had an ace in their hand. One they kept playing over and over and over again.

At first, I didn't see a problem with the arrangement. We were in the middle of an unprecedented crisis. Every other rule was being suspended—why not this one? In fact, we didn't even discuss it as an issue at the beginning; it happened the same way everything else did then—on the fly. And the public loved it. In the absence of being able to be with their own families, they got to watch one on TV. The interviews were factual and informative but included brotherly banter and teasing, each ending with three words: "I love you." Members of the media naturally inclined to criticize such a spectacle acknowledged its place in the moment. "The Cuomos aren't just feeling your pain. You're feeling theirs," wrote Ben Smith in the *New York Times* in early April. Zucker didn't just approve the arrangement, he leaned into it, telling the *Times*, "You get trust from authenticity and relatability and vulnerability. That's what the brothers Cuomo are giving us right now."

While things may have appeared rosy to viewers at home, behind the scenes the arrangement began to cause agita and became a source of consternation between the governor and me.

"Chris's producer reached out to Dani," I informed the governor one afternoon, my voice skeptical.

"What did she say?" Cuomo asked, without looking up.

"They want you on Chris's show tonight—top of the hour," I responded, winding up to prosecute my argument.

"Okay," the governor responded coolly.

"I don't think you should go on tonight," I said.

"What's the issue?" the governor asked. In the beginning, the governor had enjoyed the spots, a fun respite for him from the usual COVID crisis management.

"The schtick was great at the beginning—comforting even," I allowed, "but it's too much now. The jokes, the back-and-forth." I paused. "At some point soon, the press is going to blow the whistle on this. Let's end it before they do."

"Did someone say something?"

"We're not at a critical mass or anything," I continued. "I can just see where this is going to go, and it's not going to be good for you, and it's going to be even worse for Chris."

"Okay, I hear you," Cuomo said. "I don't know that I necessarily agree, but let's take a pass for tonight and see how it goes. Let Dani tell the producer we can't make it happen."

When I called to let Dani know we wouldn't be going on, she was relieved. She was in the uncomfortable position of having to take incoming from people at other networks who were understandably frustrated by the clear favoritism we were showing CNN. Five minutes later, my phone rang. It was Allison Gollust.

"Hey, Melissa—Allison here. You guys are doing a really great job!" I knew where this was going.

"Thanks, Allison. How can I help you?" I asked.

"So, listen, Chris's producer just pinged me. Apparently, Dani said the gov isn't available to go on tonight?"

"Yeah, sorry. We're scheduled to do Maddow tonight, and I think doing Chris the same night will cause problems, so it's not going to work," I responded.

"Well, the problem is we were counting on him for the top of the show, and not doing it will create a headache for us," she continued.

"I texted the gov about it earlier today, and he didn't indicate there'd be a problem." Of course she had.

"Yeah, about that," I replied, my voice growing firmer. "Look, Allison, the governor has a lot going on at the moment, and it's counterproductive to text him about these things directly. He doesn't know his own schedule a lot of the time, and there are a lot of moving pieces and balls up in the air. If it's possible, I'd really appreciate it if we went through the normal channels. You can text me or your producers can reach out to Dani, but going through him is not the best way to do this."

"Uh-huh," she said, her tone clipped. "You are completely screwing us, Melissa, but I got it. Thanks so much. Talk to you soon."

She hung up.

Message sent and received.

Five minutes later, Stephanie let me know that the governor was looking for me. In the short time since our call, he had received his own call from Allison Gollust. She was pissed. She believed that her text to him earlier in the day meant that he was confirmed for that night's show, and his pulling out now would cause big problems for CNN producers.

"I'm sorry, Governor, but too bad," was my response. "Dani told her producer no. I told her no. That's the end of the story."

The governor looked down at his BlackBerry. "Now Zucker is calling me."

"Seriously?!" Last time I looked, we had a chief of staff, and it wasn't Jeff Zucker.

"Look, Melissa, I know I told you I'd take a pass, but . . . ," Cuomo waffled. "I don't want this to become a thing."

"Your giving in and going on is what's going to ensure it becomes a thing," I protested.

"Melissa, he is Chris's *boss*," he answered, resigned. There are few purer relationships than the one I've witnessed between Andrew and Chris Cuomo. Andrew is twelve years older than Chris, and their larger-than-life father, former governor Mario Cuomo, was very busy working when they were growing up in Queens. What resulted was more of a father-son relationship between Andrew and Chris than a traditional sibling bond. They love each other and support one another unconditionally. But more than that, they protect each other. And they put that relationship above all else.

"I heard your point, but this is what it is right now," the governor decided. He was done arguing with me. "Let Dani know I'll do it tomorrow. Set it up with the producer." Conversation over. Point, set, match to Allison Gollust. From then on, the precedent was set in stone. If they wanted the governor on air, CNN would reach out initially through our press office, but they wouldn't take "no" or even "maybe" for an answer. Anything less than a solid commitment and either Allison or Jeff would go running straight to the governor. I typically found out about the arrangement afterward, and would then coordinate with Allison on the back end.

The governor appeared on Chris's show eleven times between March 11 and the day of our last daily press conference, triple the number of guest shots he gave almost any other news show in the country. The interviews came to an end after our last daily press briefing in June, when CNN wanted the governor on the air and I vehemently disagreed. Chris had grown exasperated by the endless debates while his show lineup hung in the balance, so we collectively decided to end the interviews.

In the fall, when the governor was trying to bring attention to what he believed was an inadequate vaccine rollout plan, he asked me to reach out to see if CNN would resurrect the interviews one more time; but at that point he was no longer the TV ratings giant he'd been, and Allison took a pass.

I was learning myself how weird and mercurial fame could be. Those of us who usually worked behind the scenes in the governor's office—nameless, faceless staff members—suddenly became recognized household names as we appeared beside the governor at daily briefings. To my astonishment, fan mail flooded in for us as well as for Cuomo.

People wrote to me as if they knew me. They sent homemade COVID masks, scented candles, Starbucks gift cards, and nail polish. They commented on my recall of facts and asked which designers made my dresses. Little girls wrote that they looked up to me, while middle-aged women penned that they respected me. For a scrawny kid from Rochester, it was both surreal and overwhelming.

At the end of March, I received a phone call from Steve Greenberg, a pollster for Siena College. Steve would typically call and give me a heads-up about the governor's ratings before they were released to the public. That day, Steve told me to sit down: In the last four weeks, Cuomo's approval ratings had soared from 44 percent to 71 percent.

I could hardly wait to call my father and share the news. His sanguine reaction wasn't what I expected.

"Well, Melissa," he said, "he's leading the world through a once-in-a-century pandemic, and he's doing an incredible job."

"I know, but I was shocked to see it confirmed that way in the data," I continued. "Anyway, Dad, I have to go, but I'll call you later."

"Wait, Melissa, don't hang up," he said.

"What's up, Dad?"

"The numbers are great, and he deserves it, and your team deserves the affirmation, but remember the lesson of George Bush."

"George Bush?" I asked, unsure of where he was going. Or even which George Bush he meant, for that matter.

"Look at his approval numbers right after we won the Persian Gulf War."

Oh, that George Bush. Operation Desert Storm. Saddam Hussein, line in the sand.

"Dad, I really don't have time to talk about a war from thirty years ago right now."

"Melissa, just look at them when you have a minute," Dad insisted.

"Okay, but let's assume I don't have time to do that today—what's your point?" I decided to humor him.

"My point is, what goes up, must come down."

I gave him the brush-off—"Got it, Dad, gotta go now, love you"—and hung up.

Was he kidding? *This* is what he was saying to me? I shook my head in fond disbelief and went back to my whirlwind.

Every minute of my workday was a flurry of activity that kept my mind so busy that I couldn't absorb the human impact of what was happening around us. That changed in the early-evening hours.

That was when I would call the families of health-care workers who had died.

When the first nurse died of COVID in New York, I called the president of the state's nurses' union, Pat Kane. Pat was from Staten Island and had worked as an emergency-room nurse for over thirty years. She had seen it all and was as tough as they came. I told Pat how sorry I was and asked for the name and phone number of the next of kin.

"Melissa, if you're going to call one, you're going to have to call them all," said Pat.

"Yes, I know, and I plan to," I answered.

"Melissa," I could hear Pat begin to tear up, "there are going to be too many."

I promised her that, no matter the number of souls we lost, I would do my best to call each family. And in the following weeks, I did. I would call and, on behalf of Governor Cuomo, convey condolences and tell them that their family member was a hero and how grateful the entire state was for their sacrifice. And then, after I hung up, I would close the door to my office, lie on the floor, and sob softly with my hand over my mouth, hoping no one else would hear.

CHAPTER 6

The Art of the Impossible

By the end of the third week of March, it was clear that we were in for the long haul. Exactly how long, we weren't sure—no one was.

With every passing day, I felt more isolated and alone. Worried about me, my father's wife, Maureen, began ordering vitamins, dropping off yogurt, blueberries, and granola, and, when my clothes had completely run out, dispatching to Target to buy me underwear, socks, tank tops, and long-sleeved shirts. Matt FaceTimed me, riffling through my Brooklyn Heights closet to pack up dozens of outfits for our press conferences, then handing them off to a New York City staffer who agreed to drive them up to me. At that point, my conversations with Matt were cordial, but superficial and rare. And there was no end in sight. Having to return night after night to the Renaissance—a room that was faintly lit by bizarre purple neon lights—was rock-bottom. I was depressed. My weight had dropped from 128 to 119 pounds; my face was pale and gaunt. Little things like a video message from my eight-year-old niece, Ashley, would send tears streaming down my face. And seemingly menial tasks became massively inconvenient: There was no way to do laundry. Or eat a proper meal—the ability to order food through room service was limited and only available during short, specific windows of time, which rarely coincided with my hours. Unsure of what was causing the virus to spread, I asked that the hotel not send housekeeping staff into my room. I purchased Clorox to scour the bathroom myself. Towels and clean sheets would be left outside my room. And in the rare instance that someone else happened to be riding in the same elevator, I would spend the next several days panicking that the person had had COVID and that I was somehow going to give it to the governor. I was too wary and dispirited to feign optimism.

"What's wrong?" the governor asked one early morning.

"Everything," I replied. "I hate this."

"Can you be more specific?"

"I hate the hotel. I hate that I can't figure out how to wash my clothes. I'm hungry because by the time I get there at night they are no longer serving food. I irrationally freak out when I come into contact with anyone there. I can't see Jess and the girls, or my brother and his fiancée, my parents—let alone stay with them. I don't even have a 'pod.' I'm just . . ."—I paused, fighting a wave of self-pity—"I'm just alone."

"Melissa, everyone is alone right now," Cuomo said, matter-of-factly.

"No, that's not true," I objected. "Jim goes home to Jenny and the kids. You go home to the girls and Larry and Matt . . ." The governor's three adult daughters—twenty-five-year-old twins Cara and Mariah, and twenty-two-year-old Michaela—had moved in weeks earlier when COVID first hit. Former secretary to the governor Larry Schwartz and the governor's cousin Matt were staying there while they volunteered on the effort as well. (Matt Cuomo, a lawyer on Long Island, was pitching in on building out hospital capacity; it was truly a family affair.)

"I know this is hard," Cuomo continued. "But you're tough. You can do this."

"Okay, yup," I cut him off—I was done engaging in the conversation. He could check pep talk off his list now. "Anyway, I have a bunch of calls to do."

Later that day, Stephanie stepped into my office, closing the door behind her.

"Okay, so we're moving into the mansion," she announced.

"Huh?"

"I just spoke with the governor, and he's worried about one of us potentially contracting COVID and then bringing it to the office," she said. "Also, given the hours we're working, it doesn't make sense for me to be driving back and forth forty minutes to Saratoga twice a day. We're going to quarantine over there."

"Don't we think that's a little bizarre?" I asked. How would this work? I had stayed in the mansion once before, in 2013, during a weekend senior-staff retreat. After dinner, the governor excused himself, and everyone politely said good night, turning in for the evening. Everyone except Steph, Josh Vlasto, Matt, and me. Instead, when the coast was clear, the four of us raided the kitchen for cheap beer, New York State wine, and ice cream, hanging out until well after midnight, savoring what we believed would be a once-in-a-lifetime experience.

"Yes, Melissa, the whole thing is bizarre," Steph conceded. "But staying at the mansion is actually not that crazy. With Larry and Matt (Cuomo) and the kids there, it really is just functioning as a hotel at this point. We will have a place to do our laundry, and there's a gym, so we can work out every once in a while, and at the very least, we know we'll get fed twice a day. It's two blocks from the capitol, so the commute couldn't be more convenient. Plus, we won't have to be alone. We'll be together. We can vent and have a glass of wine and decompress at the end of the day."

I was convinced.

The next day, I packed up my things from the Renaissance, and Steph and I moved into the governor's mansion. Room assignments were worked out with Carol Radke, the head of the household. Carol had worked in the mansion since before Mario Cuomo was governor and both knew and treated the family like family, taking extra-special care of the family matriarch, Matilda Cuomo, when she visited. The mansion is a massive old Queen Anne–style Victorian home spanning over ten thousand square feet, complete with turrets and a wraparound porch. The first floor functions mainly as an event space, where the governor hosted countless receptions and holiday parties during his time in office. It has thirty-foot ceilings, a great hall, a formal dining room, and a drawing room with a portrait of FDR hanging over the fireplace. Decorated with chairs from George Washington's inauguration and FDR's wheelchair, it feels more like a museum than a home. Upstairs is the governor's private office, a sitting room, and twelve bedrooms.

I moved into a suite named for Princess Beatrix of the Netherlands, who slept in it during a visit to Albany sixty years earlier. The room was feminine and stately at the same time and had a long history of hosting dignitaries, from Harry Truman to Albert Einstein. It boasted a large bedroom and a separate sitting room with its own fireplace. There was an en suite bathroom, multiple closets to hang my perpetually wrinkled clothing in, and an antique vanity.

The mansion staff was paired down to the bare minimum to prevent any potential COVID spread: Carol and her assistant, Sherry; Tom, the cook; and Steve, the mansion director. They were asked not to interact with anyone outside of their immediate households and every morning would arrive by 7:00 a.m. to have their temperature checked by a member of the Department of Health staff.

In those early days, every minute mattered, and it showed in my new bizarre daily routine. I would get up between 3:45 and 4:30 a.m., check emails, review the COVID numbers for the day before that had hit my inbox overnight, go to the pool-house gym to go for a run, then shower and throw on jeans and a sweater. Steph and I would then meet in the kitchen, make iced coffee, do our own temperature checks, and head to the capitol, almost always arriving before 7:00 a.m. I would show up with my hair sopping wet and tied up in a bun, and blow-dry it later in a bathroom connected to the outer office, waiting until the very last minute to throw on a dress for the day's press conference; the minute the presser was wrapped, I was back in jeans and white Converse sneakers.

The governor typically rolled in around 7:15 a.m. In the early days, Cuomo would work until around 6:30, then return home to have dinner with his daughters—a sacred time that helped to keep him level and sane—before either returning to the capitol or spending the rest of the evening working from his office on the second floor of the mansion. Steph and I typically stayed in the office and went to the mansion later, decamping to the pool house for food left for us there by Carol or Sherry. They would leave Larry's dinner for him in the kitchen, knowing that he would work religiously until 11:00 p.m. or midnight at the capitol.

We officially had our pod. It wasn't my family, but during those dark, lonely days, we became a family.

If politics is the art of the possible, dealing with COVID was the art of making the impossible possible.

At that point, in the early days of April, hospitalizations and positivity were still sky-high; the lagged effect of months of COVID invisibly running unchecked across New York State was still in its early stages. And the fear was palpable. Everyone knew someone who had gotten COVID, a reality that hit the governor's own family when Chris got sick and was relegated to living in his basement, where he continued to host his CNN show. I had a scare of my own weeks earlier when a client of my father's died of COVID mere days after the two had been in a small conference room for a meeting together. Not only was my father a diabetic, setting off a wave of fear for his health, I had been staying with him at the time and, by extension, potentially exposing the governor to COVID.

Each press conference would begin the same way, by laying out the previous day's numbers. And each day they got worse and worse. By the end of the first week in April, we reached the apex: 779 deaths reported and 18,079 hospitalized. As the numbers began to plateau in the days after, we were hopeful that New York on PAUSE had worked and that, because of New Yorkers' discipline, we had begun to flatten the curve. The only way to ensure that progress would continue was if everyone doubled down on the strategy. And we didn't exist in a vacuum. While we were urging New Yorkers to stay the course, Trump was telling people that COVID would magically be gone by Easter. The mixed messaging was counterproductive, but for the most part, Trump's voice was irrelevant in New York.

At one press conference, the governor conveyed the urgency of the moment in five soul-stirring words: "Every number is a face."

When the governor asked New Yorkers to stay home, we weren't sure what the reaction was going to be. We weren't asking people to go to war—we were asking them to isolate, but, in many ways, the human instinct to fight is more natural than being alone. Eleven days into New York on PAUSE, our worst fears were put to rest: Everyone listened. The steady stream of information the governor disseminated at our daily briefings, combined with the direct emotional appeal to take the deadly virus seriously, had worked. The entire state of New York was as still as a churchyard.

"Give the people the facts," Cuomo would say again and again, "and they'll do the right thing."

His trust in the collective wisdom and goodness of New Yorkers was proven right in the empty sidewalks of Rockefeller Center, the silent tunnels beneath Grand Central, the vacant glass towers of Wall Street. All at once, it was as if the city that never sleeps had taken an Ambien and gone into hibernation.

By the middle of the first week of April, all of the major consulting firms and academic institutions were projecting a spike in hospitalizations and intubations in New York City. Based on their calculations, New York would need up to 140,000 hospital beds and approximately 18,000 ventilators. At that time, the entire New York hospital system had 53,000 beds and about 3,000 available ventilators. There was no sugarcoating the situation: if these numbers held, the hospital system would collapse, and people would die because we wouldn't have the number of beds or ventilators necessary to keep up with the patient population. We didn't need to imagine a scenario where this could happen; all anyone needed to do was turn on the news and watch as the nightmare played out across the Atlantic, where overrun emergency rooms and lack of equipment resulted in unnecessary deaths. New Yorkers caught a glimpse of what could come when Elmhurst, a 545-bed public hospital overseen by de Blasio's administration in Queens, neared total collapse. Reports of an ill-equipped and badly understaffed, overrun emergency room, combined with chilling images of refrigerated trucks parked outside to hold the bodies of the dead, illustrated what we were confronting. And it was not a drill.

"It's apocalyptic," declared a general medicine resident at the hospital.

New York State has a combined 213 public, private, and independent hospitals statewide, each operating as its own fiefdom. They had never worked together to coordinate patient intake, staff, or resources. The only way we would have a shot at managing the crisis was if that changed, fast. The governor called Larry Schwartz, Dr. Zucker, and me into his conference room.

"Why am I reading that people are dying because of capacity issues at Elmhurst, while there are thousands of free beds in other hospitals nearby?" he asked, exasperated.

"They don't talk to each other," Larry explained matter-of-factly. "There's no centralized coordination system to ensure individual hospitals aren't overwhelmed."

"Well, there will be now," the governor said.

Within days, the governor and Larry convened the heads of every hospital across the state to launch Surge and Flex, essentially one statewide, coordinated public health system. Hospitals would be mandated to report daily into one centralized portal the number of available beds, staffing numbers, and available equipment. A war room set up on the second floor of the capitol in Albany monitored and analyzed the daily numbers, allowing us visibility into where shortages would occur so resources could be quickly shifted between nearby hospitals to manage it. The governor issued an executive order, meaning participation was not optional. But hardening the hospital system was far from the only challenge we were confronting.

Weeks earlier, the governor had led the charge to pressure Trump into engaging in a federal response, first appealing privately in a number of phone calls with the president, asking Trump to deploy the national stockpile and mobilize personnel to build field hospitals. When that fell on deaf ears, Cuomo tried a different strategy.

"I'm going to get his attention the only effective way possible," he announced one day, handing me an op-ed he had drafted. "I called James Bennett at the *New York Times*. Ask Dani to follow up. This will get Trump's attention," he predicted. The piece ran the next day under the headline: ANDREW CUOMO TO PRESIDENT TRUMP: MOBILIZE THE MILITARY TO HELP FIGHT CORONAVIRUS.

But we heard nothing from the White House. Twenty-four hours later, Cuomo had a new plan: "I want to go on every single show that will take me as quickly as possible," he said. Around that time, Trump became convinced that Democrats were going to abandon Biden and instead select Cuomo to run against him in the fall. That perception devolved into an obsession that guided his posture toward New York through-out every moment of the pandemic. Cuomo sensed it and responded accordingly to get Trump to act.

"Okay, I'll work with the comms team," I answered, making notes on the legal pad in front of me. Trump was a rabid consumer of news, and the governor knew it. If anything was going to get his attention, this would be it.

One of the shows he did that night was Chris's on CNN. He knew it would get more attention than any other platform, and attention was exactly what he was seeking. He hit Trump with a two-by-four, calling the federal response anemic.

> This has to be a national effort. There is no country that has done this that didn't make it a national effort. . . . You look at the national headlines today, every state doing their own thing. . . . It's confusing. It's chaos. They don't know which way to go.

The appearance infuriated Trump, who called the next morning, apoplectic, his voice raised and animated. The governor countered by pledging to tamp down the rhetoric if the president would get in the game and help. He then promised to go further.

"If you work with me to get us what we need, I have no problem praising your efforts," he offered, agreeing to start immediately at that morning's press conference.

"What are you doing?" I asked, exasperated. "You are like Lucy with the football with this guy. You cannot work with him. It's impossible. He's impossible."

"He has FEMA, the Army Corp of Engineers, and the Department of Homeland Security, and we have nothing. So humor me while I try to figure this out, would you?" he responded.

He called the team into his conference room to start the press briefing. A few minutes in, he held true to his word,

> I spoke to the president this morning again. He is ready, willing, and able to help. I've been speaking with members of his staff late last night, early this morning. We need their help, especially on the hospital capacity issue. We need FEMA. FEMA has tremendous resources. When I was at HUD, I worked with FEMA. I know what they can do. I know what the Army Corps of engineers can do. They have a capacity that we simply do not have. I said to the president, who is a New Yorker, who I've known for many, many years—I put my hand out in partnership—I want to work together 100 percent. I need your help.
>
> I want your help. And New Yorkers will do everything they can to be good partners with the federal government. I think the president was 100 percent sincere in saying that he wanted to work together in partnership, in a spirit of cooperation. I can tell you the actions he has taken, evidence that his team has been on it. I know a team when they're on it, and I know

a team when they're not on it; his team is on it. They've been responsive late at night, early in the morning, and they've thus far been doing everything that they can do, and I want to say thank you and I want to say that I appreciate it and they will have nothing but cooperation and partnership from the state of New York.

Within ten minutes of the briefing, Trump called back. He would immediately dispatch the Army Corps of Engineers and the *Comfort*, a 1,000-bed US Navy hospital ship to, in theory, help (the ship initially refused to accept any COVID patients and issued strict guidelines, including a list of forty-nine medical conditions that would exclude a patient from admittance to the ship). The feds would help us transform the Javits Convention Center on Eleventh Avenue in Manhattan into a 2,500-bed field hospital staffed by medical professionals from the military and National Guard. It was a step in the right direction on hospital capacity, but resources were still a massive problem.

Making it worse was the fact that the federal government wasn't coordinating outreach efforts, which pitted every state in the country against each other in the competition for scarce supplies, turning the fight for survival into a cruelly politicized version of *The Hunger Games*. The governor convened a small group of trusted aides and conveyed a simple message: "Find ventilators and get them here now." We were to follow every lead, wherever they were in the world. If they were in Asia or the Middle East, we were to find wealthy CEOs with private planes who would fly them in. If someone was selling them, we were to vet the company and buy them. Fast. Pre-COVID, ventilators cost about $5,000 each. At the height of the pandemic, that price soared to $50,000 or more. It was an international arms race.

"The cost is irrelevant," the governor instructed. "You can't place a price on the life of someone's mother or father or child, and we aren't going to."

As we scrambled to track down ventilators, the governor had an idea: In the short term, we could shift resources from hospitals upstate that currently had capacity down to New York City, where the impending crisis was expected within days. We were one New York, and we would pool our state's resources to save every life possible. The emergency powers granted to the governor by the legislature in the early days of COVID would allow us to direct private hospitals to turn over their resources—or face penalties of fines or even loss of operating licenses if they refused. It felt odd that we would need a threat to ensure cooperation, but with some hospital CEOs, we did. When one hospital operator in Buffalo—Kaleida Health—refused to comply with the order, the governor got on the phone to deliver a message: "I will personally pull your operating license." In the weeks since the pandemic began, it was the angriest I had seen him. And he meant every word. Hours later, Kaleida was on board.

At a daily briefing early that April, the governor announced the upstate emergency health directive to shift unused ventilators down to New York City, and almost instantly, the backlash began—not from New Yorkers, who by all accounts supported and understood the effort—but from politicians, mainly Republicans who represented areas across upstate. Maybe it shouldn't have surprised me after going on two decades in the foxholes of partisan politics, but it did.

The people of New York had come together in the weeks since the COVID crisis started in a way that we hadn't seen since 9/11. But now, it seemed, politicians were seeking to chip away at that feeling of unity and togetherness, more intent on divide than conquer. From that bitterness came the launch of the Upstate Lives Matter campaign in response to the governor's health order to shift ventilators downstate.

The campaign sought to weaponize a long-standing divide between upstate and downstate New Yorkers. The ill-will predated COVID by fifty years, at least.

When people around the country talk about New York, they are more likely than not referring to New York City, and that brings with it a certain resentment from people living north of Rockland and Westchester counties. Historically, upstaters felt as though New York City and Long Island got more of everything: more money, more infrastructure, more attention . . . and more fanfare. The "Upstate Lives Matter" campaign sought to exploit this well-established divide. At the worst possible time.

Enter, Elise.

Elise Stefanik was a congresswoman representing what is referred to as the North Country, starting at the base of the Adirondack Mountains and stretching up to the border of Canada. She had long been a moderate Republican, rejecting partisanship for partisanship sake and reaching across the aisle to find reasonable solutions to big problems. That was, however, until Donald Trump became president and the politics of the Republican Party shifted dramatically. Stefanik would become known as Trump's most ardent supporter, subscribing to his conspiracy theories and defending him at all costs. Later that blind loyalty would earn her the third-most-senior position in Congress, as her party replaced the Never-Again Trumper Liz Cheney with a woman who was now defining her entire political identity as a satellite of Planet Trump.

But before all of that, I knew her as "Little Elise."

Our relationship dated back to 1995, when I was a new student at the Albany Academy for Girls. My father had just left his job as political director for the Public Employees Federation, one of the largest white-collar unions in the United States, to become a partner at a New York City–based lobbying firm, Bolton St. Johns. The move meant fewer hours and a significant increase in our family's income. Almost overnight, our lives changed. We joined the country club, started taking ski trips, and learned to golf. It was then that I was transferred from public school in Saratoga Springs to the Albany Academy for Girls, the oldest all-girls day prep school in the country. At the academy, foreign language instruction began in the third grade, with nine-year-olds required to take French. Public school didn't begin teaching foreign languages until seventh grade, leaving me woefully behind my classmates when I transferred in eighth grade. As a result, I was put into a French class with kids two years younger. That was when I first met Elise. A spunky, incredibly smart, and very obviously driven student, Elise had transferred to the academy a few years earlier to escape the relentless physical and emotional bullying she was experiencing at an all-girls Catholic school. The two of us weren't close, but we clicked immediately.

As a new girl eager to fit in, I jumped at the chance to run when elections were held for middle-school student council. In the past, classmates warned, all of the same girls won. This year was going to be different: Elise and I joined forces with a group of girls coming together to form a new slate. We coined the campaign slogan—"Fresh faces"— and cut a mutually beneficial deal: A cross-endorsement that would set up the path to our individual political careers. We both won.

Elise was really my little brother Joey's friend; they were in the same grade. I looked at her as much more of a little sister, and while she and I maintained a casual friendship throughout high school, after graduation we lost touch. That is, until 2006. That was the year that I moved to Washington, DC, to work for Democratic Congresswoman Nydia Velázquez. In my first week there, while attending a party in Georgetown, I looked up to see none other than that spunky sixth-grader from so many years ago. Elise and I instantly reconnected, in spite of the fact that she was working as an assistant for the "enemy" in the Bush White House.

People would ask how Elise and I could even speak to each other, given our political differences. But we enjoyed getting together to talk about our long days, complain about our hectic schedules, and catch up over Thursday night TV when we were both too tired and overworked to either complain or talk. Over the years, we attended each other's weddings and went to one another for professional and personal advice. When I was named secretary to the governor and the state's GOP chairman issued a statement calling me a "thug," Elise bucked her own party to defend me in the press. When a reporter from *Time* magazine was writing a long piece on her, I helped Elise strategize on how best to respond. And when national media was circling with rumors that Elise and Pete Buttigieg had gone on a date and made out once at Harvard, I was the one she called to do shuttle diplomacy with the Buttigieg campaign on how to handle press inquiries. Our shared experiences and the challenges we faced as young women in a male-dominated industry created a bond that time, distance, and ideological differences were able to transcend. We had managed to tiptoe through a decade and a half of land mines of political differences . . . with one exception.

After a night out in Adams Morgan in 2007, Elise came back to my apartment with me and my then-boyfriend, Elliot, for a nightcap. Elliot brought up the subject of gay marriage. At the time, major Democratic political players, including Barack Obama, had yet to embrace the notion, instead endorsing civil unions. Elise agreed with that position, which, to be fair, was progressive for a Republican then. I had very strong opinions on the topic. I had had a number of gay friends in college whom I had seen struggle coming out, and I could never wrap my mind around the double standard. I knew Elise had close gay friends, too.

"Look, Missy, I'm not saying that I'm against the gay community or think they should be prejudged in any way, but marriage is a religious union, and the state should not dictate to the church what they should do," she said, prosecuting her argument.

"Elise, what are you talking about? Marriage is by definition a contract granted by the state. How the Catholic Church or any other religious group feels about it is completely irrelevant," I countered.

The argument went round and round, with Elise standing her ground and me getting more emotional and heated. Finally, it reached a fever pitch, and I snapped.

"What is wrong with you? Don't you get that what you're basically endorsing is as backward as segregationist laws from the 1960s? Your position basically says that your friends—your gay friends—aren't as good as the rest of us. That they shouldn't be treated the same way as the rest of us in the eyes of the law," I charged, my voice rising. "It's disgusting, Elise!"

"You know what, Missy, I don't have to sit here and take this!" Elise was crying by then. She stood up, frantically looking for her coat. I began to apologize, bargaining with her to stay and, with the help of Elliot, after a few intense minutes of cajoling, succeeded. After that, we agreed to steer clear of hot partisan topics, and our relationship remained peacefully intact.

That is, until Trump was elected. It was around that time that someone else was elected, too: Democratic Socialist Alexandria Ocasio-Cortez's stunning defeat of Joe Crowley catapulted her from unknown waitress to media darling overnight. Up until that point, Elise had been the youngest-ever female elected to Congress, a historic distinction she was incredibly proud of. When AOC was elected, Elise drafted an open letter in *USA Today* congratulating her on her victory, passing her the baton, and waxing about the importance of women in Congress lifting one another up, regardless of party. The gesture went unacknowledged.

"They're all so obsessed with her," Elise groused over dinner that February at the Chateau on the Lake, a restaurant down the street from my father's Lake George home.

"Who?" I asked, wondering if there was a specific *they* she had in mind.

"Everyone!" she proclaimed.

The undercurrent of her comments was rooted in jealousy. She disdained AOC's politics, but even more, she resented the attention she was receiving.

Eleven months later, I turned on the TV in my office. The House had brought a formal impeachment inquiry against Trump for allegedly leveraging military aid to pressure Ukraine into investigating Joe and Hunter Biden and for a conspiracy theory that Ukraine, not Russia, was behind interference in the 2016 presidential election. It was like stumbling across a weird reboot of *The Twilight Zone*, only it was on every

channel. Back when Trump had sought the GOP's presidential nomination, Elise had soundly rebuffed the notion of him representing her
party. She publicly criticized him on everything from his inflamma-
tory language on women and Muslims to his position on building a
border wall between the United States and Mexico. She called on him
to release his tax returns. But now, in the thick of the impeachment
drama, here she was, front and center with the media, day after day
doing Trump's bidding, quickly becoming the face of, and in a way
legitimizing, his defense.

"What is going on with her?" Matt asked one night over Thai takeout after a hearing.

"I don't get it—it's truly mind-boggling," I replied. He wasn't the
first person to ask my opinion of the situation, but he was the only person I was willing to have an honest conversation with about it. "She's so
much smarter than this. She has such a bright future. This is painful,"
I said.

"Well, why don't you say something?" he suggested. "You guys are
friends. You have an opinion about the situation."

"Yeah, but Elise and I haven't talked politics since the gay marriage
meltdown of 2007," I confided.

"Look, Melissa, you think she's making a mistake. Don't be hot
about it; just reach out from a place of concern. You know how this
world works. I'm sure she's surrounded by a bunch of yes men on her
staff. She'll hear you."

I slept on Matt's suggestion and, the next morning, decided to take
his advice. I picked up my phone and fired off a text to the effect of:

> I know we try to keep politics out of our friendship,
> but I've been watching the impeachment hearings
> and am concerned. You've worked so hard and
> achieved so much. I'm worried about the long-term
> reputational damage this will all have. I love you
> and wish you nothing but the best.

I wasn't sure how or if she would respond. Less than an hour later I got my answer:

> Thank you for your note. You should always feel like
> you can reach out to me.

Her performance at the impeachment hearings earned her public praise from Trump and a seat on Air Force One. Once she had a seat at the MAGA table, she leaned in hard, becoming one of Trump's staunchest defenders. She had spent her childhood outrunning bullies, but here she was surrounding herself with them, publicly worshipping the biggest bully of them all. And as she did, she became a media darling of Fox News and the *New York Post*. In a lot of ways, burrowing her way into Trump's good graces made Elise the AOC of the right. She was famous and on a fast track to party leadership. And that was that.

That is, until COVID and the afternoon that April when Rich Azzopardi, trusted adviser to the governor, asked for my take on a situation brewing with Upstate Lives Matter.

"Melissa, I need your gut," Rich implored, standing in my doorway. "It seems the upstate Republicans are not happy with the governor's ventilator mandate," he said.

"They know that people downstate could die if we don't get more ventilators there fast, right?" I pressed.

"Yes, I think they do in fact know that, but . . ."

"Are you kidding?" I asked in total disbelief. There were hospital patients literally fighting for every breath, and it was now a matter of debate whether to help them? "Are they really making this political?"

"Well, one person in particular," Rich continued. "I'll give you three guesses, but it should only take one."

"Tom Reed? Carl Paladino?"

"Your middle-school running mate. She launched the Upstate Lives Matters campaign and is on local TV saying that this administration doesn't care if upstate New Yorkers live or die, and that the governor is only sending upstate medical equipment to New York City because that's where the Democratic voting base is."

I was stunned. But more, I was hurt. Since Elise had taken on the role of Trump's top ally and obedient lapdog, she had changed her rhetoric toward Governor Cuomo. She began labeling him "the worst governor in America" and attacking him regularly on Twitter. I had tried to chalk it up to partisan politics and not to take it personally. But this was too far. How could she—my friend of twenty-five years—say those things? This administration didn't care if upstate New Yorkers lived or died? I grew up in upstate New York with Elise. My entire family lived upstate. Elise knew that. And our administration was working so hard, trying to save every possible life. She knew that, too. She couldn't possibly believe what she was saying.

That's when it hit me: She didn't believe what she was saying. This didn't have a thing to do with science or saving lives. Suddenly, I wasn't hurt anymore. I was livid.

"I know this is awkward, you two being friends and everything," Rich said, "but this feels beyond the pale."

"Rich, close my door."

Rich stepped into my office and closed the door behind him.

"No, Rich, close the door with you on the other side of it," I said. "I have to make a phone call to my old friend, Elise."

He barely had one foot out the door when I picked up my iPhone and scrolled to "Elise S," a number that had been unchanged and saved in my contacts for nearly two decades. Blind with rage, I listened as the phone rang.

"Missy?" Elise answered on the second ring.

"Elise, are you kidding with this?"

"I'm sorry, kidding you with what?" she asked, as if she didn't know.

"How could you say this administration—this governor—doesn't care if upstate New Yorkers live or die?"

"Missy, I have constituents, and if COVID reaches them, they need those ventilators."

"Yes, and if it looks like that is going to happen, we will shift resources back, but people in New York City could die now without them!" I shot back. "We are trying to save lives, and you're politicizing a pandemic. You have to retract that statement . . ."

Elise cut me off.

"I'm not retracting the statement. I don't work for you. I represent the people of my congressional district and . . ."

"Elise!" I snapped. "What are you doing? The governor represents those people, too. We represent the entire state! And you know we wouldn't do this unless we had to and that if, god forbid, COVID is a serious problem in the North Country, we will fight to save every life there, too."

"I said what I said, Missy," her tone now testy. "I'm not taking it back. This is my politics—it's different from yours . . ."

This time I cut her off, "Elise, this isn't about politics!"

"Oh, come on, Missy," she retorted.

"Who have you become?" I asked in disgust. "I am embarrassed to be associated with you."

"What?" Now she sounded genuinely hurt.

"Yes, you heard me," I wasn't backing down. "Do you know what it's like when people ask me how I could possibly be friends with you? The things you say. The way you defend Trump. How you behaved during the impeachment hearing. It's embarrassing."

"Well, I'm sorry to hear you say that, Missy," she said sincerely. "I'm proud to be associated with you."

"I'm a public servant, fighting a pandemic—you've become . . ."

"Become what?"

"A partisan hack."

"This conversation is over," she declared.

My finger was already on the disconnect button.

"You can say that again."

Politics had been driving the federal government from the beginning, but this was the first time I really felt it injected into COVID in New York. And it was the last time Elise and I ever spoke.

Not everyone subscribed to Elise's attempt to sow division. Shortly after our call, a representative from Pathways, a nursing home located just north of Albany, appeared on the news, announcing their intent to donate forty-five ventilators not currently in use to our effort. "We're here for New York State. We're doing our part and want to absolutely help," Will Wohltjen, Pathways' marketing director, declared. It was a beautiful, kind gesture and a resounding rejection of Elise's cynical tactic at the exact moment I needed it most.

It's difficult to describe how traumatizing those days were. Dr. Fauci, the CDC, and the WHO still did not know how the virus was spreading or how to stop it. No one knew if the virus could be transmitted by touch or live on surfaces and, if so, for how long. Testing was still painfully inadequate. Elective surgeries had been canceled to make way for additional capacity in hospitals. And while it was widely understood at that point that the people most susceptible to serious illness or death were the elderly and immunocompromised, there were instances of people in their teens and twenties who had contracted COVID and died. In New York City, images of mass graves being dug on Hart Island, a mile-long stretch of dirt off the Bronx, for the indigent whose families could not be found or afford a private funeral, were splashed across front pages of the tabloids. Each morning started with the same urgent imperative: every decision we made, every ventilator we tracked down, every makeshift hospital we built, could keep one more grave from being dug.

In the early weeks of April, we would fly by helicopter from Albany to New York City to hold press conferences. Every time, I was struck by the sight below of arguably the world's most-bustling metropolis replaced by abandoned blocks, peopled only by a scattering of essential workers—those we asked to run into the fire while everyone else stayed safe at home: police, transit workers, grocery store clerks, and health-care heroes. The cacophony of traffic and street vendors and tourists and aspiring troubadours was replaced by a deafening silence, pierced only by the sound of ambulance sirens. It was like a scene from a science-fiction movie. It was haunting and yet somehow beautiful at the same time—affirmation of society's willingness to sacrifice for the collective.

We were all in this together.

That is, until we weren't.

The political divide was on the brink of splitting wide open.

CHAPTER 7

Politics and the Pandemic

"The worst is over," the governor declared at our daily press conference on April 14.

Thanks to the trust, cooperation, and collective sacrifice made by 19 million people, we were successfully bending the curve: the death and hospitalization rates had not only flattened but were finally starting to decline, just six weeks since New York's first confirmed COVID case. But we were not out of the woods yet, and there was still so much unknown about COVID. We needed to inch forward, not fling open the floodgates and start dancing in the streets. Reopening the economy too soon could lead to a spike in hospitalizations, which would result in the need for more stay-at-home orders. If that happened, the progress we had made would be for naught. We would have to start over and, in doing so, lose more lives and do more harm to the already battered economy. And worse, lose the trust of the people.

Donald Trump did not care about any of that. With every passing day, the November 2020 presidential election drew closer, and Trump made it clear that he was done waiting for the pandemic to go away. Every day seemed like a surreal effort to convert a virus into votes, with Trump vacillating back and forth between ludicrous and reckless, at one point even going so far as to suggest that Americans might combat COVID by injecting disinfectant into their bodies. But now he cranked up the volume and velocity of his dangerous exhortations. Proclaiming that "the cure was worse than the disease"—never mind that there was and still is no cure for the disease—Trump started to actively undermine medical professionals and governors nationwide. He wanted to "Liberate America." Like a seven-year-old on a sugar high, Trump took to Twitter: "LIBERATE MINNESOTA! LIBERATE MICHIGAN! LIBERATE VIRGINIA!"

The phrase acted as a dog whistle to his supporters to create anarchy. Trump supporters by the thousands began to burn masks and hold protests across the country, even taking over the Michigan State House and allegedly plotting to kidnap Governor Gretchen Whitmer, whom Trump had labeled the "lockup queen."

"Some in the fake news media are saying it is the governor's decision to open up the states. . . . Let it be fully understood that this is incorrect . . . it is the decision of the president," Trump brayed from the safety of his Twitter sniper's nest.

At the suggestion of New Jersey Governor Phil Murphy, Cuomo invited governors of other contiguous states—Pennsylvania, Rhode Island, Delaware, and Massachusetts—to join our tri-state coalition of New York, New Jersey, and Connecticut. Every single one said yes, including Massachusetts governor Charlie Baker, a Republican. We called a joint Zoom press conference to unveil our new bipartisan regional coalition.

Each governor, in turn, rejected Trump's assertion that the federal government was in charge of reopening. The coalition pledged to make reopening decisions together based on hospitalizations and positivity metrics and coordinated by the potential risk presented by various industries. The Northeast had been hit harder than any section of the country, and we would use the lessons learned to guide our collective decisions. The vision of seven governors unified in message, discipline, and approach stood in stark contrast to Trump's temper tantrums, which only provoked him further.

"When somebody is the president of the United States, the authority is total," he asserted that night from the White House briefing room.

The founding fathers viewed the federal government as a potential tyrannical force, so they drafted the Tenth Amendment to the Constitution, expressly limiting the federal government's power vis-à-vis states, including in responding to a public-health emergency, and specifically giving states sovereignty on police power. The federal government had not only provided no direction at the start of the pandemic, it played no role in closing down the economy. Trump certainly had no authority to force governors to lift stay-at-home orders or reopen their state economies. Cuomo watched the White House briefing from the living room of the Albany mansion in real time.

"Dani, get me any news outlet that will take me, fast," he said.

Within minutes, Cuomo was on the phone with CNN, reciting the Constitution verbatim. "We don't have a king," he declared, assertively. The next morning he kept at it, whacking away on every cable and broadcast news station that would have him.

Trump was angry and quick to respond, "Tell the Democrat Governors that *Mutiny on the Bounty* was one of my all-time favorite movies!" He tweeted, "A good old-fashioned mutiny every now and then is an exciting and invigorating thing to watch, especially when the mutineers need so much from the Captain. Too easy!"

Huh?

I had no idea what he was referring to, but the governor, a Marlon Brando aficionado, explained: "Trump clearly hasn't seen *Mutiny on the Bounty*. In it, Captain Bligh loses the fight to maintain control over his crew, and his first lieutenant mounts a successful rebellion to overthrow him."

Despite Trump's ignorance of classic movie trivia, the point was clear: Trump wanted to stoke partisan division, pitting blue states against red states and painting reopening decisions along political lines. But he also had no idea what he was talking about, and apparently brighter bulbs at 1600 Pennsylvania Avenue (presumably in the White House counsel's office) prevailed this time. Within twenty-four hours, Trump backtracked, saying he would "allow" governors to authorize their own reopening plans. His new position was still legally incorrect, but it didn't matter. At least we were no longer on a path tantamount to dictatorship.

The majority of New Yorkers were well-disciplined and committed, at that point, to staying the course on COVID. The daily press briefings worked. They communicated presence, compassion, confidence, and humanity. But Trump's agitation was beginning to have an effect in conservative areas across the state, and, given what we had just gone through, we were nervous. One day at the end of April, I picked up the phone and dialed Jared's cell.

Jared Kushner had become an unlikely ally of ours during COVID. The president trusted his son-in-law implicitly, and Jared had the clout to move the immovable bureaucratic machinery. He and Governor Cuomo had known each other for years before Donald Trump was elected, with Cuomo even attending Jared's wedding to Ivanka in 2007. The two of them maintained a longtime relationship, and the governor honestly believed Jared was doing his best to help when we asked for it. Jared credited their positive relationship in part to the fact that, when his father, Charles Kushner, was arrested for illegal campaign contributions, tax evasion, and witness tampering in 2004, Cuomo reached out, saying, "I've had highs and lows as well. You'll be back."

Jared's roommate from Harvard had married one of my closest friends from Cornell, and as a result we had crossed paths a few times socially over the years in New York City. During COVID, we became each other's primary point of contact between New York and the White House, a relationship that could be beneficial or contentious—or both—depending on the day.

Jared's soft monotone voice came on the line.

"Hey, Melissa. How are you?" he asked politely. "What's going on in New York?"

"Things here are okay," I told him. "As I'm sure you know, we've flattened the curve and—fingers crossed—it feels like we have entered a more positive phase of this."

"Yes, that's great to hear," he responded. "I've spoken with a lot of friends, but they have mainly relocated to Florida. Did you know everything is open there?"

Shots fired.

"I did know that, yes," I answered evenly.

"And the death rate there has been much lower than in New York," Jared went on, "even without the shutdowns. Did you know that, too?" His tone was smug.

"I have read that," I said. "Although I also read that they are classifying nearly every death of those over sixty years old as pneumonia, so I'm not sure I trust their statistics, either."

"Ah, well," Jared scoffed, "don't believe everything you read, Melissa."

"Right." I didn't like the direction this conversation was going, but there was no going back now.

"So, you called me," Jared said. "What can I do for you?"

"I'm calling to ask that you talk to the president about his rhetoric," I said.

"His rhetoric on what?" Jared asked.

"All of this 'liberate' business," I explained. "I feel okay about how most New Yorkers are responding, but there are pockets of upstate and Staten Island and Suffolk County where we are starting to see noncompliance. We were the center of this thing. We can't go backward."

"Melissa, let me stop you right there," Jared jumped in, his voice sharpening ever so slightly. "This isn't the president's 'rhetoric'—it's what he believes. We've done polling, and you guys are in the wrong place on this."

"Well, Jared, respectfully," I said, "we aren't basing our decisions on polling. But Siena just came out of the field with a new poll showing that, overwhelmingly, the people of New York support how the governor is handling COVID—including our stay-at-home order."

"Sure, that's possible," Jared agreed. "But I'm not talking about New York. I'm talking nationally. Pennsylvania. Michigan. Ohio. Florida. People do not support these shutdowns there. And they want their kids back in school and the economy open. That's where our focus is now."

"What does that mean?" Was New York not part of Trump's America, all of a sudden? I wondered.

"Melissa," Jared had transitioned to patronizing, "our interests no longer align. I understand why you have to do what you have to do. You should understand that we have to do what we have to do. And the president is going to continue to push governors to get their state economies back up and running. The people have had enough already."

So had I. I couldn't believe the conversation I was having. We were in the middle of a pandemic, one that had already killed tens of thousands of people, and I was talking with President Trump's top adviser, who until recently had lived in New York, about polling in swing states? There was no point in continuing the call; I heard him loud and clear.

"Got it, Jared. I understand."

Jared was right about one thing. Our interests most certainly were no longer aligned.

It had been two months since the first confirmed COVID case arrived in New York, and after five weeks of New York on PAUSE, with the mental-health impacts of fear and isolation yet to be realized, families across the state were going stir-crazy.

Mine was one of them.

They all knew how insanely busy I was, and I was surprised one day, while I was at work, when my phone rang and my dad's number popped up.

"Hey, Dad—everything okay?" I answered. "I'm totally swamped."

"Yes and no," he began apologetically. "I know you're crazy, but can you please talk to your grandfather?"

My heart skipped a beat. "Oh no, what's wrong?" I asked.

"Melissa, he doesn't understand. He doesn't understand why he can't live at his house. He doesn't understand why we won't let him leave. And he doesn't understand why he can't go walking at the mall."

It had been just over a month since my father drove to Rochester, New York, to pick up Nonno, who had just flown back from West Palm Beach, where he had wintered for the past twenty years. Like families around the world, we were concerned about the possibility of

Nonno getting COVID and didn't want to take any chances. He was living alone and my father wanted to be able to monitor him more closely and make sure he had what he needed, mainly food and his diabetes medication, without having to interact with other people in stores and potentially risk contracting the virus.

My father's family has a history of Alzheimer's, and my grandfather had started to feel its effect creeping in, ever so slowly, over the last few years, the decline growing steeper and quicker with the loss of my grandmother. Corradina and Gaetano had been lovebirds for fifty-five years. They had met after World War II, when my grandfather's family emigrated from Naples, Italy, to New York. There were a number of cities that immigrants were encouraged to live in upon arriving at Ellis Island, and Rochester, a medium-size city in upstate New York, was one of them. If there was any better explanation for how our American roots ended up being planted in Rochester, we never heard it.

Nonno got a job at a men's clothing manufacturer, where he met a seamstress with a smile that lit up any room she walked into. Corradina "Dina" D'Angelo was a native Sicilian whose family had also settled in Rochester after the war. She and my grandfather were both devout Roman Catholics, raised middle-class, aspiring to realize the great American dream. But it was their Italian heritage that sealed their bond with three core values: family, food, and guilt.

Dina DeRosa was smart, hardworking, warm, and classically beautiful. She loved cooking, parties, Italian soap operas, cannoli, nail polish, jewelry, and, most of all, her family. Just over five feet tall, she was a giant. Our pillar.

Her only child, Giorgio, was the center of Dina's universe—and he could do no wrong. When he grew up and got married, it was a given that when he and my mother, Melody, were struggling to make ends meet, they would live under the same roof with Nonno and Nonna, who helped them raise Jessica, Joey, and me for the first few years of our lives. That house would forever be my heart's home base.

Next to my father, I was my grandmother's favorite, her nickname my own middle name. I inherited her cheekbones and work ethic, and she would lovingly harangue me to focus more on family and less on fun or work. As soon as I hit my twenties, the first question out of her mouth whenever she called was whether I was dating anyone. Confirmation that I was still single elicited an audible sigh. "Melissa, how many times do I have to tell you?" she would say. "If you want to find a boyfriend, you have to stop drinking wine and learn to cook."

My grandparents did absolutely everything together for over half a century, and very rarely did you see one without the other. They watched soccer games together. Worked together. Cooked together. Played bocci and cards together. They grew old together.

One August afternoon in 2012, they were leaving a family wedding. My grandfather was anxious to get home and walked ahead of her as they crossed the street. He didn't see it happen, but he heard it. My grandmother screamed as she braced for the car to hit her. The driver, who wasn't paying attention, was going over 30 mph— and Nonna's tiny body was thrown more than 15 feet. They didn't pronounce her dead until they reached the hospital, but there's no way she'd survived for more than a few seconds after impact.

Nonno was never really the same again. He was alone, and he was lonely. His memory had started to fade. My father encouraged him to keep up a routine. Nonno began going to the mall every morning for exercise. He would run into people he knew, giving him a sense of social interaction, and stretch his legs while he sipped his coffee. It was one part of his day that he relied on. It gave him a sense of control and predictability.

With the pandemic, malls had been closed since the second week of March—a concept that my grandfather could not understand. At first, he thought my father was lying to him, and so nearly every day, my dad would drive him to the mall so Nonno could see for himself that it was deserted and locked. As the days wore on, he got more and more agitated. He wanted to go to his own home. And he wanted to go walking at the mall. He wouldn't take no for an answer anymore, and Dad was hoping maybe I could get through to him.

"Sure, of course, Dad," I said, setting down my BlackBerry and temporarily ignoring the frequent additions to my unending email queue. "Put him on."

"Hello?" Nonno asked, sounding confused.

"Nonno! How are you?"

"Jessie?"

"No, Nonno, it's Melissa."

"Oh! Melissa! How are you, dolly?"

"I'm okay, Nonno. Just very busy at work."

"You work so hard," he said. "I'm so proud of you."

"Aww, thank you, Nonno," I continued. "Nonno, Dad said you were upset about not being able to go to the mall?"

"Yes, he won't let me." His voice dropped to a whisper. "I don't know why, but he won't let me go back to my house in Rochester. The plants have to be watered. I have things to do there."

"Nonno, it's because of COVID."

"Che cosa, COVID?" he asked. After he retired, his English got worse, and he and Nonna primarily communicated in Italian. These days, he would switch back and forth between English and Italian without even realizing it.

"COVID, Nonno. It's a very terrible virus. It's killing tens of thousands of people, and it's very dangerous. Everything is closed, including the mall."

"The mall is closed?"

"Yes, Nonno. And Dad is worried about you—we're all worried about you—that's why he's having you stay with him for a while."

"When can I go home, Melissa?"

"I don't know, Nonno. But I hope it's soon."

"Okay, dolly."

He didn't understand what I was saying, but he yes'd me, anyway.

"Don't be too tough on Dad," I added. "He loves you. And I love you, too."

"I love you, dolly. Bye-bye now."

After I hung up the phone, I couldn't stop thinking about my grandmother. She and I hadn't spoken for two months when she died—the result of guilt manifesting into avoidance. I had broken off an engagement to my then-fiancé, Elliot, earlier that year, and my grandmother was devastated. Her generation didn't engage in that kind of frivolous behavior: if they said yes to spending the rest of their life with someone, they meant it. I could never figure out how to properly explain my decision to my grandmother, and each time we spoke, the only thing I could hear was disappointment in her voice. So I stopped returning her calls. And then suddenly on one August afternoon, the ability to talk to her was taken away from me. Imagine if Nonna could see me now, thirty-seven years old and on the brink of a failed marriage. How disappointed she would be in me . . .

Matt and I were navigating COVID the same way we were navigating our relationship—separately but civilly, carefully avoiding any deep discussion or close scrutiny. The original plan worked out with our couples' therapist dictated that, at the conclusion of our three-month separation, we would make a real decision on how to move forward. COVID threw a wrench in that plan, pushing "us" to the back burner once again. After returning from San Francisco, Matt initially moved back into our three-bedroom Brooklyn Heights town house. Every couple of weeks, he would surface with the need to have "the talk," but I was always too busy with a call or a press conference or a fight with the White House. It never seemed like the right time. My whole personal life felt like it was detached and stored in some distant, unspecified future, my maybe-husband, my maybe-children waiting— or not—somewhere down some unmarked road. It's weird how people talk about living in the present as some transcendent self-awareness achievement. I was doing exactly that during COVID—living in the hyper-present. It was a long way from zen, but in a way, I was relieved to be so deeply immersed in helping to manage the state of New York and grateful for the free pass it granted me not to manage myself. But the clock had run out. I finally gave in one May afternoon and agreed to have the talk. No more delays.

It was the middle of the day, but I headed back to my bedroom for our scheduled call. I couldn't bear to be in the office for this one. I knew what he was going to say before words came out of his mouth. "Matt, I can't handle this. With everything else that's going on right now . . . please . . . it's too much," I pleaded, tears streaming down my face.

But Matt was done. He loved me, but he was no longer in love with me. He wanted to move on. He would respect my desire to keep things quiet for a few months longer, given the outsized attention I was receiving in the press, but he asked that we get the ball rolling. Lawyers. Negotiations. An agreement.

When we hung up, I lay back in bed and started to sob. My mind wandered back to when we'd first met. I was joining the administration as communications director, and he was the newly promoted press secretary. Only eight months his senior in age, I was his boss, but really he was my partner. We strategized on everything together and acted as each other's sounding board before engaging with reporters. We spent hours in my office, meticulously laying out press rollout plans for the governor's State of the State address, and bonded over our shared love of *The West Wing*. We backed each other up in senior staff meetings. At some point, he asked if I wanted to grab a drink at Docks, a restaurant located on the first floor of our office building. Drinks became dinner. We had dinner thirty-two consecutive nights after that. He told me about his parents, two of the city's most well-regarded lawyers, who had met decades earlier while working as prosecutors in the US Attorney's Office for the Southern District of New York. Matt told me I reminded him of his mother, a smart, driven workaholic who shattered glass ceiling after glass ceiling in that job, and who herself would later become a US attorney. I told him about my failed engagement. How I knew from the moment I said yes that it wasn't really what I wanted. I let my guard down with him, and he became my best friend, until one night when he told me he wanted more: He wanted to be my boyfriend.

"I'm sorry, Matt, but technically I'm your boss. I care about you, I really do, but I've worked too hard for this job to jeopardize it. Maybe someday, but not today."

He was crushed. He went home to his mother and told her what had happened. "We'll figure this out, Matt. It will be okay," she assured him.

Several days later, he called. His mother had put him in touch with a lawyer who had done a review of the state's public officers law.

"There's no rule against dating in the office, including someone who is technically your supervisor," he told me. "The lawyer I hired has drawn up an opinion for your review."

How romantic. He was going to leave the office in a few months to work on the governor's reelection campaign, and then he would transition into the private sector. Our boss-employee situation would be temporary, he told me. Assured in writing that I wasn't doing anything wrong, I took the leap. Several months later, we were living together. A year after that, he proposed on a beach in Mexico. Eight months after that, we were married at the Sagamore Resort near my father's house in Lake George. Matt was my rock. A real partner.

Not long after that, I could sense something was wrong. Matt was working for Uber, while I was still toiling away in the public sector. The glue that held us together had been work, and we were no longer working together.

"Matt, what do you want from me? This wasn't exactly deceptive marketing. You met me at work. I came as advertised!" I said during one contentious exchange.

He hated my long hours and that all I wanted to talk about was New York politics. He needed more attention, more affirmation, more time. Less than a year into our marriage, he found that attention elsewhere. And when I found out, it broke me. I got on a plane to Mykonos—a trip we were supposed to take together to celebrate our one-year anniversary—and I cried until there weren't any tears left. For a period of time, I could no longer feel. I was dead inside. Unwilling to admit defeat, I told Matt I would try to get past it. But the two of us were never the same afterward. As much as I wanted to pretend, I couldn't. Matt spent the next two-and-a-half years trying to fix it: Surprise gifts from business trips to Paris. Homemade dinners. He attempted to anticipate my every need and meet it. It didn't matter. My guard was up, and no matter what he did, I wouldn't let it down again. He met me more than halfway, but I could never forgive him. Deep down, I knew he was right and it was time to officially end what had unofficially ended years earlier, but I didn't want to. I had thought Matt would be my everything. Now we were nothing. And in that moment, feeling its full weight, my heart broke all over again.

Just then, my phone began to ring. It was my assistant, Tracy. I was late to a meeting with the governor to discuss the state's reopening plans.

It was time to go back to work. So appropriate and so seemingly impossible. Except this is what I did.

I walked into the bathroom to splash cold water on my face. *Pull it together, Melissa, you don't have time for this.* I called my lawyer but, other than him, didn't tell a single soul about my conversation with Matt for two months. Instead, it lived, both alive and deadening, in my chest.

That afternoon as Dr. Zucker, Rob, Jim, and I huddled with the governor in his conference room to discuss reopening plans, I kept thinking of how many people around the state and the country, like my grandfather, badly needed a return to some semblance of normalcy.

The immediacy of the emergency was behind us, but the threat wasn't. We were all now trapped in an uncertain, turbulent limbo; the sort of perpetual snow-day coziness of learning how to bake bread, bingeing Netflix, and finishing 1,000-piece jigsaw puzzles was well past its expiration date. The national unity that had existed during the height of the pandemic was waning. Decisions were being questioned, fingers were being pointed, and politics were increasingly the primary driver of what should have been public-health judgments. Masks, school closings, rules in public spaces—all had become social hot buttons. And with every passing day, it was getting uglier.

Businesses began to violate shutdown orders, while videos of fist-fights over masks went viral on the internet. Maskless college kids flocked to beaches and bars to celebrate spring break, leading to bursts of superspreader events. States with Republican governors were following the White House's lead, abruptly canceling stay-at-home orders. Even some in our Northeastern multistate coalition were beginning to waver.

"At some point, you have to let Jesus take the wheel," remarked Delaware's chief of staff on one particularly tedious conference call.

The loosening of restrictions was politically expedient and, in much of the nation, wildly popular. But with images of mass graves being dug on Hart Island still fresh in our memory, New York was not going to take any chances.

Everyone knew that people needed to get back to work. They needed to get their hair cut and their teeth cleaned; all those newly adopted puppies and kittens needed to be neutered or spayed. And, as silly as it may sound, people needed to go to the mall. But the question was how to do it without inadvertently causing a resurgence of COVID.

Cuomo had clear instructions: "Reopening decisions must be based on the facts. No politics. No spin. No emotion. No conspiracies. Just the facts and the data and the science." We were to open as quickly as we could, *as safely* as we could.

Rob and Jim had been working with our outside consultants and the health department to come up with a metrics-based, phased reopening plan. Minus any serious guidance from Washington, the governor wanted to enlist international experts to approve our reopening plans. Rob and Jim recruited Dr. Michael T. Osterholm, director of the Center for Infectious Disease Research and Policy at the University of Minnesota, and Dr. Samir Bhatt, senior lecturer at Imperial College London, to work with us. They would provide technical advice and analysis throughout the state's reopening process and help track our progress.

Our approach was regional and gradual. Internalizing the lessons of the last two months, we would ensure the hospital system had the capacity—a vacancy rate of at least 30 percent—to absorb a potential resurgence of new cases. We would mandate that each region have the ability to perform a weekly average of thirty virus tests per 1,000 residents a month, to feel confident we had an accurate picture of the depth of the spread, and to hire at least thirty working contact tracers per 100,000 residents to ensure that any regional outbreaks could be identified. Once each region hit metrics based on those criteria, they could begin to reopen—waiting two weeks before graduating to the next phase, so there was time to monitor any potential COVID uptick. The order in which businesses would reopen was prioritized based on economic impact and risk of infection; it began with construction and manufacturing, plus retail stores were allowed to reopen for curbside pickup, followed by services like barbershops and salons, then restaurants and hotels, before we finally reopened venues that facilitated mass gatherings, like movie theaters and amusement parks. Permitted capacities were cut in half, with everything requiring social distancing and masks. Reopening would begin in areas least impacted and continue until New York City finally threw open its doors.

On May 15, the same day Trump officially announced Operation Warp Speed, a public-private partnership with the goal of accelerating the development, manufacturing, and distribution of COVID-19 vaccines by the end of the calendar year, the first regions of New York State began to reopen. We braced ourselves, unsure of the human impact the decisions we were making would have. Were we really ready? What if infections spiked and hospitals collapsed? Would more people die? And, just as we entered the next phase of the crisis, the Monday-morning quarterbacking began.

Reporters were getting testy. We were still holding daily press briefings, but now that the urgency of the first two and a half months was behind us, the mood in the press corps shifted. The patience afforded to us early on, in the dark days of the unknown, was replaced now by accusations and blame. The question-and-answer portion of each presser was hostile, dominated by reporters shouting questions over one another that had no relevance to the news of the day—instead focusing on what had gone wrong and why.

"Why didn't you shut down businesses earlier, Governor?"

"Why is the death toll so much higher in New York than it is in California?"

"In retrospect, did your decisions contribute to more deaths?"

Our office had a reputation for being hard-charging. We didn't run from that characterization; we prided ourselves on it. We viewed every circumstance—a legislative fight over marriage equality, the annual budget negotiations, or rebuilding LaGuardia Airport—as a battle, and we fought for every inch. It didn't make us many friends with the people on opposing sides, but we were effective and were famous for getting things done. That mentality carried over to the way we engaged with the press. We fought for every comma and every word, sometimes calling editors at 11:00 p.m. or 6:00 a.m. to argue over the way something was phrased or demand a correction on a detail we believed was factually inaccurate. The fights were often contentious, sometimes crossing over into being nasty. In retrospect, the approach we took with the press was damaging and far too often unnecessary. When everything is an emergency, nothing is an emergency, and as we doubled down, they resented it. Many people who have never worked with the media have the idealized perception that the press operates from a place of pure objectivity. The reality is that reporters are human beings just like everyone else. Social media has made this more apparent. If media outlets have policies to rein in reporters on Twitter, you wouldn't know it. Their personal opinions are often on full display there and inevitably seep into their regular coverage.

But COVID felt different, and their accusatory questions felt devoid of any acknowledgment of the once-in-a-century nature of the circumstance. It was as if the press corps, who themselves had been frightened by the unknowns of COVID only weeks earlier, had collective amnesia. The tone of the questions was accusatory, as if they hadn't lived through what had just happened alongside us. They knew we were building the plane as we were flying it, and that we were doing it without any tested blueprint or guidance from the federal government. And they knew that New York City's density, combined with the arrival of COVID months earlier than initially detected, was the storm that created the situation we found ourselves in, but they weren't acknowledging any of it.

At that point, our office's always-contentious relationship with the *New York Times* was in freefall. The *Times's* frosty relationship with the Cuomo family dates back decades. Their editorial board was made up of what Mario Cuomo would call "white-wine liberals," essentially highbrow Manhattan elitists whose view of the world was rooted in idealism, not realism, and who themselves were detached from the everyday struggles of middle- and lower-class New Yorkers. They looked down on the Cuomos, Italians from Queens—a reality that played out time and again when election season came around. The die was cast when the *Times* endorsed New York City Mayor Ed Koch for governor over Mario Cuomo in 1982.

While it would not be factual to say our interactions with the *Times* were ever positive, when the pandemic was initially raging, it was not hostile. But now, the truce was over. After one particularly difficult press conference at which the governor and the *Times's* Albany bureau chief had an especially nasty exchange over the Health Department's nursing home health guidance, the governor snapped back.

"Well, you have to remember the facts. I know you're the *New York Times*, but facts are still facts, right? Even at the *Times*, okay?" he said, his tone curt and frosty.

After the presser wrapped up, I couldn't get the exchange out of my head. I knew we were headed back to a dark place with the *Times* at the exact moment we needed their objectivity and understanding.

My instinct was to try to fix it ASAP. I picked up my iPhone and called the reporter; we needed to take the temperature down. Acknowledging that everything locally was closed (Albany had yet to meet the metrics necessary to reopen bars and restaurants), we settled on going to his house for a socially distanced chat in his backyard. His house happened to be catty-corner from the Executive Mansion.

We spent over an hour catching up. The conversation was friendly; we talked about our personal relationships, discussed what the governor's legacy would be from COVID, debated the term "shelter in place," and compared California's response to New York's. The banter was spirited but positive, even when we disagreed with each other's perspective. Judging by the clip of his wine consumption, he appeared to be enjoying himself. While I had intentionally held myself to two glasses, he had finished a second bottle. The reporter's son arrived and waved hello from the back porch before disappearing into the house. I looked down to see my phone ringing. It was the governor, and it was the second time he had called in the span of twenty minutes. Time to leave. I felt good that I had reset the *Times* relationship.

"Okay, this has been fun. Thanks so much for having me. I have to get back to the real world," I said picking up my purse to leave.

"Wait, are your eyes blue or green?" the reporter asked, leaning in closer.

"Blue," I responded, feeling like the situation had just taken a turn in the wrong direction.

"Are you sure?" he asked, slurring his words. "I think they look green."

"Nope, blue. They've always been blue," I said definitively. It was absolutely time to go.

As I stood there, wrapping up the debate and attempting to say goodbye, he put his hand around my wrist and pulled me toward him.

"Don't go, Melissa. It's still early. Stay longer," he said, his grip around my wrist tightening.

"Jesse, I'm sorry, I have to go," I said, my voice strained.

He continued to hold onto my wrist for a few seconds longer, again pleading for me to stay. I could smell the alcohol on his breath. I pulled my arm free, grabbed my purse, and jetted for the door, waving good-bye, and walked quickly through his house back out to the front walk, the mansion in welcome sight.

I felt unsettled and couldn't quite believe what had just happened. I immediately picked up the phone and called my colleague and trusted friend Rich Azzopardi.

"Are you okay, lady?" he asked. "You've got that sound in your voice like there are black helicopters hovering overhead," he said.

When I explained what happened, he immediately went into defense mode.

"I should never have let you go there alone," Rich said, beating himself up. "I knew something like this could happen."

Despite our decision to divorce, I felt compelled to tell the story of what happened that afternoon to Matt, and within days a handful of other coworkers, trying to make sense of the situation. Everyone reacted the same way: not surprised. Two years earlier, in 2018, Jesse McKinley had gotten into an argument with one of the governor's female campaign staffers while out one night; he was so drunk and grew so aggressive that he had to be removed from the bar by the bouncer. Four years before that, he grew so drunk—aggressively hitting on a young female in our press office—that he sent her an apologetic email the next morning.

While I may have been one of the most powerful women in New York, the *New York Times* wielded a particular power over me and my office; it is a complicated, asymmetrical power dynamic. That night I received a text from Jesse. I looked at it, contemplating how to respond. To me, it was an obvious attempt to take my temperature, to level set.

In the weeks that followed the incident, the reporter fell uncharacteristically mute at our press briefings. His accusations about whether or not the governor shouldered responsibility for the death of New Yorkers for not shutting down fast enough were replaced by his near silence during question-and-answer sessions—to me, a tacit admission that he knew he had done something wrong.

Around the same time the press was transitioning to Monday-morning quarterbacking, extremist members of the legislature were, too. While the Far Right focused almost entirely on politicizing COVID in nursing homes, the Far Left circled around when we made our decision to close New York State.

We had announced our total stay-at-home order on March 20—nineteen days after our first confirmed COVID case. At the time, New York was just the second state in the country to announce total closure, behind only California, which, despite having confirmed COVID on January 26, had announced their "shelter in place" policy on March 19, one day before us. We had to drag the legislature kicking and screaming to give the governor the authority to close businesses and impose quarantine, even dispatching Dr. Zucker to do a series of closed-door meetings with the legislature in order to make the case for why such broad authority could be necessary. And when we had started making major decisions, including closing schools in New Rochelle's "containment zone," we received affirmative pushback from members of the legislature, including from the Democratic senate majority leader. When we made the move to put New York on pause, we did so without any federal guidance whatsoever in a moment of unprecedented chaos. But that was then, and this was now. And now, legislators were second-guessing everything alongside the media.

"Did you see this tweet from Biaggi?" Rich asked one afternoon at the end of May.

"Ugh. What does *she* want?" I asked, bracing myself for State Senator Alessandra's Biaggi's latest salvo. I opened my phone and scrolled through Twitter. And there it was,

> New York: so we are clear, Cuomo's considered, official
> answer to growing questions of how COVID has been
> handled, is: "No one told me to be ready for this. No

one said this would come from Europe." Leaders don't rely on "others" to see looming threats. Esp such visible ones. Did we not elect *you* to see the threats coming? Why did *I* know in February that the threat to NY was growing, but you didn't? This is misdirection.

It was such horseshit. Biaggi had never said anything publicly or privately about knowing COVID was coming. She was part of the same skeptical conference that was reluctant to even approve the governor's ability to make such sweeping decisions. And back when we were making the tough choices no one else wanted to make, she and her colleagues cowered in their homes, afraid just like everyone else.

Underscoring the absurdity, she had just visited our office days before her tweet to deliver baked goods to thank our staff for their hard work. But this was par for the course with Biaggi, whose hypocritical behavior toward our administration had become customary.

Alessandra Biaggi was the granddaughter of former Congressman Mario Biaggi, who famously worked with the Mafia and Frank Sinatra to try to stop the filming of *The Godfather*. The senior Biaggi had resigned after being convicted of bribery and sent to jail. Alessandra had worked as a mid-level lawyer in our counsel's office for less than a year in 2017, a job she secured with one call to Cuomo's then secretary Bill Mulrow, who had known her family well for years. During her campaign for state senate, she wrapped herself in the Cuomo record and our accomplishments, proudly wearing our administration's lapel pin and exaggerating her role in signature policy initiatives like codifying *Roe v. Wade* in New York, despite the fact that neither the majority of the senior staff, the governor, nor I had ever had any meaningful contact with her.

After winning, our office reached out to offer her a courtesy meeting with Cuomo and me in her new capacity as state senator–elect. Cuomo hadn't formally met her before and asked her what her long-term goals were. She said she had her eye on a congressional seat in the

Bronx then held by Eliot Engel. Cuomo posed a question, "Alessandra, remind me, when did Engel get elected?"

"You know the answer to that, Governor," she snapped, her face flushing red with fury. Eliot Engel had replaced her grandfather Mario when he went to jail decades earlier.

Cuomo truly didn't remember. "I don't—that's why I'm asking," he responded. Not knowing Congressman Biaggi's sordid history myself, I was just as confused by the exchange. Not long after the meeting, I understood. Bill Mulrow called. He had gotten an irate call from Alessandra's uncle. She felt the governor had been intentionally disrespectful in asking about her grandfather. When I relayed this to the governor, he phoned Bill himself, explaining that it wasn't his intention and asking how to fix it. Bill promised to try to clear the air but explained unequivocally that we had struck a nerve: the Biaggis were not happy. Since that meeting, Alessandra had reinvented herself as a far-left agitator, attacking Cuomo in the press on a near-daily basis. She called the governor corrupt for hosting a fundraiser during budget season, when she had done the exact same thing days earlier. And she routinely floated that she would primary the governor. Here she was doing it again. But this time it was about COVID, intimating we had cost people their lives. This time, it wasn't political; it was life and death.

Looking at Biaggi's string of tweets was the last straw. Fuming, I sent a text, "You are both full of shit and a pretty terrible person." The text was hotter than necessary, and it was one of those interactions that, as soon as it was over, I realized was clearly a mistake. The same way the governor had snapped with the *Times*, I snapped with her, both exchanges foreshadowing the collision course we were on with the legislature and the media.

CHAPTER 8

Black Lives Matter

JUST WHEN I HAD BEGUN TO FEEL HOPE THAT WE WERE TURNING the corner, on the brink of reopening New York City's badly bruised economy, a different kind of firestorm hit, a powerful inferno that was part public-health crisis and part social-justice crisis—the latter threatening to undermine three months of progress toward overcoming the former. And it happened not in New York, but 1,200 miles away, in Minneapolis.

On the evening of May 25, forty-six-year-old George Floyd stopped by a convenience store to buy cigarettes. He was still sitting outside in a car with friends when the clerk called 911 to say he suspected a customer had just paid with a counterfeit $20 bill. Police arrived and yanked Floyd out of the car and ordered him to the ground, where he was handcuffed and shoved face-first into the sidewalk. Derek Chauvin, a forty-four-year-old white police officer, pinned Floyd's neck down with his knee for roughly nine minutes, while two others assisted in restraining him and another prevented alarmed onlookers from rushing to Floyd's aid. Floyd pleaded for his life, telling the officers over and over again that he couldn't breathe. They didn't listen. He fell silent. Chauvin kept his knee on Floyd's neck throughout the nine-minute ordeal, even after it was evident he was dead.

The gut-wrenching murder of another unarmed Black man in America at the hands of law enforcement was documented on camera phones by bystanders. Almost immediately, those videos went viral. The preceding months of isolation and conflict had turned an already-fractured nation into a tinderbox of pent-up anxiety and frustration; the murder of George Floyd was the flame that produced a coast-to-coast conflagration.

In the week that followed, protests broke out in cities across America, with demonstrators warning, "No justice, no peace."

To New Yorkers, the horrific scene was like a traumatic flashback. Seven years earlier, Eric Garner, a forty-three-year-old Black man from Staten Island, was put in a prohibited chokehold by two law-enforcement officers who suspected him of selling loose, untaxed cigarettes. Garner told officers "I can't breathe" eleven times. They didn't listen, either.

The city's medical examiner ruled Garner's death a homicide. Nonetheless, a grand jury empaneled in Richmond County decided against indicting the officers involved.

It was an all-too-familiar cycle of injustice for the Black community—deadly violence perpetrated by law enforcement in response to a petty crime, and exactly no accountability.

Demonstrations erupted in New York City in response to the Garner murder and generations of unchecked police brutality. At the time, Governor Cuomo worked with Reverend Al Sharpton and the Mothers of the Movement—a group of women whose African American children have been killed by police officers or by gun violence—to broker peace. He signed an executive order naming the state attorney general as a special prosecutor for police-related civilian deaths, the first measure of its kind in the nation. It provided some temporary comfort that action was being taken. The outrage had dissipated in New York, and the press had moved on.

Until now.

Five days after George Floyd's horrific death, I was spending my Saturday night working on my laptop in the pool house at the mansion alongside Stephanie Benton. There had been mass demonstrations the night before in New York City, where ugly clashes between the police and protesters had been recorded by bystanders. It was bad.

The videos had gone viral on Twitter, leading to further outcry about what appeared to be gratuitous police brutality. The governor and I had helicoptered down to the city earlier that Saturday to address the situation. Cuomo announced that he had asked the attorney general to investigate the NYPD's conduct, and that he supported demands by criminal justice advocates for transparency of police disciplinary records. But any hope that these actions would help heal the raw wounds of protesters was overly optimistic. The protests raged on.

Thousands of unmasked people suddenly gathering on the streets after months of staying at home threatened to compound the crisis. The situation was prime for an unprecedented superspreader event that could swiftly undo whatever progress we had made in containing COVID.

As I sat there in the pool house, unpacking the events of the past few days, I got a call from Mike Kopy, our director of Emergency Management. A thirty-two-year veteran of the state police, Kopy was exactly the person you wanted in that position: a no-nonsense professional who could cut through the red tape, mobilize, and get the job done. And he was as nonpolitical as they come. When my phone rang and he was on the other end, it was almost never good. But regardless of the scope of the crisis—a pipe bomb sent to Bill and Hillary Clinton's residence, a flood in the Mohawk Valley, a runaway barge in the Hudson River, a security breach perpetrated by an agent of the Iranian government—he was unflappable, calmly explaining the issue, proposing a solution, and executing the plan.

"Kopy?" I answered "Everything okay?"

"No, Melissa, I wish that it was, but it's not."

"What's wrong?" I could hear unaccustomed tension in his voice, an emotion Kopy rarely conveyed.

"I just got off the phone with police chiefs across the state— Buffalo, Rochester, Syracuse, Albany, New York City," he reported. "It's a mess. The protests have turned violent. They are burning police cars, vandalizing private property, and throwing bricks through windows.

The local PDs cannot get the situations under control, and there's a fear that if they exert force, they will only provoke the crowds and exacerbate the situation."

As Kopy was speaking, I could hear faint chants coming from outside. I covered the receiver of the phone and whispered that I'd be right back as I headed to investigate. Stephanie mouthed, "Is everything okay?" and I nodded. An unspoken lie; I didn't believe that at all.

"Melissa, I know you're in Albany right now," Kopy was saying, "You should know that not far from the mansion, protesters have surrounded a police substation and have started pelting officers with rocks and bricks. I'm coordinating with the governor's security detail on the situation there, as well as the mansion, and closely monitoring the capitol."

I walked through a long narrow hallway and opened the sliding glass door at the front entrance to step outside. The chants grew louder. As I walked toward the gate, I could see that hundreds of people were gathering out front. Protests outside the mansion were a near-daily occurrence and generally consisted of a few dozen people chanting about anything from hydrofracking to Medicaid spending. This did not feel like a protest. It felt like a mob. An angry mob. And as their chants grew louder, I feared they were out of control.

My heart began to pound.

"What do we do, Kopy?" I asked him, temporarily shutting out my own proximate concerns and returning to the original purpose of his call.

"Alert the governor," he told me. "I think we should consider recommending a curfew to the upstate mayors and offer backup. Unfortunately, there's not much more we *can* do beyond that at the moment that won't make the situation worse."

"What does Corlett say?" Keith Corlett was the superintendent of the state police. I had learned early on that there are all kinds of land mines when dealing with various levels of law enforcement. Everywhere you look is a potential turf war. In situations like this, where the state could be perceived as encroaching on local PDs, it was easier for Kopy to be the heavy, allowing Corlett to maintain his collegial relationships with other law enforcement. I knew I could rely on Kopy to run point. He assured me the superintendent was already on board, and I promised to call him back after I briefed the governor.

I stood outside for a few seconds longer as I tried to collect my thoughts. From the start, my job was a series of firsts: but after the first subway breakdown, first hurricane, first bomb threat, and first pandemic, I had my frame of reference. A protocol. A playbook.

I had never been through one of these. *Another first.*

As I turned to walk back inside, my sister called. Jessica lived with her husband and two young daughters in Albany. I assumed she had heard about the chaos downtown and was looking for answers. Not having any, I side-buttoned the call. Within seconds, she texted: "Melissa, WTF is going on? We just turned on the news, and it looks like downtown Albany is burning—Alexa and Ashley are afraid—what do I tell them?"

I took a deep breath and went back inside, where I found that the governor had joined Stephanie and his daughters. He could immediately tell by my expression that something was wrong.

"What's going on?" he asked.

"That was Kopy."

"Okay, and . . . ?"

"And," I paused, "it's bad. He says every major upstate municipality and New York City are spiraling out of control. It sounds like none of the local PDs can manage the chaos, and it's getting violent," I said. "And I don't know what to do."

I had a rule of principal management when it came to the governor: Go to him with a problem when the fire was out or when it was raging out of control. I could count on one hand how many times in eight years it had been the latter.

"Let Kopy and Corlett know that I'm about to call them," Cuomo said. "In the meantime, call the upstate mayors. Ask what they are seeing on the ground. Get Emma on the phone. Offer state police and National Guard backup. Ask if they have considered a citywide curfew. Tell them I am here to help in any way that we can and that I plan to call them each individually for a status update shortly."

"Okay," I said, turning around to dial Rochester mayor Lovely Warren.

"And Melissa?"

"Yes?"

"Do it calmly. It's going to be okay."

"Okay," I answered rotely.

"Melissa? Look at me," he urged.

I nodded.

"It will be okay."

"Okay," I said, fighting back my rising panic.

"Let's get to work," he said solemnly.

We spent the next six hours talking to mayors and police chiefs across the state, deploying law enforcement assets and monitoring the pandemonium. Every mayor took us up on the offer of state police backup—the exception being New York City mayor Bill de Blasio.

Finally, at 2:00 a.m., I went up to my room. Unable to sleep, I sat cross-legged on the white bedspread, monitoring Twitter and email—MSNBC on in the background—with both my BlackBerry and my iPhone beside me.

Just then, I heard chants start up again. The crowd that had gathered in front of the mansion hours earlier had marched downtown, tipping over cars and smashing windows in their wake. They had even hijacked a tractor trailer and set it on fire in the middle of the street, a mere three blocks from the capitol. And now they were back.

My bedroom faced Eagle Street, the front side of the mansion. I got up and tiptoed over to the window, pushing the curtain aside just enough to see what was going on.

The crowd had shrunk to a few dozen, and it seemed they had a very specific agenda. They started setting off firecrackers and throwing bricks over the walls along the perimeter of the mansion. A sudden fear gripped me: What if, instead of a brick, one of them hurled a Molotov cocktail over the wall and hit the house?

I called Vinnie Straface, the head of the governor's protective unit. Why weren't the governor's security detail or the Albany PD or the state police doing anything? I wanted to know. Vinnie insisted they were on it and explained that the worst thing they could do was use force on the protesters—that it would only inflame and embolden them and make the situation worse. Exasperated and disoriented, I picked up the phone and called the governor. He was still wide-awake downstairs.

"Do you hear this?" I asked, my voice shaking.

"Yes, but it's going to be okay. You need to calm down."

"How can I calm down? How can *you* calm down?"

"Because. I lived through the Crown Heights riots. I was in LA after the Rodney King verdict. I've experienced versions of this. Sometimes, there's so much justified anger that it boils over. Sometimes, this is inevitable," he said. "We hear the pain, we work to drive it to a place of constructive hurt."

"I'm not going to sleep," I said.

"Of course you're not. Neither am I. But sometimes it's our job to not sleep. Stay up. Make calls. Control what you can control. And be ready by seven a.m. to discuss what we say in the morning. The people of this state are going to need to hear from us."

I actively tried not to be scared, but I was. Scared for the people in neighborhoods that were being looted. Scared for my sister and her kids. Scared of what felt like a situation spiraling out of control and the unknown of what would happen next.

The protesters stayed until around 5:00 a.m. The next morning, there was spray paint along the exterior of the brick walls and broken bottles strewn along Eagle Street. A car on the corner had been set on fire. All of this a fraction of the destruction that had occurred all across the state.

That morning when I arrived at the office around 7 a.m., exhausted and overwhelmed, I was officially dragging. It had been three months since COVID started, and I was running on fumes. I reached for my iPhone and texted my therapist: "Hi there—long time! Any chance you have five mins for me this morning?" Almost instantly, he texted back: "You've been on my mind. Yes, let's talk. How about 11 a.m.?" I felt a wave of relief: "THANK YOU! Call then!" I looked up to see Stephanie in my doorway. Rob and the governor were in the conference room, waiting for me. I reached for a legal pad and my phones and hurried over to join the huddle for our daily briefing.

COVID was not what was on people's minds that Sunday morning. We discussed the situation and decided we needed to make an impassioned appeal directly to the protesters. Peaceful protest—righteous protest—was justified, but resorting to violence and destruction could not be tolerated. It undermined the legitimate outrage over George Floyd's murder.

To make matters worse, it was clear that the White House, desperate to change the subject from COVID and a flailing economy, viewed the chaos as an opportunity. It was almost as if Trump and his inner circle were happy that the protests had turned violent. The president himself had tweeted: "When the looting starts, the shooting starts," a racially charged dog whistle from the civil rights era used by segregationists and white police chiefs in the 1960s. To Trump and his advisers, this was a gift: a wedge issue that had fallen from the sky to rally suburban voters and white women four months before the election. It was obvious what they were doing, and it needed to be called out. We decided to do exactly that.

I looked down to check the clock: 11:05. I was late.

"Sorry, guys, I just need one minute. I'll be right back." By the time I reached my office, my phone was vibrating; my therapist was calling me.

"Doctor, I'm so sorry—thanks for taking the time," I answered.

"No problem, Melissa, how can I help you? Are you doing alright?"

"That's the thing," I replied. "I've been okay for the most part, but between the sleep deprivation and the stress and anxiety . . . I don't know, it's just all starting to wear on me."

"Yes. Well, Melissa, you're human," he said. "Think of it as if you're a rubber band. Rubber bands stretch and go back to normal, but if you don't let them and you keep pulling, over time, when they are stretched too far for too long, they lose their elasticity. They get thinner and thinner, and at some point, they snap. We need to listen to our bodies."

"I was hoping that maybe there is something you could prescribe," I said. "In college, sometimes I would take an Adderall when I got really tired in order to do all-nighters during finals. Would it be possible to get something like that?" My call wasn't about talking through my feelings or state of mind—I didn't have time for that. I was in search of a quick fix, a magic pill that could keep me going and focused.

"Melissa, Adderall treats ADD," the doctor told me. "I've been seeing you on and off for years, and I can tell you with 100 percent certainty that you do not have ADD. The answer is not drugs to keep you awake; the answer is to listen to your body: You need a break, you need food, you need to sleep." *Easy for him to say.* "You can't keep going at this pace—no one can—it's too much. I'd like to start getting you scheduled for regular sessions." I could hear knocking, followed by Steph's voice calling to me through the door. The governor was asking for me.

"I'm sorry, Doctor, I have to go," I said. "I'm sorry I asked, and, yes, I hear you."

"Melissa, do you actually hear me? This is important."

Steph cracked the door open and popped in, "Sorry—he just asked for you again."

"I'm sorry, I'll be right there," I responded.

"Be right where?" the doctor asked, confused.

"Sorry, Doctor, I wasn't talking to you, but I really do have to go now. Thanks for squeezing me in. I hear your points, I really do. Bye now." I hung up, feeling defeated. I knew myself, and I didn't have much left in me. But there wasn't any other option than to keep going.

I grabbed a mini bottle of Diet Coke from the mini fridge next to my desk and went back to wrap up with the governor and Rob.

At the press conference that morning, we sat flanked by state police, rather than the members of the health team who had been our partners for months. Our press conferences were still being carried on cable news every day, and while it was a different crisis, to be sure, we knew the eyes of the nation would be on us.

CHAPTER 9

Say Their Name

"Violence never works," the governor began.

"It dishonors Mr. Floyd's death," he continued. "Mr. Floyd was not violent. Mr. Floyd was compliant. Mr. Floyd wasn't even charged or accused of a violent crime. There was no violence. That's what makes the killing more outrageous."

And then Cuomo glared into the camera and called out the White House's tactics: "When you are violent, it creates a scapegoat to shift the blame. It allows the president of the United States to tweet about looting rather than murder by a police officer. It allows the federal government to politicize what is going on and come up with theories blaming the Left and the extreme Left that only furthers the politics of division."

As the sun set that Sunday night, we weren't sure what to expect. The reaction was mixed: Upstate cities that imposed curfews and doubled their police presence saw a return to mostly peaceful protests, with violence and criminal activity dropping dramatically. New York City, however, was an unmitigated disaster.

Overnight, crowds in the city swelled into the thousands as protests that began days before turned into rioting and looting. Store windows were shattered across Manhattan as opportunists seized on the chaos to rob high-end designer shops. Police cars were set on fire, and the Bronx was literally burning. To make matters worse, local law enforcement was completely out of its depth. Even Gotham City's massive force (the nation's largest by far) lacked the manpower to manage a crisis of this magnitude, with some police responding by driving into crowds and pulling down people's masks to pepper-spray them. Videos of anarchy across the city went viral, causing both sides to dig in deeper.

Over the weekend, the additional resources we deployed across upstate to the localities who had taken us up on our offer of support had proven effective. None of them were in the worsening firestorm that was engulfing New York City.

In the city, de Blasio made clear that, despite the deteriorating situation, he neither needed nor wanted support from the state police or the National Guard. The governor kept the channels of communication open, speaking directly with rank-and-file members of the NYPD and their union officials to get their perspective on what was going wrong. Every few hours, we would make another overture to City Hall, and every time the answer was the same: thanks, but no thanks. To overrule the mayor, Cuomo would have to take the extraordinary step of removing him from office and taking over control of the NYPD. That would have been an unprecedented move in the middle of a dual health and public-safety emergency, and we never seriously considered it.

But that Monday morning—after another long, ugly night—it was clear that continuing to let the mayor do nothing was not an option.

The governor and I barely spoke on the tense flight down to New York City. Tone in this press conference was everything. If it appeared that Cuomo was telling de Blasio what to do, the story would shift from the riots to the long-simmering feud between the two men, and the message would be lost. But if we didn't put pressure on the city, they'd continue the losing strategy they'd been employing for days.

Once we arrived at our Manhattan headquarters, Cuomo instructed me to call Emma in the mayor's office. She and her boss needed to understand our current position; we wanted no surprises, but they needed to know we wouldn't continue to stay silent much longer.

Emma answered on the first ring, her voice sounding defeated from the last three days of chaos. I could also hear her trepidation, anticipating that, minutes before our press conference, I was about to drop a bomb.

I told her that, based on conversations the governor was having with law enforcement on the ground, he believed strongly that the NYPD didn't have enough police officers on the street. Nor were the rank and file being managed properly; they needed clearer instruction on when to use force, when to ask for backup, and when to make arrests. Cuomo also thought a citywide curfew was necessary. These were all local decisions, and technically the state did not have the authority to overrule the mayor, but we could not and would not stand by silently any longer.

Emma was not in a position to agree to anything without consent from both the mayor and the police commissioner. She asked that the governor refrain from applying public pressure on City Hall before he and the mayor could confer. I agreed but reiterated that the governor did not consider the status quo effective, and something had to be done. He would speak with de Blasio immediately after the press conference.

At the presser, Cuomo presented the daily COVID numbers and used his platform to try to urge calm, particularly in New York City, which continued to be a major problem. With the city set to reopen in exactly one week, he cautioned, all of the work New Yorkers had put in to curb the pandemic could be wiped away as a result of the maskless crowds surging in the streets. The governor also expressed concern about the impact the chaos would have on the thousands of people who had fled the city during the pandemic. Businesses had been operating remotely, and people who could afford it had headed to second homes in the Hamptons, Connecticut, and Florida. We needed the workforce to come back at full strength, but why would those who had relocated do so if shattered storefronts and burning police cars were what they would be coming back to? Finally, Cuomo warned that violence and looting would give the critics—and the antagonist in the White House—carte blanche to falsely paint all the protesters as criminals, undermining the whole Black Lives Matter movement and shifting the subject from the real issue of police brutality, systemic racism, and the injustice of George Floyd's death. He then floated the idea of a possible curfew, but stopped short of making any pronouncements. He said he would be discussing the issue with the mayor.

We were wrapping up the question-and-answer portion of the press conference when Trump pulled the pin on a Tweet grenade and tossed it into the universe: governors across the country should send in the military to take down any additional protests, the president declared. Then he took it a chilling step further: "If a city or a state refuses to take the actions that are necessary to defend the life and property of their residents, then I will deploy the United States military and quickly solve the problem for them."

It didn't take a genius to know where this was going. Trump had delusions of Patton grandeur and would love nothing more than to send tanks and camouflage-clad soldiers into cities across the country—a scenario that would unquestionably trigger more chaos and lead to further bloodshed.

As we hurried up the flight of stairs back to the governor's thirty-ninth-floor office, Cuomo told me to text Emma. "Tell her I need to speak with the mayor. Now."

The subject of the NYPD and de Blasio was historically fraught. He won his original campaign for mayor on the platform of undoing "stop and frisk," a signature policy of the Bloomberg administration whereby officers could stop, temporarily detain, question, and "pat down" civilians they suspected of potentially having contraband or other weapons. While Black New Yorkers make up roughly 24 percent of the city's population, they accounted for approximately 55 percent of those stopped under the policy. Ninety percent of those stops did not lead to a summons or arrest—in other words, the policy led to thousands of law-abiding citizens being stopped on spec and undergoing the humiliating and sometimes frightening experience of being questioned and searched by the police for no reason at all. While de Blasio viewed his position as an attempt to make policing fairer, the NYPD rank and file felt his rhetoric was anti-police, a situation made worse when he appeared on ABC News's *This Week* and talked about teaching his biracial son to be wary around law enforcement because of his race. Two weeks later, two officers were assassinated while sitting in their marked patrol car in Brooklyn, and all hell broke loose. Officers turned their backs on de Blasio as he spoke at a funeral for one of the officers. The head of the officers' union said de Blasio had blood on his hands. And, in active protest, police officers stopped working, with arrests plummeting 66 percent the following week compared to the year prior.

Complicating matters, de Blasio fancied himself the standard bearer of the Far Left, and, in the years that followed, that meant staking out a position that actively opposed police presence. Cuomo and de Blasio had come to verbal blows three months before COVID, when the governor began a crusade to combat rising crime on the subway, in part, by deploying 500 additional police officers. It was the latest chapter in the saga of the extreme Left versus Andrew Cuomo, one that had been underway since he was first elected in 2010. The mayor vocally opposed the plan, siding with Democratic Socialist Alexandria Ocasio-Cortez and the Far Left against the governor, and called on his MTA board appointees to vote against it. While the governor succeeded in gaining approval for his plan, it was another proof point for officers that de Blasio did not respect them or understand the job they had to do.

Now, amid mass chaos following George Floyd's murder, the far-left wing of the party was taking its support for the protesters a step further, wrapping itself in a new political slogan: Defund the police. It was ill-advised and stupid, but that didn't stop extreme-left elected officials from taking up the mantra. The mayor took it a step further, attempting to lead the charge by announcing he would cut $1 billion from the NYPD operating budget and another $500 million from its capital budget. Now de Blasio was caught between the reality of needing officers to ensure the city didn't devolve into complete pandemonium and not wanting to alienate his political base. The governor knew it and was hell-bent on not allowing de Blasio's politics to interfere with public safety.

So now here we were, in our Manhattan office, with de Blasio and the police commissioner on speaker.

"Mr. Mayor, Commissioner Shea. Not to state the obvious, but we have a problem, gentlemen," the governor began.

The conversation quickly took on a tone that could be described as "blunt congeniality." Cuomo began asking pointed questions about troop deployment. The press had estimated that some 5,000 protesters had been on the streets the night before. Police Commissioner Dermot Shea now reported that he had only 4,000 officers on duty. The governor's eyes widened in disbelief at what, to him, amounted to a staggering admission of malpractice. Shea had just confirmed what the governor had been told and feared; the city had deliberately minimized deployment.

"You have thirty-eight thousand officers in the NYPD. With all due respect, where are they?" he demanded.

The commissioner begrudgingly acknowledged that he could deploy additional officers if that's what the mayor wanted. We then moved on to the elephant in the room: the New Yorker in the Oval Office who would be looming over the city, actively stoking the conflict. Trump was unpredictable and dangerous, and we needed to work together to make sure that whatever he did, said, or tweeted would not further undermine our efforts to get the situation under control.

The conversation ended with an agreement: Shea would double the officers on duty that night to 8,000—a number the governor pushed them to but still believed was woefully inadequate. Additionally, Cuomo and de Blasio would issue a joint press release ASAP announcing a citywide curfew, the first of its kind in seventy-five years. The timing of the curfew was a point of debate. Too early could send the message that peaceful protesters wouldn't be able to have their voices heard. Too late would render it meaningless. We jointly decided that the order would go into effect at 11:00 that night and would be effective until 5:00 the following morning. Essential workers would be exempt.

We would respect tradition and the law; the state would not send in the National Guard without a request from the mayor, but they would be on standby.

We were headed straight back to Albany. This was a big announcement, and Cuomo wanted to explain the rationale for it to the public. He wanted to go on air with radio host Alan Chartock to discuss it. He knew the press would be listening, and this would ensure necessary context got into their stories. I texted Rich Azzopardi to lock it in and get the advisory out to the press.

Chartock was a longtime public radio personality, dating back to the Mario Cuomo administration. When the governor went on his show, it was always with a message to deliver. Chartock did his interviews without any consideration for how the Albany press corps would interpret them, which they found absolutely infuriating. Instead, Chartock catered to his listeners. He would grill the governor on news of the day, but also ask questions about his love life, his dog, and his workout routine. Cuomo was comfortable with Alan—sometimes too comfortable, from my perspective. The dynamic between the two provided a forum for a free-flowing, unscripted conversation. Some days, the approach was advantageous to us, but at other times, it would require three days of damage control.

The governor spent the flight back to Albany with his earbuds in, eyes closed, listening to a playlist his daughters had put together for him on his iPod; I could hear a refrain from "Take It Easy" by the Eagles leaking through. We didn't speak for a single minute of the flight. I could tell he was thinking it all through. But as soon as we began our descent, he opened his eyes, looked at me, and asked, "Are we set?"

I nodded, simultaneously texting Rich to confirm in real time that what I was telling the governor was true.

As we stepped off the helicopter and approached the cars on the ground, I received a text from Dani: trouble was brewing with City Hall. I got in the passenger seat of the car, pulled the seat belt across my chest, and sighed.

"What now?" the governor, who was literally in the driver's seat, asked.

"Dani just texted. City Hall hasn't signed off on our joint statement. If this isn't out in the next few minutes, I don't think you can go on Chartock. If you make the announcement before the release hits, it will only create a feud story about you big-footing the mayor, and then the actual news will be lost."

Cuomo continued to stare straight ahead out the windshield.

"Call Emma," he instructed me. "This was something we agreed to over an hour ago and said we would immediately announce. This curfew goes into effect in a few hours. I'm not criticizing him for the piss-poor job he and his police chief did keeping the city safe this weekend. I'm not calling them out for their inadequate deployment of law enforcement. I'm not even calling him out for not enforcing the mask mandate that will allow the city to reopen in seven days. All I am trying to do is avoid further chaos and stop Trump from marching on New York. It's enough already."

I dialed Emma, who claimed that the press office had the statement but was "tinkering" and she would be right back to me. I informed her the governor was going on the air momentarily and would discuss the mutual agreement, whether the statement was signed off on or not.

Minutes later, we were in the living room of the mansion. The phone next to the navy blue velvet couch rang. It was the front office. They had Alan Chartock for the governor. And the statement wasn't out yet.

"Melissa, what is going on?" Cuomo demanded as he listened to the hold music. "It's been an hour and a half already!"

"I've been going back and forth with Emma," I said, exasperated. "But honestly, this isn't about politics or the press reaction. The public needs to know what the hell is going on. Announce it. I'll do whatever I can to move this statement in the next few minutes."

I stepped outside of the living room, closing the door behind me and dialed Emma . . . again.

"Melissa, our team is just . . ."

"Let me stop you, Emma. The governor is on the radio. He's going to announce the joint agreement. It should have been announced an hour ago. I love you—I really do, and I sympathize with the insanity that's been swirling around both of us, but for the love of Christ, can you *please* just send the statement out?"

"Okay, okay. I'm on it!" she promised.

Two minutes later, the statement and the governor's comment hit at almost exactly the same time. I allowed myself a sigh of relief. No harm, no foul. And, hopefully, no media-driven, feud-story distractions.

Wrong.

Dani was on my phone the second Cuomo was off the air. "City Hall is upset that the governor discussed the announcements on Chartock," she said. "They feel like we should have waited—it was their news, too." Rome was burning, and this is what City Hall was worried about?

I pinged Emma, but she didn't respond. I told myself it was not actually a big deal and turned my attention back to the actual crisis as opposed to the self-created one.

That afternoon, there was more news out of Minneapolis. The results of two autopsies performed on George Floyd were released. Cause of death: homicide. As word trickled out, crowds in cities across the nation grew larger and angrier.

With upstate under control, our team was 100 percent focused on New York City. The crowds were getting more and more aggressive, and so was the NYPD. Looters again ran through Midtown Manhattan, smashing windows and grabbing whatever merchandise they could. And there were no police within sight to stop them. I watched the television footage in shock. Where were the additional law-enforcement bodies we had agreed to hours earlier?

As I started to call Emma, NY1 cut to a live phone interview with the mayor, who was responding in real time to the looting not by sending in additional troops, but by announcing that the city would continue the curfew the following day but start it three hours earlier—at eight o'clock in the evening—and extend it through the week, until Sunday. That was not what we had discussed or what we had agreed. The move enraged the peaceful protesters—exactly the reaction we had sought to avoid.

Why was he projecting out six days when we didn't know what tomorrow would bring? The city hadn't discussed this with us before going forward. Now the decision lay squarely on the shoulders of the mayor.

The next morning, Cuomo summoned Rob and me to his conference room. Kopy was on speaker. We learned that a high-ranking member of the police union had reached out directly to the governor that morning with disturbing information: he believed that de Blasio, fearful of more police clashes with protesters going viral on video, was purposefully not deploying additional bodies. As a result, knowing they were outnumbered, officers were unwilling to take on the looters.

Cable news ran wall-to-wall coverage of the iconic Macy's storefront in Herald Square and Rockefeller Center, both covered in smashed glass. New York City residents were afraid. And the president was still posturing like a deranged despot.

"We are out of options, guys," the governor told us. "Today is the day. This is out of control. New Yorkers cannot take another week of this. The city is too fragile. And if we don't push de Blasio to act—I mean really act—Trump is going to send in the military."

"Do we actually think he would do that? Isn't this just grandstanding?" I asked.

The governor shook his head.

"Melissa, he's a crazy man. And you cannot predict what crazy people will do, because they don't act rationally. Who knows? But we can't let it happen, and none of this is fair to the people who live in the city and are just trying to go about their lives."

"I agree with you, Governor," Kopy, who had been on the ground in New York City the night before, piped up.

Rob and I nodded in agreement. City Hall had just proven that they would not truly address the situation. Cuomo scribbled a few points down on a small index card in front of him, slid his pen back into the inside breast pocket of his suit jacket, and looked up.

"Steph, are we ready?"

"Yes, Governor. PowerPoint is loaded."

"Okay, guys. Let's go."

Rob and I locked eyes as we turned to walk into the Red Room. We weren't sure what exactly the governor was going to say when the cameras were rolling, but it was clear he was done holding his tongue.

"The facts of the New York City situation are this: the mayor of New York City says he doesn't need the National Guard and he doesn't think they would be helpful, and he can do it with the NYPD," the governor said, winding up. "First, the NYPD and the mayor did not do their job last night, I believe that. Second, you have 38,000 NYPD people. It is the largest police department in the United States of America. Use 38,000 people and protect property. Use the police; protect property and people. Look at the videos; it was a disgrace! I believe that. I believe the mayor underestimates the scope of the problem. I think he underestimates the duration of the problem, and I don't think they've used enough police to address the situation. Because it is inarguable that it was not addressed last night."

He acknowledged the difference between protesters and looters, and emphasized that he wasn't attacking the rank-and-file police, rather the improper way they were being managed and deployed. He didn't mince words, articulating publicly what he had been saying privately for days.

Officers on the street want to clearly know what the mission is and "have to be given the confidence and the support" to carry it out, Cuomo asserted. His next comment was aimed directly at Shea and de Blasio, repeating: "You have 38,000 police officers, deploy them."

City Hall was furious. But the mayor now realized both the practical and the political reality: the chaos was doing more damage to him than offending the Far Left would. That night, the streets were flooded with NYPD. Arrests and looting dropped dramatically. That mattered far more than any bruised egos or negative press about the "feud" between the governor and the mayor.

The rest of the week was a constant seesaw; some nights were more peaceful, while others continued to be rife with chaos. There was anger from peaceful protesters who felt muzzled by the early curfew, and fear from essential workers—mainly immigrants and people of color—who were being stopped and aggressively questioned by law enforcement on their way home. NYPD was frustrated with the lose-lose situation they were in every night, and an already traumatized city was trapped in a perpetual state of anxiety.

By Thursday afternoon, the governor was restless. He called Beth, Jim, and me into his conference room.

"We need actual answers here, guys," he said.

"In terms of . . ." I started to ask.

"Reform," he cut in. "The nation is angry. They should be angry. Hell, I'm angry!" he continued. "They have watched the same videotape over and over again: Black man dead, white police officer walks. No accountability. Let's seize the moment and actually do something with it. Get input from stakeholders. Consult the Mothers of the Movement. Call Reverend Sharpton. Make sure there's a path to get the legislature on board, and come back to me this afternoon to show me what you've got."

Jim, Beth, and I came back hours later with a four-part plan for legislation that we considered straightforward and based on common sense: make police disciplinary records transparent, ban chokeholds, make false race-based 911 reports a hate crime, and appoint the attorney general to act as a standing special prosecutor for any civilian death involving law enforcement. Iterations of many of the proposals had been floated for years by advocacy groups but were always considered to be pie in the sky, the political will never there to push them through. Until now. The governor did his usual pressure testing, asking dozens of questions ten different ways, made a number of adjustments, and signed off.

"What should we call the plan?" he asked.

We hadn't had time to figure that out but promised to come up with something and get back to him.

That night, the governor, Stephanie, and I had dinner on the back patio of the pool house at the mansion with Cara, Mariah, and Michaela. The conversation was dominated by George Floyd, the protests, and the history of racism and slavery in the United States. I often used the girls, who were smart, curious, and part of a generation that increasingly wielded influence, as my own improvised focus group throughout COVID. That night, I explained the package we were planning to announce the next day. They asked questions and poked and prodded, but ultimately all gave their seal of approval.

One problem, I told them. We still didn't have a name for the package.

"Why not name it after George Floyd?" Michaela suggested.

"I thought about that. But this is so much bigger than George Floyd," I responded. "It's what your dad has been saying all week—it's George Floyd but also Breonna Taylor, Eric Garner, Ramarley Graham, and on and on."

"Well, then, isn't that it?" Michaela responded.

"Isn't what . . . oh, yes. That is it—thank you!" I leaned over and gave Michaela a big kiss on the cheek, took a sip of Diet Coke, snapped my laptop shut, and headed inside for an 8:00 p.m. conference call with the team. We had our policy proposal, and now we knew what to call it. The governor would use our next briefing to announce the "Say Their

Name" police reform agenda, and New York would lead the nation in meaningful change.

The next morning, we were putting the final touches on the day's PowerPoint for our daily press briefing, when Stephanie interrupted, iPhone in hand.

"Have you guys seen this?"

"Seen what?" the governor asked.

"This." Stephanie hit play to show a graphic video of a Buffalo police officer shoving a peaceful seventy-five-year-old protester to the ground, his head hitting the pavement with an audible crack.

Cuomo immediately asked Stephanie to get the Buffalo mayor on the phone and told me to find out the name of the injured protester and which hospital he was in.

"If he's conscious, I'd like to talk to him," he added.

Minutes before our press conference, the governor spoke with Buffalo mayor Byron Brown and seventy-five-year-old protestor Martin Gugino. He conveyed the same message to both: what happened was incomprehensible, the state stood ready to assist in any way possible, and he would be calling for the district attorney to investigate the incident. Rob and I stood in the governor's conference room, attempting not to eavesdrop while getting anxious looking at the clock. As I heard the call wrapping up, I walked over and popped my head into the doorway.

"Governor, it's 11:28—are you ready to go?"

"Yes. Wait, no. Stephanie, can you please ask the press office to add the footage from Buffalo into the slideshow."

I was too taken aback to hide my surprise.

"Wait—are you sure?" I asked. "That video is really disturbing."

"Yes, it is. Which is why the entire nation should see it."

Within minutes, we were seated at the briefing table. After ticking through the daily COVID numbers, the governor unveiled the "Say Their Name" agenda and played the video.

"Mr. Floyd's murder was the breaking point of a long list of deaths that were unnecessary and which were abusive," he said. "That is a fact, and people are saying, 'Enough is enough.' Reform works for everyone's interest here. Stopping police abuse vindicates the overwhelming majority—99.9 percent—of police who are there to do the right thing and *do* do the right thing every day. It restores the confidence, the respect, and the trust that you need to make this relationship work."

As the sun set that Friday night, the protests were largely under control. There was little to no looting in the city, and the rest of the state was peaceful. The mayor lifted the curfew that Saturday morning—one day early.

We turned our focus back to COVID. If the numbers held, we would be in a position to reopen New York City that Monday morning. Maybe, just maybe, I allowed myself to think as I climbed into bed that night, spent and exhausted to the core, we could soon put both crises behind us.

CHAPTER 10

Sprinting to the Finish Line

It was 4:30 a.m. and I was wide awake. But for the first time in three months, it wasn't because of anxiety or pure fight-or-flight adrenaline. I woke up excited. In seven short hours, we would be at our 100th consecutive daily press briefing, announcing what the world had been waiting for: New York City—once the global epicenter of the COVID pandemic—was officially reopening.

Nothing could keep me down. Not the last week of mayhem. Not the last four months of uncertainty. Not even the out-of-control dread from never knowing what could come next. Nope. That morning, I sprang out of bed, ready to take on the world.

I threw on a white tank top and the navy Lululemon spandex leggings I stole from my sister six months earlier and laced up my sneakers. Flipping through my iPhone to find the best upbeat playlist, I headed for the gym. At that hour, I had the gym to myself. I grabbed the remote, turned on MSNBC, and stepped onto the treadmill. Just then, I got a Gmail calendar notification: "Matt's Bday :)" Ugh. So, it's the 100th day of COVID, NYC's reopening, and my estranged husband who just told me he doesn't want to be married to me anymore's birthday. Great.

As I started running, my mind wandered back to a few weeks earlier, when I was in the gym with Larry.

"Good morning, Melissa."

I kept running, smiled, and pointed at my AirPods—the universal signal of "I can't hear you."

"Hi there!" I waved.

"Melissa, do you have a minute?"

I nodded and removed my right earbud.

"Hey, Larry. Sleep okay?" Maybe if I kept it light, I could deny away the rain that was no doubt about to fall on my sunny little parade.

"Yes, I slept fine. Melissa, I am concerned. And I hope I'm not overstepping, but as former secretary to the governor, I feel I have to say something."

"Of course, Larry, what's up?" I increased the treadmill running speed from 6.5 to 6.8. Like I could run away in place from whatever was coming.

"Nursing homes. The Republicans are pouncing at a national level. This isn't about the policy—they are playing on the politics. You have the public . . . for now. But the minute the crisis is really over, there will be a void, and Trump and the Republicans will look to kill you. And nursing homes is where they are going."

This wasn't news to me.

"No, I know, Larry—that's a really good point, and Dr. Zucker is working on a report with DOH to dissect what actually happened in nursing homes and dispel the politics." Specifically, the report was going to analyze from a health standpoint how COVID spread into nursing homes.

Larry worried aloud that nursing home operators would try to ensure that the blame for the spread of COVID among their patients would fall anywhere but at their own feet. They would help push the narrative. Trump saw it and was seizing on it. And the governor had so many enemies on the Far Right and the Far Left. "You need to be ready."

"I hear you, Larry." I could feel the anxiety creeping in. I increased the speed to 7.0. "And I agree 100 percent." I promised to check in with him later that day, put my earbud back in, and ran for another twenty minutes. Buzz officially killed, I stepped off the treadmill, waved to Larry at the weight bench, and walked out of the pool house.

Thinking back to that conversation, my mind was reeling; I knew Larry was right. And the nursing home report—where was that?

As rapidly as we had been issuing executive orders and the federal government was putting out new health regulations, the state's Department of Health was issuing health guidance and directives, sometimes as many as five a day. The best way to describe the dynamic is fog of war. There were federal and state actions happening simultaneously, seventeen crises occurring on top of each other, and decisions being made as expediently as possible. All of them done with the best possible intentions.

Executive orders come from the governor's office, and each one requires two signatures—those of the governor and his secretary. Cuomo's and mine. When we issued them, I would spend hours going through every detail, personally signing off on each one before going to the governor for approval. But our Department of Health routinely issued directives independently, in consultation with members of the COVID task force, and while it would run legal traps through counsel's office, it didn't have to go to the governor to issue its guidance or mandates. And occasionally that yielded unpleasant surprises. One of those surprises occurred seven weeks earlier.

"Hello?" Linda had answered, half asleep in the wee hours of April 22.

"Have you seen this?!" On a scale of one to ten, I was at fourteen, and it wasn't even 5:00 a.m.

"See what? I'm still waking up," she said.

"The front page of the *New York Post*!" I shouted, my voice continuing to rise. Linda Lacewell had come to Albany at the beginning of March to join the governor's COVID task force. As superintendent of the Department of Financial Services, Linda Lacewell earned her reputation for being meticulous and effective, and she was often deployed to get to the bottom of bureaucratic messes. She had spent weeks untangling problems at the Department of Labor when the unemployment system crashed in the early days of the pandemic.

"Hang on, I'm pulling it up." Linda was awake now.

"Wait, I'll save you the trouble," I snapped, beginning to read aloud:

New York State just issued a drastic new guideline urging emergency services workers not to bother trying to revive anyone without a pulse when they get to a scene, amid an overload of coronavirus patients. While paramedics were previously told to spend up to 20 minutes trying to revive people found in cardiac arrest, the change is "necessary during the COVID-19 response to protect the health and safety of EMS providers by limiting their exposure, conserve resources, and ensure optimal use of equipment to save the greatest number of lives," according to a State Health Department memo issued last week.

"*What*?" Linda had now joined me in the parallel universe of tabloid outrage.

"I'm going to stroke out!" I said, exasperated. "This has to be fixed!"

"Okay, calm down; we'll figure this out," she said, trying her best to bring my blood pressure down.

"The governor goes on TV every day, saying that we're going to fight as hard as we can to save every life that we can, and DOH issues a directive telling EMTs not to try to revive patients?!" That one took half a day, but it was reversed by the time the sun went down. It was the second time in as many days the governor would be blindsided.

The first time was during a press conference on live national television on April 20, when Bernadette Hogan of the *New York Post* posed a question.

"What is the state's policy regarding admission or readmission to these nursing homes?" Bernadette had asked. "Whether or not one of these people have tested for the virus. There was a state directive that said that people cannot be denied readmission or admission. Just wondering what the state policy is right now, again, judging the high number of deaths that are coming out of these areas."

Rob Mujica and I exchanged glances on the dais, unsure where this was going. The governor looked at both of us, clearly wondering the same thing.

"If you are tested positive for the virus, are you allowed to be admitted to a nursing home, is the question?" Cuomo asked.

"Or readmitted," Bernadette clarified.

Cuomo turned to the dais and responded: "It's a good question. I don't know."

Dr. Zucker jumped in: "The policy is that if you are positive, you should be admitted back to a nursing home. The necessary precautions will be taken to protect the other residents there."

Bernadette wasn't done and came back with a follow-up question.

"Is that safe, though, and does staff have the capacity to treat those individuals? Is that the best place, again, judging how rapidly the virus spreads and also this is a very vulnerable population, as you guys have expressed multiple times?"

"And that's why we're working closely with the nursing home, both the leadership and the individuals who are working in the nursing home, to protect those individuals who are coming back who had COVID-19 and were brought back to the nursing home from where they came," Dr. Zucker, our health commissioner, explained.

Back in the governor's office after the press conference ended, Cuomo turned to us as soon as we were inside the door. "What was Bernadette talking about in there? What was that with nursing homes?"

Our administration had sought to be as aggressive as possible when it came to COVID in nursing homes. Before we even had our first confirmed COVID death, the governor banned visitation and mandated temperature checks and PPE, while DOH directed that COVID-positive patients be separated from the facility's general population.

In mid-March, the federal Centers for Medicaid and Medicaid Services (CMMS) issued guidance that stated that a nursing home should—not may or could, but should—continue to accept patients from hospitals where COVID-19 was present. The March 25 admissions policy was based on that federal guidance: nursing homes should not reject a medically stable patient "solely on the basis of" their confirmed or suspected COVID-19 status; the same thing also applied to hospitals.

The thrust of the order was not dissimilar to federal directives issued in the 1980s when the AIDS epidemic was playing out and there was a fear that people who were HIV-positive would be denied care because of their health status. However, it wasn't that simple, because New York State law went further. While nursing homes could not discriminate, New York law stipulated that they also could not accept any patient that they could not adequately care for. In the context of the COVID-19 pandemic, adequate care required, at a minimum, adherence to detailed guidance issued to nursing homes throughout the unfolding crisis. That included rigorous infection-control procedures, providing adequate PPE, and being able to safeguard other residents. And New York was far from alone. Eleven other states issued similar guidance to nursing homes following federal direction, including Republican strongholds Utah, Arizona, Indiana, and Nevada.

None of it mattered. Unbeknownst to us, COVID-19 was already present in New York, including in its nursing home and long-term-care facilities, for more than a month before the state's first confirmed COVID-19 case, silently infiltrating our communities after arriving from Europe in January or early February. The heroic efforts of New York's nursing home employees to control the spread of the virus got a late start, in part because the federal government failed to recognize the spread and take action to close international travel, and in part because of the unrecognized risk of asymptomatic spread early on.

Facing harsh criticism for his mishandling of COVID-19 himself, Trump seized on nursing homes as an opportunity to flip his narrative. And he was not to be underestimated. Trump was a master marketer who excelled at sensing people's feelings—particularly their fears and anxiety—and exploiting them. Trump knew that the families of nursing home patients were under tremendous stress. The families knew that

COVID was viciously attacking the elderly in these congregate facilities but were effectively powerless to do anything about it. Trump sensed the anxiety and gave it a political target. There was someone to blame. Government messed up, and that's why your loved one died. It wasn't that he was incompetent and the federal government blew it; it was that governors—specifically Democratic ones (and ignoring the Republican ones who did the same)—enacted deadly policies that killed your grandparents. The vitriol was reserved for governors who had been highly critical of Trump: Gavin Newsom in California, Gretchen Whitmer in Michigan, Phil Murphy in New Jersey, and Tom Wolf in Pennsylvania. But no one had a bigger bull's-eye on their back than America's governor, Andrew Cuomo.

Standing in the governor's office after the presser, Zucker explained that the March 25 health order was put in place when the major concern was the collapse of the hospital system, like the heart-wrenching scenario that was unfolding back then in Italy. The goal was to ensure that patients who were medically stable and understood not to be contagious but still testing positive (or whose status was unknown due to lack of testing capacity) would not end up taking badly needed hospital beds unnecessarily for days or weeks on end. He added that other directives were put in place to ensure everything was done safely and by the book.

The worst-case scenario that the Health Department's March 25 admissions advisory was aimed at never came to pass. Because we bent the curve when we did, there were always additional hospital beds. Nursing homes had other options available to them.

The governor looked at Jim, Rob, Dr. Zucker, and me. "Guys, you see where the *Post* is going with their questions," he said. "This won't be about the merits or the reasoning for the policy. We need to be able to clearly explain this, and if we need to change course and disregard federal guidance, do it."

The initial decision was made to immediately issue additional clarifying guidance to nursing homes statewide to reenforce what their responsibilities were in terms of providing patient care, and to reiterate that no DOH guidance, including that of March 25, superseded their legal obligation: if they could not safely provide adequate care for a patient in their facility, legally they could not accept them.

Two and a half weeks later, when we had enough testing capacity, we took additional precautions, directing nursing home staff to be tested twice a week. We also went a step further, mandating that hospitals could no longer discharge a COVID-19 patient to a nursing home until the person had tested negative for the disease.

None of it mattered. Trump was driving the narrative on nursing homes now. The press and the Far Right smelled blood, and they were ready for a feeding frenzy. A report DOH had initiated in May was, in theory, supposed to answer the question of how COVID spread into nursing homes. Zucker and Cuomo had discussed the idea when the press first started to hammer us on the March 25 DOH order, which was being twisted into some villainous, nonexistent executive order forcing nursing homes to take contagious COVID patients and thereby endangering the lives of countless vulnerable seniors in assisted living across the state. Dr. Zucker, a distinguished veteran of the World Health Organization and the Department of Health and Human Services, maintained it was the right public-health decision. Zucker believed a real examination of the facts would show that it was the staff and visitors who brought COVID into the nursing homes through asymptomatic spread long before we ever knew COVID was here. As it turned out, Zucker was right.

A statistical analysis of nursing home data found that infected nursing home staff members were the primary driver of COVID in nursing homes. The conclusion was reached based on the timing of employee infections correlating with the timing of peak nursing home resident deaths across the state—meaning, as the caretakers got sick, nursing home patient deaths followed. Staff in infected areas of the state got COVID at the same rate as the general public and unknowingly introduced it to their workplaces. It was also likely that an unknown number of visitors brought COVID into nursing homes before testing was available or visitations were suspended during the two months the virus had silently spread undetected across the state. The finding was consistent with what states across the country were seeing, regardless of their admission policies. Where COVID was prevalent, staff members had infections and unknowingly brought it to work with them.

Any endorphins my dawn workout had generated had beaten a hasty retreat. I braced for the official start of my workday.

Mental note: put in a call to check in with the group. And Matt's birthday. What should I do? A call? Text? Does he want to hear from me?

I threw on my favorite white sleeveless dress and thick, navy blue belt and headed to the living room. Steph and Rob were already there, eating breakfast and working away on the day's PowerPoint for the daily briefing.

"Rob, you don't happen to know where the health team is on the nursing home report, do you?" I asked.

"I don't, Melissa, sorry."

"No problem—I'll figure it out."

Just then, the pocket door to the room slid open.

"Good morning, good morning!" The governor was certainly in a good mood.

"Well, someone woke up on the right side of the bed this morning," I said.

"It's a good day, Melissa," he boomed. "It's a good day for this country. It's a good day for the people of this state. Let's make sure Dani has the subway set, please."

Shit. I had completely forgotten that he wanted to ride the subway to the office.

The MTA had presented a daunting challenge since the pandemic began. Early on, health experts believed that COVID could live on a surface for up to two days. Stainless steel supposedly allowed the virus to be the most viable for the longest period of time, and subway cars are almost entirely stainless steel. Making matters more complicated, essential workers relied on the subway to get to and from work, and so shutting them down was not an option. New York City's subways are the only public mass transit system on the globe that runs twenty-four hours a day. The governor worked around the clock with Sarah Feinberg, the interim president of the New York City Transit Authority (an operating agency under the MTA), to come up with a plan to keep the system running safely. Sarah, a former administrator of the Federal Railroad Administration under President Obama, was tough as nails and as smart as they come. Sarah was in her early forties, blond, and beautiful, traits that sometimes caused insecure men to underestimate her, a mistake that generally came at their own expense.

"We can contract with all of the cutting-edge companies out there, but the reality is that we can't disinfect the cars the way any of them are proposing if there are people on them," Sarah had quickly concluded, noting that it wasn't just the essential workers who would be riding, but homeless New Yorkers as well. Many had decamped from perpetually crowded shelters onto subway cars, figuring it was safer to live there.

In the end, the only way to ensure subways were cleaned would be to empty them, and the only way that could happen was if, for the first time in history, we temporarily shut them down every day from 1:00 a.m. until 5:00 a.m. The NYPD and MTA police would empty out every single one of the roughly 6,500 cars in the system; homeless people would be offered rides to nearby shelters. Sarah worked with Rob and our state operations director, Kelly Cummings, to put together a plan that offered buses or for-hire vans to provide transport to any essential worker who needed to travel to and from work during that time, and we would disinfect every car in the system every twenty-four hours. It was a colossal undertaking, but we managed to make it work. The governor riding the subway this morning was a symbolic but meaningful gesture to drive confidence in the millions of New Yorkers who hadn't ridden it in three months. It was safe, and New York was back.

"Umm, yes, one second . . ." I stammered while the governor waited for my confirmation that everything was ready.

"I just spoke to Dani, Governor," Steph interrupted. "She's all set with the pooled video and photog, and she's already advanced the ride again this morning."

Phew. Thanks, Steph.

Cuomo smiled. "Great. Okay, let's get going, people."

We were going to be early, but there was no slowing him down.

When we landed at the 34th Street helipad, the governor met Dani and headed over to the subway. Rob and I climbed into a separate car to go directly to the office to prep for the briefing.

"Melissa, I saw today is Matt's birthday. Any plans?" Rob asked innocently.

"He's actually in Connecticut, and I'm obviously underwater with work, so we'll celebrate when things calm down."

"Gotcha," Rob said. "Well, wish him a happy birthday for me."

"Will do."

As I sat in my office prepping for Q and A, I looked down at my phone, distracted. I had texted Matt birthday greetings an hour earlier, but still no reply. I texted again: "Call me when you're up!" I knew there was no fixing us, but I wasn't ready to lose the friendship, too. I clicked on the Twitter icon and shot off a tweet:

> Today is day 100, the day NYC officially begins to reopen.
>
> It is also @MatthewLWing's birthday . . . so lots to celebrate!

My assistant stuck her head in the doorway to let me know the governor was ready.

Still no response from Matt. I silenced my iPhone, grabbed a Sharpie and some note cards, and walked down the hall.

The governor was sitting at his desk, making final changes to the PowerPoint slide when Rob, Dr. Zucker, and I walked in together. He glanced up.

"Steph, why don't you come in here, too?" Steph got up from her desk and joined us. "Big day today, team. Big day." I hadn't seen him like this in as long as I could remember. He was vibrant, happy, excited even. "You'll remember this day for your entire lives," he told us. "History will remember this day." He stopped for a minute, took off his glasses, and looked back up again. "I'm proud of you. I asked a lot of you every single day, and you guys never once let me down. Take a minute and appreciate that." We smiled and, in that moment, as a team, looked at each other, understanding the gravity of what we had been through and where we were today. "Okay," the governor said, looking at his watch, "minute's over—let's get to work."

We all headed down to the thirty-eighth-floor press briefing room—the same room we had sat in ninety-nine days earlier when we had announced the first confirmed COVID case in New York. So much had changed in that brief period of time. Tens of thousands of lives had been lost. Families torn apart. Businesses decimated. And in the face of it all, this state of 19.5 million people, our state, showed the world that the strongest four-letter word truly is *love*.

The governor sat down, announced the official reopening of New York City, and, looking into the camera, beamed: "I am just so proud of how New Yorkers have responded. We can be a tough crew. New Yorkers heard the message; they did what they had to do . . . it was frightening, but New Yorkers did it."

As we left the office that day, we weren't sure what would happen next, but we were confident that, whatever it was, New Yorkers could get through it. We proved that together we could get through anything.

Afterward, on the helicopter ride back to Albany, I broached the idea of ending the daily briefings and shifting to as-needed mode, but the governor seemed reluctant to let go.

The governor pulled out his iPod, put in his earbuds, leaned back, and closed his eyes.

"Okay, let's think about it," he finally agreed. "But for now, let's figure out what we need to say tomorrow."

Just then, I felt my phone vibrate. It was Matt. *"Hey—thanks for the note—and congrats on the City reopening—huge achievement!"* I exhaled and closed my eyes.

We continued the briefings for another eleven days, using them to show progress on projects around the state, taking the press pool on the road as a tool to inspire confidence that New York was coming back and would be better than ever before. We opened the bike-and-pedestrian path on the Governor Mario M. Cuomo Bridge and unveiled the long-awaited new Terminal B Arrivals and Departures Hall at LaGuardia Airport.

We focused on social progress, too, signing the "Say Their Name" reform package the day after the legislature passed it, alongside Reverend Al Sharpton, NAACP President Hazel Dukes, Senate Majority Leader Andrea Stewart-Cousins, Assembly Speaker Carl Heastie, and members of Mothers of the Movement. It was a huge victory for protesters and police reform advocates and unequivocally the right thing to do. It was also another instance of New York being first, the most-sweeping package of reforms enacted by any state since George Floyd's murder.

The morning of June 17, the governor summoned me to his conference room, where he was going through the day's COVID numbers with Rob and Dr. Zucker.

"Melissa, could you step into my office for a minute? Excuse me, gentlemen; we'll be right back."

He asked me to close the door to his inner office behind me. I had no idea what he wanted to talk about.

Sitting behind his desk, the governor looked up at me.

"It's time to end the briefings," he said bluntly. "I think I'll announce it this morning. What do you think?"

I was taken aback.

"Wow. Okay. Yes, I agree, I'm just surprised. We hadn't talked about this for a week and a half, and so I just thought . . ."

"No, I know," Cuomo acknowledged. "I didn't think New York was ready before. I think information is comforting. A routine is comforting when you're going through a trauma. I didn't want to abandon people. But it's time now. New Yorkers are ready."

"Okay, I'm with you, I agree," I paused. "How are we going to get it out there? Are you just going to blurt it out?"

"I don't think I 'blurt,' Melissa," he said, throwing me the half-smile he uses when he thinks I'm being a wise guy. "But, yes, I will announce it at the end of today's press conference. Let's set the last briefing for Friday, and we can discuss later today what we think the right vehicle is."

He got up from behind the desk, extending his right arm out toward the door—his way of indicating that the conversation was over.

The governor let the team know that he would announce the end of the briefings and made sure everyone agreed. Everyone did. He asked Jack Davies, a whip-smart up-and-comer in our press shop, to load the PowerPoint, and we walked into the inner office to enter the Red Room. Just then, Cuomo stopped and gestured to the doorknob, "Do you know that this is the same doorknob that's been here since FDR was governor? Think about that—how much history is in this room." We all knew the fabled history of the fabled doorknob because he had told us many, many times before. But we nodded and smiled anyway, appreciating his respect for the legacy of the building, the leaders and staffers that came before us, and the enormity of the moment we were living through. "Okay, let's go." He opened the door, gesturing for the team to walk in—always the last to enter, holding the door for every one of us.

"We did what we had to do, my friends, and we did it together, and we did it every day, and now we're going to move on to other things," the governor began. The last daily briefing would be on Friday, he announced, and from then on, only as necessary. It was time to move forward, and the governor was right—New Yorkers were ready.

After the presser was over, the governor and I sat and discussed what the last briefing would look like. We agreed that it should be different from all of the others; we were in a different moment, and the message and setting should reflect that.

"What if you do a direct-to-camera from behind the desk?" I asked, picturing a White House–style address from behind the same oversized mahogany desk used by Mario Cuomo and FDR.

"You don't think that's too much?" he asked.

"No," I insisted. "After everything this state has been through, I don't think it would be possible to be 'too much.'"

"Okay. Ask Steph to come in. I'm going to work on a draft." It was settled.

The governor spent the next day and a half writing draft after draft of the script for his final daily COVID briefing. While he would turn to the speechwriting team for facts, quotes, and historical background, much like his father, his words were always almost entirely his own.

The morning of the final briefing I woke up at 5:30 a.m.—the latest I had slept since March 1. I checked my BlackBerry, skimmed the clips, and called our chief of staff, Jill DesRosiers.

"Hey, lady. Are we all set for today?"

"Yep," she assured me. The crew was already at the capitol. They'd tested the lights and the feed. The look-back video was done and loaded, to be shown after the governor's remarks, and the press team was ready with the satellite information.

I exhaled. "Thanks, Jilly. I really couldn't do this without you."

"None of us could do any of this without each other, Melissa."

I hung up, put my head back down on the pillow, and started to think about the last 111 days. What we had been through. Standing up the test sites, the fights with the White House, the constant wail of ambulance sirens. I thought about Pat Kane and the health-care workers. I thought about the upstate nursing home that sent ventilators downstate to show Elise Stefanik and the world that we were one New York. I thought about graves on Hart Island and the thousands of volunteers who came from out of state to help, and the essential workers who showed up every single day to keep the state going. And just then, overtaken by the enormity of it, by depression, pride, and sheer exhaustion, I started to cry. I had held it together as best I could, sprinting to the finish line over the last 111 days, but I couldn't hold back anymore. And rather than fight it, I gave in, letting myself feel all of it.

When I arrived at the office, the governor was already there. He and Steph were going back and forth, in typical fashion, wordsmithing until the very last minute. True to form, Jill was right. Everything was set and ready to go.

I popped into the office to look at the camera shot when the governor stepped in behind me.

"What do you think? Are we ready?"

"I want to play around a little with what's going to be on the desk for the shot," I said. "Go focus on the speech."

Cuomo nodded and looked into the camera to see the shot for himself.

"It's almost right—just needs one thing," he said. The governor crossed the room, picked up the Andrew Cuomo bobblehead doll that had been given to him as a gag gift years earlier and carefully placed it on the desk, where it would be clearly visible in the camera shot. "There you go, Melissa. I fixed it for you. Now it's perfect." He grinned. I smiled back. *Well, apparently he still has his sense of humor.*

The governor delivered the briefing in one take, clocking in at just over nine minutes.

"We showed that in the end, love does win," he declared. "Love does conquer all. That no matter how dark the day, love brings the light. That is what I will take from the past 111 days. And it inspires me and energizes me and excites me. If we could accomplish together what we did here, this impossible task of beating back this deadly virus, then there is nothing that we can't do."

When he was finished, there wasn't a dry eye in the room. He walked around his small office hugging the cameramen and technicians, thanking them for their hard work over the last 111 days. "It's the people behind the camera, the ones that work without recognition, who truly get the job done. Thank you."

He turned and walked into the conference room, "What did you think?"

"It was perfect," I responded. "You did it."

"No, *we* did it. *New Yorkers* did it." He turned to pick up his black leather briefcase, a signal that he was ready to head out. "I'm going to go see Michaela. You guys will be over soon?"

"Yes, we're all set for 1:00 p.m."

"And we invited everyone?"

"Yes, we invited everyone."

Cuomo was very big on group gatherings; he felt it was important to bring everyone, from executive assistants to senior staff, together to make sure the entire team understood that they were appreciated and included. I never liked going to staff events; outside of a small group of senior staff that I worked most closely with, I was incredibly introverted at the office and have never been good at forced socialization. But that afternoon, overtaken with pride and gratitude, I was looking forward to it.

The core team from the executive chamber who worked on COVID gathered at the pool house—everyone tested and outdoors. Having been holed up in our individual offices, socially distanced and masked for the last several months, it was the first time we had all been together since February.

People referred to them as "pool house parties," but they more closely resembled the ending of a work conference—dinner entrées under heat lamps, a roving photographer, hearty New York State wine, and a podium, because for our administration, a party wasn't a party without a series of speeches.

The governor asked Rob, Jim, and me to make toasts in honor of the team. True to form, Jim played stand-up comedian, using sarcasm to lighten the mood. Rob was stoic and unflappable; having worked in state government at all levels for twenty-five years, he had seen it all and wanted to make sure the staff, especially the younger members of the administration, had a proper appreciation of their role in a once-in-a-century crisis. The governor, ever the student of history, spoke passionately about the importance of the role of government—the real-life impact of the machinery and what government can accomplish when it is competent and the people running it display an unrelenting work ethic.

When it was my turn, I could feel the emotion rising up through my throat. I didn't typically show emotion at work; I grew up being taught that if I did, especially as a young woman, I would be viewed as weak or hysterical. But that afternoon, I gave up trying to control how I felt. I removed the oversized black sunglasses that had been acting as a headband to hold my hair back, and put them on my face to cover my eyes.

"I don't really know what to say to you," I could feel my voice shake. "I woke up this morning, and I don't know why, but I started to cry. What we did. What *you* did. The way that the nation and the whole world turned to you to comfort them, to keep them safe. You never said no; you always found a way to get to yes. You worked eighteen-hour days under crushing pressure—life-and-death pressure—and you never complained for even a minute." At that moment, I broke Dad's cardinal rule and let them see me sweat. I started to tear up for the second time that day, this time not curled up in bed, but standing in front of all of our staff.

I couldn't find the words to express my gratitude, so I borrowed another New York governor's. "FDR said that courage is not the absence of fear, but rather the assessment that something else is more important than fear. I never fully understood that quote until the last 111 days," I said. "But I do now. All of *you*, the people standing here, define courage—*you* are courageous. We talk a lot about 'essential workers'—the people who went to work to make sure everyone else could stay home. *You* are our essential workers. *You* make the government work."

After making the rounds with Michaela, posing for photos with the staff, and individually thanking every person there, the governor headed back into the main house while a few of us lingered, sipping New York–brewed beer, talking, and laughing. We knew it was highly likely that we would battle a second wave of COVID at some point, but for a brief moment, we allowed ourselves to breathe.

That night, I headed up to my dad's house in the Adirondacks to spend the weekend with him and his wife, Maureen, my siblings, and nieces. It was the first weekend I had spent outside of Albany since the pandemic began, and while I should have been relieved, I felt guilty and a little bit lost. The intensity of the past 111 days had filled my every waking hour, and while the daily briefings had provided the nation with a sense of stability to navigate the pandemic, the truth is that they provided the same for me. And while it had only been one day, I could already feel a void. It turns out I was a typical New Yorker—one who needed those briefings every bit as much as our constituents did, as much for the human contact and continuity as for the information. I was both glad they were over and I missed them already.

CHAPTER 11

No End in Sight

I WAS LYING IN A LOUNGE CHAIR ON THE DECK OVERLOOKING LAKE George when my phone rang. It was the governor, calling on speakerphone with his daughters in the car—a classic move he often pulled with senior staff that prevented any real dialogue.

"Where are you guys?" I wondered.

"We're going for a little drive, maybe find a little brunch," Michaela answered in her sweet, sing-songy voice.

"Oh, look at you—living the life of leisure," I teased.

"Oh, yes, that's me, cool dude in a loose mood," the governor shot back.

"Yep, that's you alright. What can I help you with, Governor?"

"So, the girls and I were talking this morning, and they think that it's time to do the book. What do you think?" he asked.

"Oh yeah?" I responded noncommittally.

Mariah jumped in. "Melissa, don't you think the whole country could learn from what New York just went through? It could be like a playbook for governments and citizens to follow. COVID is just starting to get bad in other places."

"It's an interesting idea," I allowed, "but don't you think it's too soon? We are still living this, and . . ."

"Meliss, hang on, we're going to lose you," I heard the governor say. "I'll call you later. But think about it."

The line went dead.

"Who was that?" My father was standing in the doorway with two large coffees.

"The governor and the kids."

"I thought he was going to leave you alone this weekend," he said, leaning down to set my latte on the small table beside me.

"He is," I semi-lied. "They were just saying hi."

Dad wasn't going to let it go that easily. "Melissa," he scolded, "you have to take a break. You're supposed to be up here to take a break. That means not having the phone surgically attached to your ear, and it means not talking to the governor and your team every hour."

"Yes, Dad, I hear you." He turned to walk back into the house.

"Hey, Dad?"

"What do you think about the governor publishing a memoir about the first three months of the pandemic?"

"Absolutely he should do a book," he answered. "The whole world hung on his every word. He got everyone through this thing."

"What do you think about him doing the book *now*?"

"Now?"

"Yeah, sort of as a road map for other states and the public to learn from."

"I think it is a spectacularly bad idea."

"Why?" I asked coyly.

"Because it will be viewed as a victory lap, and we are still in the middle of this thing. They will come to kill him. This will give them the cudgel."

"Who's *they*?" I wondered.

"The press, the Right, the Left. Everyone. No one liked that he got this attention. There's a lot of jealousy and a lot of anger. They will say it's arrogant and premature and use it as an excuse to dissect every decision."

Gut checked. I knew he was right. I just didn't appreciate how right he was.

So I put my concerns on the back burner. Just because the daily briefings had ended didn't mean the pandemic had. We were still fighting this thing. The fire was contained but not under control. On most days, it seemed like we were digging miles of trenches and dousing dozens of flare-ups.

Just as it seemed that New York had finally beaten back COVID, the South was spiraling, and Republican governors there could not have cared less. Twitter was abuzz: "Breaking News out of Miami-Dade County, FL—a major hospital now at capacity amid the big #COVID-19 spike in Florida."

We were four and a half months from the 2020 election, and Republicans had chosen their path, pegging COVID restrictions as tyrannical and inciting protests against local officials attempting to impose them. They labeled the crisis a hoax and actively took executive action to ban mask mandates. Sometimes, I found myself wondering if these swaggering Republican governors viewed COVID spiking in their states as political badges of honor, as if refusing to close businesses or require social distancing made them badasses.

Watching the situation play out in disbelief, the governor directed Zucker and our senior team to come to him with a recommendation on how to protect our progress.

"Dr. Zucker, can you give us an update on what's going on across the country?" the governor asked on a conference call with Beth Garvey, Rob Mujica, Kelly Cummings, and me that morning.

"It seems that the actions that certain governors have taken, along with the messaging around not wearing masks, has resulted in a spike across a number of states," Zucker reported. "I'm sure you've seen the videos of people partying in nightclubs with no restrictions. It's really an irresponsible mess."

"Wonderful," Cuomo said with bitter sarcasm. "Anything else?"

"Well, there's a theory that because it's the end of June and it's so hot in places like Florida, Texas, Arizona, people are actually being driven indoors and that air conditioners circulating the air in closed spaces could also be contributing to the spread," Zucker continued. "The health community isn't positive, but that could be a contributing factor."

"And how bad is the spread?" Cuomo pressed.

"Well, Governor, to put it simply: it's bad. Hospitals in a number of states are now on the verge of collapse."

"Christ," the governor responded. "Were they not paying attention to what happened here over the past few months?"

"Rob, do you want to jump in here?" I interjected.

Rob had been speaking with the multistate coalition. With air travel not being restricted and people flying freely throughout the country, there was a real risk that the people from these states with rising infection rates would bring it back to the tri-state area and we would end up back where we were in February and March.

"Guys," the governor implored, "what are we doing here?"

That was my cue. "Governor, Paul, George, and I have been talking, and I think there is a real appetite for making a joint decision around some kind of quarantine policy." Paul Mounds and George Helmy were the chiefs of staff for Governor Lamont in Connecticut and Governor Murphy in New Jersey, respectively. I had had no relationship with either of them before March of that year, but over the course of the crisis, the three of us had become each other's sounding boards—supporting one another and always giving each other honest advice. There were only fifty people in the country who understood the pressure of being chief of staff to a governor during that period, and despite having no face-to-face contact with one another, we held each other close.

"Isn't that exactly what we opposed back in March when Rhode Island threatened to quarantine New Yorkers?"

Beth explained that the Constitution gives states broad authority when it comes to health emergencies. The key was that any mandated quarantine would have to be data-based so that, when challenged, we could affirmatively show that the states that people are traveling from are a real risk to the health and well-being of New Yorkers.

"Okay," Cuomo replied, "what's the proposal?"

We'd been working with our health department and the health departments of the surrounding states, and after a tortured and protracted back-and-forth, we reached consensus: We could impose a mandatory fourteen-day quarantine for any person arriving from a state with a positive test rate higher than ten per 100,000 residents over a seven-day rolling average or a state with a 10 percent or higher positivity rate over a seven-day rolling average. We would update the list once a week to avoid daily confusion.

Cuomo asked the crucial question that was on everybody's mind: "And how will we actually *enforce* this order? It'll be meaningless if the public doesn't believe there will have to be compliance."

Kelly had the answer ready. She had been talking to the Port Authority, the heads of all the upstate airports, and the airlines to come up with a system to track incoming passengers. While New York State doesn't control the airspace, once someone steps foot off the plane and into a New York terminal, we have legal authority. We would use the National Guard to collect forms for anyone who stepped foot in New York from one of the states on the quarantine list and do random checks to follow up during the fourteen-day window. Anyone breaking the quarantine could be fined or confined. It wouldn't be perfect, but it would send a message and, perhaps, dissuade people from coming to New York from one of the highly impacted states, while also disincentivizing New Yorkers from traveling out of state if it meant they would have to quarantine for fourteen days when they come back.

Cuomo directed me to run the plan by my counterparts in Connecticut and New Jersey; he would reach out to the governors of both states directly himself afterward. I was also to contact Alexander Cochran and Sarah Paden, the well-connected heads of our DC office. Alexander had worked for Cuomo since his HUD days, while Sarah had played a major role in managing the governor's successful 2018 campaign—he trusted them both implicitly. Alexander and Sarah were tasked with putting out feelers to see if any mayors or governors in any of the states where COVID was spiking needed help. Cuomo was the longest-serving governor in the nation and had been serving as vice chair of the National Governors Association. If Trump wasn't going to step up, he reasoned, he would.

"The country sent us volunteers and supplies when we needed it," the governor reminded us. "It's time we do the same."

We had officially come full circle. Only three months earlier, Florida was attempting to ban New Yorkers from traveling there. Today, anyone coming from Florida would have to quarantine for two full weeks before traveling freely around the Empire State. We had been ambushed by COVID silently for months when we were hit hardest. By contrast, governors in red states across the country had a front-row seat as our hospitals teetered on the verge of collapse. And they had apparently learned nothing.

The next morning, as I sat at my desk preparing our first press conference since we had ended our daily briefings only five very long days earlier, segment after segment on cable news showed hospitals across the South and the West reaching capacity and about to collapse. It was triggering for me. My heart began to race, and, without even realizing it, I clenched my fists. The images on TV were of hospitals in faraway places, but I saw Elmhurst and refrigerator trucks holding dead bodies.

My ringing iPhone startled me back to the present. It was our communications guru, Mimi Reisner.

"Oh my god, Melissa! Did you see?"

My stomach clenched, a muscle memory from being in fight-or-flight mode 24/7 for months on end.

"*Harper's*! The digital issue just hit." Mimi had been singularly focused on our messaging campaign to persuade the country to mask up and stay home but had diverted a sliver of her attention to help me navigate press incoming.

I pulled up the *Harper's Bazaar* site. There it was, their July "Voices of Hope" issue.

Months earlier, in the dark days of March, I had intervened when hospitals across the state banned pregnant women from having someone accompany them in the delivery room when giving birth, overruling them and mandating that at least one person of the woman's choosing be allowed in the room for support. It was one of those moments when I felt the power of my position and a responsibility to be a voice for women. Afterward, model Christy Turlington reached out. She was active in maternal-health issues and asked if there was more we could do to give women choices when giving birth during COVID. I consulted with our health team and women's policy point person, and together we launched the COVID-19 Maternity Task Force to put the best minds on the topic around a virtual table.

A few weeks later, Christy emailed. She was slated to be on the cover of the July issue of *Harper's Bazaar* and wanted to take a nontraditional approach, spotlighting women she viewed as "Voices of Hope" during COVID. She was reaching out to ask if I would be willing to be a part of it.

While I was honored, I was concerned it would appear frivolous while so many New Yorkers were struggling. I went back and forth but ultimately agreed. It would be a chance to showcase the work our administration was doing to protect women during the pandemic. And it wouldn't be a big deal: a Zoom interview and a photo. Two weeks later, boxes from New York City were delivered. Fifteen different dresses and a dozen or so pairs of designer shoes to choose from. "Please select the outfit that best communicates your style and passion," read the note from the marketing editor at *Harper's*. Manolo Blahnik, Prada, Christian Louboutin. It was bizarre.

Just before the issue was set to go to print, one of the editors called. They had decided to change course: *Harper's* would issue six different versions of their July issue, putting each one of the women Christy had selected on a rotating series of different covers. Not what I had signed on for, but this was the direction the editors had decided on. At that point, I had been featured in *Elle* magazine and the *New York Times* style section, but nothing that came close to this.

That morning, in the middle of yet another unfolding crisis, there I was on the cover of *Harper's Bazaar*, standing on the steps of the capitol wearing a black Prabal Gurung dress and white Jimmy Choo sling-back stilettos. I winced.

"Mimi, does this look ridiculous?"

"Melissa, it's incredible! Do you know how many women work their entire lives and never get to be on the cover of *Harper's*?"

"Yes, but I mean with everything going on . . ."

"No, no, *no*! This is a real recognition of our hard work and everything we've done—*you've* done—during this pandemic. Lean in!"

Cindy appeared in my doorway. "Melissa, sorry to interrupt. I have Kelly on the phone. A few of the airlines don't want to comply with the travel-quarantine policy the governor is announcing today—she says it's urgent. Oh, and the governor is asking for you in his office."

Shortly after, we were back on television for yet another briefing. Joined by Phil Murphy and Ned Lamont on Zoom, Cuomo announced a tri-state policy that all individuals traveling from states with significant community spread of COVID-19 would have to quarantine for a fourteen-day period from the time of last contact within the identified state, effective at midnight the same day. We were four months into the emergency, and there was still no end in sight.

CHAPTER 12

There's a Problem

COVID WAS NOW WELL BEYOND NEW YORK AND WAS RAGING across the nation. There was a massive leadership vacuum at the federal level that was getting worse with every passing day. The rest of the world had taken notice, too: Europe had just imposed a blanket travel ban against United States citizens, and other countries across the globe were considering similar restrictions. COVID was winning this war so far, and no one had learned the lesson we hoped they would from watching New York fall first and fall hard, before fighting back. The governor, prodded by his daughters, became more convinced that now was the time to publish a book. He envisioned a guide for governments and citizens, a mix of lessons learned and personal narrative. I understood the reasoning, and there would certainly be an audience for what he was describing, but we would be putting a giant target on our backs.

"Talk to a few people about it and see what they think," Cuomo said, asking that I engage some of our outside advisers to see how they saw the idea.

In New York, while we had largely tamed the beast, we began to see something both in the numbers and anecdotally.

It was summer in the city. People had been cooped up for months. They were hitting reopened bars and restaurants with abandon. The streets were filled with maskless New Yorkers ignoring any and all social-distancing requirements. Mayor de Blasio wasn't doing anything about it. The prevailing way of life as we knew it was: two steps forward, two steps back. But I worried it might be three back.

As I sat in my office contemplating our next move, my phone rang. It was our chief of staff, Jill.

"Melissa," she said soberly, "there's a problem."

"What's going on?" I asked, suddenly alert.

"Tom just called me." Tom Feeney was our head of logistics and events. He was as unflappable as they came, a trusted, steady hand. He reported to Jill that a bunch of the junior staffers were out drinking the night before.

"Okay, and?" I prodded.

"Apparently, Charlotte Bennett was there." Jill went on to tell me that Charlotte said she thought the governor had hit on her.

"Wait, who's Charlotte Bennett?" I couldn't pick Charlotte Bennett out of a lineup.

"She used to be a briefer. She's the one I mentioned to you."

I flashed back to a conversation weeks earlier with Jill. Between the George Floyd protests, the looting, and New York City's reopening, I had only been half paying attention. From what I could remember, there was a briefer who said she didn't feel comfortable doing her job anymore and had requested a reassignment to a job she had previously asked for weeks earlier. If it should have set off any alarm bells, it didn't. It was COVID, and every day someone on staff was asking to be reassigned: some asked to work on subject areas they were passionate about, while others didn't feel physically safe coming into the office and requested to work from home. Some, battling the mental health effects of what we were confronting, took a leave of absence. At the time, I didn't give Charlotte's request much thought.

"What does 'hit on her' mean exactly?" I pressed.

That was all Tom had said; he didn't elaborate.

In eight years in the governor's office, this was another first for me. All at once, the refrain "I don't know what to do" began to reverberate in my head. This was secondhand information about a conversation that took place over cocktails. Was it a complaint? An exaggeration? A joke among friends out drinking? Hitting on a young female briefer?

Everyone can and should define their own personal boundaries, but it didn't comport with the Andrew Cuomo I knew. Whatever this was, I knew we needed to find out.

"Jill, get Judy," I instructed. Judy Mogul was special counsel to the governor. She was a veteran of the Southern District of New York's US Attorney's Office and a highly regarded civil litigator, and her judgment was unimpeachable. She would know what to do.

Judy had proactively reached out to Charlotte to get to the bottom of what had happened. My understanding was that, five months earlier, in January of that year, Charlotte had gone to the mansion to deliver some documents to the governor. As Charlotte told it, she handed him the papers and exchanged pleasantries when he asked her to tell him something about herself. Charlotte responded by announcing that she had been a victim of sexual assault as an undergraduate. A women's studies major with a degree from Hamilton College, she had since become a political activist around sexual assault and came to the administration because of the work Cuomo had spearheaded to confront sexual violence on university campuses.

Instantly, I knew where this was going. The governor had a family member who had been sexually assaulted in school. He'd helped her fight the system to demand accountability and had become passionate about the topic of sexual assault on college campuses—obsessed, even. He'd read every book, article, and study he could find, gone through family counseling with her, and ultimately championed the nation's strongest campus sexual assault legislation. And any time sexual assault came up or someone identified themselves as a survivor, he became the self-anointed "counselor in chief." He'd start asking questions about how he could help, how they were dealing with their own trauma, and how it was impacting their lives and relationships. I'd seen him do it many times over the years with sexual assault victims, including with women whom he'd just met. Personally, I thought it was too much, and I'd let him know that more than once: "When someone tells you they're a sexual assault survivor, you say, 'I'm so sorry for what you've gone through' and then you offer to connect them with an expert." But Cuomo disagreed. He insisted on being affirmatively supportive, and he believed that my reaction was cold and unfeeling.

Charlotte hadn't seen the governor again until that May, when there was one morning when she came into the office to drop off materials and he was already there. He started making small talk with her, asking what was going on with her life, where she'd been and so on. She told him that she'd moved up to Albany months earlier to help out during the crisis, that she felt lonely because her parents wouldn't let her come visit due to the pandemic and she didn't have many friends on the staff. She had come and gone a handful of times with documents for the governor, and they would engage in small talk. Sometimes it was friendly banter, and sometimes it was more personal in nature; the governor would ask about her friends on the staff, how everyone was treating her, and how she was spending her time outside the office.

This part didn't surprise me at all. Cuomo had a way of engaging with staff at all levels. He would ask questions as a means of showing that he was interested in them, and often teased people— men and women—about their social lives. He would even jokingly attempt to play matchmaker, suggesting that, if they were open to it, certain junior staffers date one another. Chuck Schumer did the same, although more successfully. The *New York Times* devoted an entire article to Schumer's matchmaking and the dozen couples in his office who had married, saying Schumer "keeps close track of office romances, quotes marriage-friendly Scripture ("God to man: be fruitful and multiply"), and is known to cajole, nag, and outright pester his staff (at least those he perceives as receptive to such pestering) toward connubial bliss."

At one point, the governor supposedly asked Charlotte who she was sleeping with.

Wait, what? I was taken aback.

Charlotte then clarified her initial assertion and said that he'd actually asked her who she was "hanging out with." And I thought to myself, *How do you get from "who are you hanging out with" to "who are you sleeping with"?*

Charlotte also said that, when she told the governor she was working on a speech to deliver at Hamilton College, he offered to help and encouraged her to "own her truth" that she was sexually assaulted. She felt like he was taking over her speech. He'd ask if, in the aftermath of her own trauma, she was engaged in healthy relationships. Charlotte said that, among other things, when they talked about COVID, he supposedly told her that he was lonely and that he missed hugging people.

Charlotte also relayed that a few Saturdays earlier, after a press conference, Stephanie and I had left her alone to assist the governor with administrative tasks. Charlotte said she believed this was the governor's doing in order to prove that he could be alone with her.

Where did she get that from? The Saturday Charlotte was talking about, Steph and I had asked to leave. We had been in the office around the clock for days, and we needed a break. We wanted to get out of the office for a while. And the governor hadn't determined who would staff him; Stephanie did, based on who was available.

Now I really didn't know what to make of this. I compiled a mental checklist of the parade of horribles and began to tick through them.

Did she say that he touched her? Absolutely not. Did she say that he propositioned her? Made any advances? No and no. Charlotte said that while the governor had not taken any unwanted steps, she believed he was "grooming her," and that she caught it early and took herself out of the situation. The only time I had ever heard the term *grooming* was in the context of pedophilia. *What was going on?*

We hung up, and I leaned back and let out a long breath. My phone rang, and AMC popped up on the caller ID. Andrew Mark Cuomo. He was calling to check in on the next day's press conference and, up until that point, was oblivious about this new issue.

I dialed Judy back and conferenced her in. I could tell by the governor's tone that he thought I was overreacting.

Judy hung up to get to work consulting with other lawyers on how to handle the situation.

The following morning, I read the top stories in all of the New York papers and skimmed the nationals. It was Groundhog Day. Cities that had reopened were considering measures to close again. Hospitals were filling up. Trump was inciting chaos. I snapped my laptop closed, showered, and headed to the office, edited the day's press release, and reviewed the PowerPoint.

When we arrived at the New York City office, I felt a knot in the pit of my stomach. We had ended our COVID daily press conferences only twelve days earlier, and here we were, back again, to announce that we were delaying the reopening of indoor dining for New York City, a damning acknowledgment that the progress we made was already in jeopardy. When the governor started to wrap up the press conference, I slid my chair back, stood up, and slipped out of the room while both he and Dr. Zucker were still talking. I walked back to my office and shut the door behind me. Just then, I could hear knocking.

"Melissa?" Cindy, my New York City–based assistant, said. "It sounds like the gov is ready to head out. The troopers are asking that you meet him at the elevator."

I grabbed my BlackBerry, iPhone, and makeup case to leave. I reached into my bag, feeling around for my oversized black sunglasses. When I got to the elevator, Cuomo was standing there with two of the troopers.

As we got into the black Dodge Charger waiting for us in the loading dock, I could feel the angst inside me begin to bubble up.

"How do you think that went?" the governor asked.

"Huh?" I answered.

"The presser. What did Azzopardi say? Does he think the press plays this straight?"

"I didn't talk to Azzo, Governor," I answered, staring blankly out the window, looking at masked New Yorkers walking down the sidewalk on Second Avenue.

Sensing something was wrong, he turned to me, "Melissa, what is wrong with you?"

I whipped my head around.

"What's wrong with *me*?" I asked rhetorically.

"What's that supposed to mean?" he questioned, on a completely different page.

"We were supposed to be done with these press conferences. We were supposed to be reopening. We were supposed to be getting past this. And now, on top of everything else . . . Charlotte Bennett?!" I responded, exasperated. "Why, why, why did you engage with her?"

"Melissa, she confided in me that she was victimized. She is struggling and needs support."

I had seen this before.

A year earlier, in July 2019, Cuomo had held a press conference at the capitol as part of a campaign to change the statute of limitations on rape in New York from two years to five years. To bring attention to the issue, he invited members of the sexual assault advocacy group Time's Up to appear alongside him. When it was her turn to speak, Oscar-winning actress Mira Sorvino, one of the first women to accuse the film producer Harvey Weinstein of sexual harassment, choked up as she revealed for the first time publicly that she was a survivor of date rape. After the press conference, she was visibly emotional about the disclosure, and the governor was concerned about her. He invited her to come in and sit down. The two spoke for nearly an hour and exchanged contact information. From time to time, the governor would reach out to her to ask how she was doing, if she was okay.

Afterward, I asked what they had been talking about. "What Mira went through is a painful, terrible thing, Melissa. My heart breaks for her," he said.

"Yes, Governor, and I know what you lived through, and I know it comes from a good place. But it's not your job to engage with her— you should really just help her find someone to talk to," I responded. At the time, he thought my reaction was cold and insensitive.

A year later, riding through Manhattan, we were back where we started.

"You and I see these things differently. Charlotte told me she was a victim of assault," he protested. "After a person tells you that, how do you *not* make sure they are okay? Check in on them? Ask questions? I looked at her and saw a young woman in pain. My family has gone through this before. You have family members that have been victimized by sexual assault; *you've* gone through this before."

The car made a left onto East 34th Street toward First Avenue. We were three blocks from the helicopter. The governor stopped at a light and turned to face me again.

He was emotional, "I can't believe you are acting like this, Melissa!"

I was at my breaking point. The death and destruction of lives from COVID. The opening and potential re-closing. Trump. The crime. My marriage. The weight of the decisions I was making. The sheer emotional and psychological toll. The pressure and fatigue. All of it together was too much. And sitting there, all I could think was, there was no end in sight. *This is never going to end, this is never going to end, this is never going to end.* The blood rushed to my face. I needed a break— from COVID, from the press, the protesters, the White House, and from the thousands of decisions we were making that were constantly being guessed and second-guessed. I looked down at my bag sitting on the floor next to my feet and reached for it. I was at my wits' end. I needed air and time and space.

"I'm sorry, Governor. I need a break," I said. And with the car idling, I took off my seat belt and got out, shutting the door behind me.

I had no plan. But there I was, walking aimlessly down the sidewalk in a black-and-white polka-dot dress, stilettos, and giant sunglasses. How subtle.

My mind was running through a list of people I could call—someone outside of my professional orbit, a real friend, an old friend. Most of my college and high school friends had relocated during the height of the pandemic and hadn't come back; I couldn't think of a single person who would be around that I could talk to. I'd never felt more alone.

As I kept walking, Robin Fisher, one of my oldest friends from Cornell, popped into my head. She was a New York City diehard, born and bred. She detested the Hamptons and deemed the people who fled the City during the darkest days to be traitors. She was also a workaholic, a force to be reckoned with in the commercial real estate industry who was back at her desk the first minute businesses were allowed to reopen. And her office was in Midtown.

"Missy?"

"Robo! Oh my God, it's so good to hear your voice."

"You too, bella! It's been so long! Where are you?"

"I know this is last-minute, but I decided to hang back after today's presser. I'm currently walking across town on 35th Street. Are you around? Can we grab lunch?"

"Fuck, yeah!" Robin used expletives in her sentences the same way teenage girls use "like."

"Really? You can sneak out?"

"For you, anything! I'll text you the name of a restaurant near 38th and Lex with outdoor dining. Be there in twenty!"

When I reached the restaurant, Robin was already there. When she stood up, I saw what looked like a small basketball in her belly. I had completely forgotten that one of my dearest, closest friends was six months pregnant. *Where the hell had I been?*

As I walked closer, she came toward me, arms wide open.

"Can we do this?" I asked tentatively.

"Shouldn't you know what's okay and not okay?" she retorted.

"Ha, I guess I should."

"Well, I don't give a fuck one way or another." Robin wrapped her arms around me. It was the first real hug I'd had since before COVID began. Finally, a friend. "Take off those god-awful sunglasses and let me look at you!"

I slid the glasses off, placing them on the white linen tablecloth, and looked up at her.

"Jesus Christ, dolly, you look like shit. What happened?"

"The last four months happened." As the words crossed my lips, tears started to well in my eyes, and the waitress appeared, seemingly out of thin air.

"Hi there, can I take your order?" She smiled and then zeroed in on me.

"She'll have a glass of sauvignon blanc."

"Robin, it's so early, and I haven't slept," I objected rotely.

"Come on, Missy! I haven't seen you since January. This is a celebration!"

Suddenly, the waitress joined the conversation. "Wait a minute, are you Melissa DeRosa? From the governor's press conferences?" It was the first time I'd ever been recognized like that. It seemed ridiculous and bizarre all at once. It wasn't like I was an elected official or a celebrity.

"She sure is!" Robin replied, beaming like a proud parent.

"I watched you and Governor Cuomo for 111 days straight. You got me through COVID. I can't believe I'm meeting you!" the waitress gushed. Robin egged her on.

"Do you want a picture with her?"

I wanted to hide under the table.

"If you don't mind?" The server sidled up next to me.

"Of course I don't," I said self-consciously, praying no one else would identify me while we were posing for the picture.

Over lunch, Robin and I caught up. She didn't give a damn about Trump or Jared Kushner or Bill de Blasio—and she didn't ask. She cared about me. Was I lonely? Overworked, overtired? How could she help? We FaceTimed our friends Lacey and Lisa, and we laughed. It was a world away from where I had been, and it was exactly what I needed.

"Okay, bella. I hate to break this up, but I have a 3:00 p.m. meeting," Robin announced, looking down at her watch. "Can you stay in New York City tonight? If you don't want to go to your apartment, you can stay in one of our guest rooms. Joe would die to see you!"

I thanked her but reluctantly begged off. "That's so sweet, honey, but I think I have to head back. I already feel like the last few hours have been incredibly irresponsible." I gestured to the three empty wineglasses in front of me.

"Listen to me, Missy. If anyone needs a little bit of a break, it's you."

I smiled, and we hugged one more time before she took off down the sidewalk, back toward her office. I sat at the table a few minutes longer. Now what?

Who else might be around? Anyone else I should try to see while I'm here? I scrolled through Twitter—an attempt to see what I had missed while I'd been checked out for the last few hours—and saw a tweet from an old friend, one I had been meaning to talk to since my incident with that *New York Times* reporter weeks earlier. He would be in the city working, and I wondered if he was free to catch up? I started to dial.

Nick Confessore is a Pulitzer Prize–winning national investigative reporter for the *New York Times*. Most people knew him from his appearances on MSNBC. I knew him from a dozen years earlier when he was assigned to cover Albany when Eliot Spitzer was governor.

The first time Nick and I met was at a bar called Savannah's in downtown Albany. I was twenty-six years old, working as a lobbyist. He was thirty-four and looking for leads. John Cordo, my boss at the time, introduced us, saying, "I think you two would get along very well."

He was right. Nick and I clicked from the beginning. After a short time, the group we were with peeled away, and Nick and I were left alone. We talked for hours. We knew a lot of people in common and found out quickly that we both enjoyed the art of a good argument, ending the night debating politics over vanilla crème brûlée. We had stayed close ever since. It was a difficult line to walk at times; he had very strong opinions about my boss, just as I felt his colleagues could be biased and unfair. But we made it work. A decade later, he had become one of my most-trusted confidantes.

When I arrived at the Upper East Side haunt Nick had selected, he was already seated. As I approached, he caught my eye, stood up, and wrapped me in the second real hug I truly needed that day.

"Ahh, sporting a COVID beard, I see?" I teased.

"Didn't you hear? It's all the rage," he said with a smile. "How are you, friend?"

"I'm okay. How is Anna? The kids? Everyone good?"

"As good as we can be, given the circumstances," he said. "What's happening up in Albany? Do you ever get to come home?"

"Actually, I've been wanting to tell you one thing that happened up there," I said. "It involves your newspaper."

I recounted my encounter with the Albany bureau chief a few weeks earlier.

"Honey, I'm so sorry; that's terrible," Nick sympathized.

We talked about the reporter's rumored history with women and alcohol and how it actually wasn't that surprising that such an incident had occurred—"which doesn't make it okay," Nick made clear. It actually makes it worse, I thought to myself. How many other women had he acted like this with? Just then, my purse started to vibrate. Annoyed by the interruption, I reached down to find my iPhone. Instantly, the respite of the last few hours washed away, and I was snapped back to reality.

"Nick, I'm sorry," I said. "I really have to grab this."

"No worries, I'll be here." He picked up his iPhone to work as I walked away.

Charlotte had read the employee handbook and, as I understood it, suggested that she did not think that the governor had engaged in conduct that fell within the sexual-harassment definition. She said that she did not want this to go any further. While she was assured that she could continue her job as a briefer if that's what she wanted, she said that she was happy with the health team; actually, she called it her "dream job" and said she considered the governor a friend. She stated unequivocally that the governor did not touch her or proposition her.

While some of their conversations, as relayed by Charlotte, were personal in nature, she had initiated some of them and was comfortable with them up until the point that she wasn't. Charlotte said that, in her judgment, things could have taken a turn in the future, but that she had removed herself from the situation before they did.

What just happened? Was this all blown out of proportion? I felt like I was on a roller coaster, desperately wanting to get off and being told I had no choice but to be strapped in for the ride. As I tried to gather my thoughts, I looked at my watch. It was time to go.

I said goodbye to Nick. We hugged for a few seconds and promised to talk more, and then as quickly as I had arrived, I was gone.

"Back up to the capitol, Melissa?" the driver asked. "Traffic is light."

I unbuckled my seat belt, lay down across the back seat of the SUV, and silenced my phones, thinking, "Maybe when I wake up this will all have been a bad dream."

And then, overtaken by emotional and mental exhaustion, I closed my eyes and fell asleep.

CHAPTER 13

The Perfect Storm

COVID CASES HAD DROPPED TO AN ALL-TIME LOW, REGIONS ALL across the state were settling into a new normal, and people were getting back to work and reentering malls and restaurants. We were focused on strategies to revitalize the badly bruised economy and entice New Yorkers to return home to the city they had fled months earlier. But just as the pandemic was waning, another problem emerged. Things were beginning to feel like a fun house perched on a seesaw; maintaining balance was an impossibility.

The weekend of July 4 was bloody and chaotic.

New York City saw fifty shootings over the holiday weekend. Nine people were dead and forty-one others wounded. Adding to the tension, the noise of illegal fireworks exploding throughout the city could be heard all night long. While a far cry from the crime the five boroughs were known for in the '80s and early '90s, the holiday toll represented an alarming wave of violence, coming on the heels of a surge in crime we had endured since lockdowns were put into place months earlier. Murders were up by 23 percent citywide for the year, and the month before had been the most violent June on record since 1996, contributing to the ever-growing perception that New York City was spiraling out of control.

The increase in crime was being met by a demonized and demoralized police force. Hailed as heroes in the days after 9/11, since the George Floyd murder and subsequent protests a month earlier, the NYPD had been vilified and were resentful.

In the face of the Defund the Police movement that had swept the nation on social media and had become a rallying cry of Gen Zers and far-left/socialist protesters, combined with the number of anti–police misconduct bills passed in New York and signed into law, the NYPD had all but given up. Many of the top brass and those in union leadership took the position that the police had been put in a no-win situation. The vocal minority on the Far Left actively vilified them. If they attempted to arrest or question someone, it would be caught on iPhone video and put out on social media without context. At the same time, they believed that if they used tactics to intervene in a crime that included any use of force, the new city laws put on the books by de Blasio would send them to jail. As a result, some officers refused to get out of their patrol cars when they saw a crime occurring. The message was clear: The city no longer had their back, so why should they have yours?

It was already the perfect storm. The only thing that could make it worse was the intervention of President Trump. Over the weekend, it was becoming increasingly clear that Trump, whose reelection odds were getting dimmer by the day, was flailing. He had pushed states to reopen recklessly, which predictably caused an increase in COVID's spread and the number of people testing positive, with or without symptoms. That, of course, in turn resulted in more closings. COVID was rising in almost every region of the country outside of the Northeast, and Trump's incompetent response was being widely blamed. Over that July 4 weekend, he attempted to explain the spike away; tweeting the line "If we didn't test so much and so successfully, we would have very few cases."

It was an incredible display of incompetence meets delusion, as if not knowing cases were present would somehow make the virus less deadly. And with politics taking priority over people, rather than attempting to responsibly confront the health crisis, Trump instead desperately sought to change the subject to anything other than COVID. Late in the day on July 5, it seemed he had found the distraction he craved.

"Chicago and New York City crime numbers are way up," he tweeted Sunday evening. "Shootings up significantly in NYC where people are demanding that @NYGovCuomo & @NYCMayor act now. Federal Government ready, willing, and able to help, if asked!"

Once again, Trump saw an opportunity—not to unify the country or heal division but to change the subject and show who's boss. He zeroed in on Democratic cities across the country, striving to portray my party as coddling protesters and soft on crime versus Republicans, who cracked down on chaos and supported the police and suburban women.

I called to give the governor a heads-up: "Trump's tweeting at us again."

"What now?" he asked.

"About the shootings in New York City over the weekend. He poses it as an option and doesn't come right out and say it, but it feels like he's threatening to send troops in."

"Oh yeah?" Cuomo responded. "On what legal authority?"

"Who knows, but since when has the law ever stopped him?" I reminded him. "Want to address it in tomorrow's briefing?"

"No," Cuomo was firm. "He wants us to do that. That way we're talking about what *he* wants to talk about instead of what he should be focused on. I'm going to talk about the president tomorrow but about COVID, not this."

To say the relationship between Trump and Cuomo at that point was fraught is the understatement of the century. A few weeks earlier, the governor, Rob Mujica, and I flew down to DC to meet with Trump, Jared Kushner, Mark Meadows, and Elaine Chao to discuss a number of priority infrastructure projects Cuomo wanted to fast-track—the Second Avenue Subway extension into Harlem, repairs to the dangerously decrepit Gateway Tunnel from New Jersey to Manhattan, and providing an AirTrain to and from LaGuardia Airport. The governor planned to appeal to Trump's ego as a "builder" and his desire to "supercharge" the reopening of the economy.

The meeting was set to take place two weeks before Albany's legislative session was due to wrap up, and we were in negotiations with the assembly and the senate over a number of end-of-year priorities. When we arrived, I was stuck on a tense conference call with LouAnn and Shontell. Cutting it off prematurely would not have gone over well, so I opted to skip the meeting with the feds and finish negotiations with the state houses from the front passenger seat of the Suburban. A little over an hour later, Rob and the governor climbed back into the SUV.

"So, boys, how'd you do?" I asked after Rob slammed his door shut.

"Rob, you want to take this one?" the governor said, buckling his seat belt and adjusting the rearview mirror.

"It didn't go well," Rob reported from the back seat. They were barely inside the Oval Office before Trump started screaming. Just before they arrived, one of Trump's sons had received a subpoena from the New York State attorney general's office as part of their investigation into alleged large-scale fraudulent financial practices at the Trump Organization. Trump, who regularly leaned on the US Department of Justice to do his personal bidding, could not comprehend that Cuomo wasn't behind it. And just like that, the meeting was over before it began.

"For a minute there, I thought he was going to kick us out of the Oval Office," Rob said, ending his recap. From that point on, communication between our two offices was practically nonexistent.

Weeks earlier, Trump had threatened to deploy federal agents to New York City, but we had been able to stave him off. This time, with Trump more desperate than ever, we weren't sure we would be as lucky. While the rise in crime over the preceding month was disturbing, the citywide protests had subsided. The violence that New York and other big cities saw playing out was largely attributed to economic desperation exacerbated by the pandemic. It was not organized or methodical. From a crime-prevention standpoint, Trump's threat of big-footing the mayor and NYPD was nonsensical. But it wasn't about that. Rather than engage Trump directly, we decided to ignore the president's latest antics and stay laser-focused on COVID. If Trump wasn't going to act like a leader, Cuomo was ready to step up to fill the void being sorely felt by so many states across the country.

"Melissa, let's get a call with Alexander, Kelly, and Jill."

"What's the topic?" I asked.

"I want to reach out to other governors and mayors around the country who need help. We can send supplies, share best practices. I'd even take a SWAT team to spend the day helping out if it's needed," Cuomo explained.

"Really? You're not concerned that people will say it's not our place?" I countered dubiously. "Can you imagine what you would do if a governor of another state came to New York to do our job?"

Cuomo was insistent. "I don't really care what people say. When we needed help, we weren't shy about asking, and the people of this country stepped up. Now others need help, and it's our turn."

"Okay," I tried again, not yet ready to abandon my devil's advocate role, "but you're not worried we'll get criticized for leaving New York in the middle of the pandemic?"

He had a ready answer for that, too: "It's in New York's best interests that the rest of the country get this virus under control. We know Trump isn't going to do anything except make the situation worse. It's on us to step up and help."

As the governor of New York threw the weight of his office into engaging elected officials, recruiting doctors and nurses, and finding medical equipment to deploy across the country, the nation's putative commander in chief was focused on the civil war he was hoping to spend the summer both stoking and then taking credit for extinguishing. The culmination of Trump's strategizing came on July 8, when, to great fanfare, the president and Attorney General Bill Barr announced Operation Legend, named after four-year-old LeGend Taliferro, who was shot and killed in a domestic violence altercation while he slept in Kansas City, Missouri. The goal of Operation Legend was ostensibly to use federal resources in unprecedented fashion to "fight the sudden surge of violent crime" in American cities, starting with Kansas City. Within days, agents from various federal agencies—the FBI, DOJ, the DEA, Homeland Security, the US Marshals Service—were dispatched.

Trump was a sideshow, but a destructive one. And like any bully, he was looking for a reaction. Cuomo's decision to actively ignore his antics on Twitter appeared to be working: We didn't give him the attention he so desperately sought, and so he looked for it elsewhere. In the interim, we were given time and space from being in his crosshairs to focus on COVID. While red state governors mocked mandates, Cuomo tapped Jane Rosenthal, CEO and founder of Tribeca Enterprises, to develop a national ad campaign to educate and encourage the public to "mask up." And while Trump was focused on politicizing the virus, we spent our time developing partnerships with mayors around the country.

In the middle of July, Atlanta Mayor Keisha Lance Bottoms appeared at one of our pressers to put pressure on the governor of Georgia on mask and social-distancing requirements. Cuomo also deployed a swat team of operations and medical professionals to Houston to erect sites to provide free access to COVID testing. A few days later, we announced that the governor, senior staff, and medical professionals would travel in person to Savannah for a daylong conference with local government officials on how to tackle COVID. It was uncanny; the absentee federal and state leaders were too self-involved to even notice at first that we were on the ground doing the jobs they should have been doing. But then, after ten days of reprieve, it appeared that our national travel had landed us back on Trump's radar.

Rich spotted the incoming salvo. "He's tweeting about crime in New York again," he reported, handing me his phone.

"The Radical Left Democrats, who totally control Biden, will destroy our Country as we know it. Unimaginably bad things would happen to America. Look at Portland, where the pols are just fine with 50 days of anarchy. We sent in help. Look at New York, Chicago, Philadelphia. NO!"

"Oh, good. This again." I handed Rich back his phone and turned to my computer.

"Do we want to say anything?" Rich wanted to know. "A couple of reporters are asking."

"I think we keep ignoring him," I replied. "You?"

"Yeah, I agree. Just want to make sure you saw, just in case."

"Just in case what?"

"I don't know—you saw what he did in Kansas City," he said. "He just rolled out a full-on military operation in Portland. The guy is clearly flailing."

"Yeah, but the mayor in Kansas City asked for his help—why I'll never understand, but he asked," I pointed out. "And Portland is about the ongoing protests. We haven't had organized protests in New York for weeks. He wouldn't actually send troops to the city; this is just another tantrum."

Rich was less convinced.

"I don't know, Melissa. You know Andrew Cuomo is in this guy's head. He's doing these pressers with mayors in red states. We announced he's traveling to Georgia tomorrow, and now, all of a sudden, Trump is tweeting about us again?"

"What are you saying?" I pressed him.

"I'm saying I just don't believe it's a coincidence," Rich answered. "If you're Trump and your numbers are tanking, and you look up and see Cuomo playing the role of president, what's the best way to get him to knock it off? You magnify a problem in his backyard and use whatever authority you have to look like you're doing Cuomo's job."

I could see his point but still couldn't fathom Trump actually following through. "Yeah, but this isn't about protests anymore; this isn't organized crime. It's street crime. It's terrible, and it shouldn't be happening, but it's not about the governor—it's NYPD and de Blasio territory. What on earth would federal troops do to stop it?"

"I'm not saying it makes sense," Rich conceded. "It's just my gut, so I wanted to say something."

The next day, with the national press focused on Andrew Cuomo and the mayor of Savannah, Trump made another announcement: He would restart daily COVID briefings. During a break between sessions in Georgia, my phone rang; it was Rich.

"Melissa, have you seen this? Trump just said he's going to restart his daily briefings." The daily briefings Trump held in the early days of the pandemic had largely been discontinued since late April, roundly criticized as a vanity exercise. Trump regularly used his press conferences to tout misinformation, criticize Democratic governors for the COVID situation in their states, and suggest that elected officials who were not appreciative of his efforts would be deprived federal assistance.

"I saw," I said. "As if they were so helpful the first time."

"Yeah, that's not my point, Melissa," Rich said.

"What's the point?" I was happy to stay in just-ignore-him mode as far as Trump was concerned.

"Come on," Rich scoffed. "It hasn't crossed your mind that Trump is doing this because the gov, you—the whole team—is in Georgia right now doing his job?"

"I think he's doing it because his numbers suck and maybe someone around him is telling him to stop playing GI Joe and focus on the real national crisis that's going to cost him the election," I countered.

"I just have a bad feeling about this," Rich concluded. "I think he's refocused on the boss."

"Well, luckily there's nothing he can do to us," I assured him.

That evening, as the helicopter began its descent into Albany, I opened my Twitter app to see what we had missed in the air. Trump had just addressed reporters from the Oval Office:

"I'm going to do something—that I can tell you. Because we're not going to let New York and Chicago and Philadelphia and Detroit and Baltimore and all of these—Oakland is a mess. We're not going to let this happen in our country. All run by liberal Democrats."

"Fuck," I muttered under my breath, not wanting to wake the governor, who was napping in the seat next to mine.

"What's wrong?" Rob whispered. I x-ed out of that story and kept scrolling. Another one popped up, I clicked.

"Rich was right." I handed Rob my phone to show him a local news story that had just hit: TRUMP THREATENS TO SEND FEDERAL AGENTS TO POLICE NYC: "I'M GOING TO DO SOMETHING." Rob read the headline and handed me back my phone.

"This is just more posturing, Melissa; he's been saying this for weeks," he said.

"Yeah, no, I know. It's fine." I slid my iPhone back into my oversized tote and glanced over at the governor, who had just opened his eyes. As the helicopter touched down, he removed his earbuds and leaned forward.

"What do we know, Meliss?"

"All good, Governor," I responded. "I've been texting with the mayor of Savannah, who is thrilled with the trip and said it was incredibly useful for him and his team. Our guys on the ground are busy setting up mobile testing sites. Otherwise, it's pretty quiet." The trooper on the ground opened the door, the noise from the propellers drowning out our conversation.

"Quiet is good, Rob!" the governor ironically yelled, leaning up, and gesturing to Rob to have him lead the way out of the chopper. "We like quiet. Let's go."

I got into the passenger side of the car the governor was driving, shut the door, and leaned back, closing my eyes. Yes, quiet *is* good, but when was the last time there was quiet? It felt like every time the situation was under control that year, another fastball was thrown at our head. And I couldn't get Rich's voice out of my head. Trump had started sending federal agents into Portland days earlier, resulting in reports of agents in unmarked vans pulling up and grabbing people off streets. It was like a scene out of a bad '90s crime movie. In Oregon, it was making protesters double down, leading to more anger, outrage, and mayhem. If it happened in New York City, hundreds of thousands of people would revolt and no one—not the NYPD, the National Guard, or the feds—would be able to control it. It would be an unmitigated disaster.

Back at the mansion, I headed to the pool house and pulled my computer onto my lap. I spent the next few hours actively trolling Twitter, refreshing news sites, and calling around to contacts in the national press; no one was hearing anything. After a while, I closed my laptop, turned off MSNBC, and closed my eyes. I needed to sleep. And maybe, just maybe I was right and Rich *was* just being paranoid.

Late the next afternoon, Dani hurried into my office.

"Melissa, are you seeing this?" she asked as she grabbed the remote off my desk and surfed to CNN. The sense of uneasy calm I'd talked myself into vanished in an instant. News was leaking out in real time that the president was planning to deploy 150 Homeland Security Investigations agents to Chicago and "possibly other Democrat-run cities" the next day. The agents were expected to stay in Chicago at least two months and would be making arrests for federal crimes.

I stood up, grabbed my bag, and headed for the door.

"Where are you going?" Dani called after me.

"To talk to the governor," I responded. Cuomo was working from the mansion that afternoon, and by the time I arrived, he was already sitting down for dinner with Cara, Stephanie, Michaela, and two of her friends visiting from New York City.

"Look who decided to grace us with her presence," he taunted as I walked in.

"Ha ha, look who has a sense of humor," I bantered back, trying to be light and positive in front of the girls.

"Come on, tardy lady; grab a plate while that food's still warm," he urged me.

"I'm actually not that hungry," I said. "Can I talk to you for a minute?"

"Everything okay?" Michaela asked, picking up on the undercurrent.

"I'm sure it is," I told her. "I just want to flag something for your dad."

Cuomo rose from his chair at the head of the table and gestured to the living room, sliding the heavy wood-paneled doors closed behind us.

"What's wrong?" he asked in a hushed tone.

"I'm sure nothing, but Trump keeps pushing and pushing on send-ing federal agents into Democratic cities, and you know how he is with New York, and they just leaked that they're moving in on Chicago tomorrow. I just, I don't know . . ."

"Is the press saying anything about us?" Cuomo wondered.

"Not yet, but you know he would love nothing more than to invade the city. Hit de Blasio, hit you, rain chaos down on all of the people who despise him. Plus, he'll get to say he's doing it because he stands with law enforcement, even though you know it will get their back up," I said, adding, "I wouldn't be surprised if Giuliani is in his ear . . ."

"Okay, I'm sure it's just bluster, but make some calls, see what we can find out," Cuomo instructed. "I'm sure it's nothing."

He headed back to the family dinner table while I walked up to the pool house, plopped into a lounge chair, and started dialing anyone I could think of. I called Emma in Mayor de Blasio's office, my contacts at the NYPD, the head of the state police, and nearly a dozen reporters in New York and Washington. No one had heard New York would be on the list, but that didn't mean anything. Finally, I decided there was no use in trying to figure this out behind the scenes; it was time to go through the front door.

Jared answered on the second ring, "Melissa, how are you? What can I do for you?"

"Hi, Jared, I was just calling to check in," I began.

"What's going on in New York?"

He knew exactly why I was calling. "Well, I obviously saw the leak about Chicago and the president's comments on other Democratic cit-ies, specifically citing New York a few times," I said. "I couldn't imag-ine there was a world in which he—you guys—would send federal agents into New York City, but I thought it best to just have the direct conversation."

"I don't know why you think that would be such a crazy thing to do, Melissa," his usual soft monotone voice had an edge.

"Excuse me?" I stood up and started to pace.

"I'm saying, you just said you couldn't imagine we'd do it, but I'd argue it would be irresponsible not to," Jared elaborated.

Fuck.

"Jared, let's cut to the chase," I said. "Are you saying you guys are going to announce you're sending feds into New York City tomorrow?"

"I'm saying it's certainly on the table, Melissa. It's the president's home city, and we can't trust de Blasio to get things under control. We've called on Andrew to use the National Guard for over a month, and he seems unwilling to do it, so what other options do we have?" He was trying hard to sound like the voice of reason.

"Jared, I don't even know what we're talking about," I argued. "The protests are over—the gun violence we're seeing in the city isn't organized. What on earth would the National Guard do at this point?"

"I'm just saying, it doesn't seem you are willing to step in where de Blasio is failing, and we have friends and family in that city, and the president is not going to sit on his hands," Jared warned.

I couldn't believe it. They were going to do it. My pulse started racing.

"Jared, do you understand what will happen if you send federal agents into New York City?"

"I can't imagine it would make matters worse," he replied.

"Jared, I promise you: it will be worse. And I need you to listen to me," I added. "The people there hate you. They hate the president. They hate your administration. They will view whatever you do as a declaration of war . . ."

Jared cut me off. "Melissa, law enforcement feels they've been handcuffed, and I think they'd welcome the intervention . . ."

This time, I cut him off. "Are you kidding me? The NYPD—no matter what whoever you're talking to on the inside is telling you—will freak out. They don't welcome other law enforcement on their turf on a good day, let alone in the middle of all of this! You'll end up with a pissing match between law enforcement and hundreds of thousands of protesters, who will then clash with that law enforcement. There will be violence, there will be mayhem, and it will be *your fault.*" My voice had risen to a near-shout without me even realizing it. How could I get through to him?

"Melissa, I think you've made your point loud and clear," Jared said primly. "I don't think this conversation is productive any longer."

"This isn't politics, this is real life, and the kind of chaos you will cause . . ." I paused and took a deep breath. "Jared, you break it, you buy it, and I promise you, you do not want to own this, and the president does not want to own this."

"Okay, Melissa, fine! I hear you!" Jared, who never raised his voice, had reached my decibel level.

"What does that mean?" I demanded.

"It means I hear you loud and clear. Good night!"

To his credit, Jared—for the most part—was a reasonable actor steeled in a mosh pit of flame throwers. If anyone could get to the president, he could, but he had to be convinced. I had had dozens of conversations with him over the previous several months, some more heated than others, and I knew when what I was saying was effective and when it wasn't.

"Hey, are you okay?" Steph had been sitting under the awning next to the pool house, having a glass of wine, and had witnessed the very animated conversation.

"They were going to do it: they were going to send the feds in—I'm almost positive—and they were going to announce it tomorrow," I said, dropping down in the chair next to her.

"And now they're not?" Steph sounded worried.

"I don't know, but I don't think so," I said, replaying what had just happened in my head.

"Well, in that case, you deserve this, lady," she said, producing another wineglass and filling it to the brim with sauvignon blanc.

"Quite the Albany pour there, thank you," I remarked, picking up the glass to cautiously clank Steph's before taking a sip. We wouldn't know for sure until the morning, but at that moment, I felt confident that, at the very least, we had bought some time.

The next day, as I sat in my office, the news broke. As leaked less than twenty-four hours earlier, President Trump announced plans to expand Operation Legend. I scrolled furiously through Twitter, looking for the list of announced cities—and there it was: Albuquerque, Chicago, Baltimore, and Philadelphia. *Thank God.* I picked up the phone to call the governor.

"Trump released the list of cities he's sending troops into, and we're not on it," I reported.

"Okay. Now it's time," Cuomo said.

"Time for what?"

"I'm going to call the president," he said.

"To what end, exactly?" I asked, worried the governor was about to do something to poke the bear.

"This back-and-forth has to stop," Cuomo declared. "To him this is all about the polls, and it's getting dangerous. He has to understand that I'm not the enemy. I have to give him a reason to understand that— and if we do it right, New York can benefit from it."

The governor called Trump that afternoon and spoke the only language that mattered to the president: politics.

Cuomo understood the electoral calendar better than anyone. It was well known that the president had been seething with jealousy over the governor's popularity during the height of the pandemic and believed him to be a potential threat. The president bristled under the constant criticism and interpreted everything Cuomo did and said as a personal slight. Cuomo promised that we would stand down so long as Trump kept an open line of communication and promised not to send troops to New York City.

There was another request, too: Not only did we not have to be enemies, Cuomo suggested, but we could mutually benefit from a partnership on infrastructure. At the end of the day, Trump presumably was going to come back to New York, so why not return as a champion of his fellow New Yorkers, able to point to something substantial he had done for the people here? Jared and I were to work out the particulars, but the president and the governor reached a verbal agreement that day to get the Gateway Tunnel, the long-stalled AirTrain to LaGuardia, and the Second Avenue Subway expansion to Harlem built.

Appealing to reason may have been an exercise in futility with the forty-fifth president of the United States, but appealing to ego worked like a charm.

The next day, after ticking through the COVID numbers, including the lowest hospitalizations since the middle of March, Cuomo announced at the daily briefing that President Trump had agreed not to send troops to New York City. It was a fragile peace, but one both sides were committed to upholding . . . at least for the moment.

CHAPTER 14

Can You Believe This?

As July melted into August, things seemed too good to be true for us. While the rest of the country grappled with hospital shortages and scrambled for PPE, New York's COVID rates continued to remain at the lowest levels since the pandemic began. People were dining outdoors, socializing, planning trips, and looking forward to some much-needed post–Labor Day normalcy.

With the presidential election on the horizon, government officials nationwide morphed increasingly into agents of their preferred candidates. But, due in large part to the peace agreement reached between Governor Cuomo and President Trump weeks earlier, we mostly stayed out of the political fray. We concentrated instead on bringing businesses back to full strength, preparing for any potential COVID spikes by solidifying our stockpiles and closely monitoring daily numbers, and prioritizing the governor's infrastructure plans.

With the latter in mind, I called Rick Cotton, the executive director at the Port Authority, to give him a heads-up about another call we had coming up with Jared Kushner's team. We needed to get moving on the AirTrain approvals, the Second Avenue Subway, and the Gateway Tunnel funding.

"Sure, Melissa, but don't you think this is getting a little ridiculous?" I wasn't surprised to hear his concern after the three calls we'd had over the previous week and a half had gone nowhere.

"Jared will be on the call this time, and he assured me that everyone necessary to actually get these things going will be, too," I said. "We have to keep pushing."

"Okay, it's just starting to feel a little like he's Lucy and we're Charlie Brown." The irony was not lost on me. I generally played the role of Trump administration skeptic, and Rick could tell I didn't necessarily believe what I was saying, either.

"I know, I hear you, but I spoke to Jared yesterday, and he understands he has to move the DOT bureaucrats right now," I said. "Let's give it one more shot before I go back to the governor and tell him this is going nowhere. Then I promise we can stop doing these insipid calls."

I hung up and headed to the mansion, where Steph and the governor were working on Cuomo's speech for the upcoming Democratic Convention. The governor had just finished dictating his most recent version when I found them outside under the awning of the pool house.

"Steph, can you print that out for me, please?" he requested, without looking up.

"One for Melissa, too?" Stephanie suggested, acknowledging my presence.

"No, it's not ready for her yet." The governor said shaking his head.

"How are we doing out here, guys?" I asked brightly, interjecting myself into a conversation I wasn't invited to.

"Fine, fine, fine, just working on this speech," Cuomo answered, reaching for a cigar.

"Wow, we're a full five days from when you're supposed to record this—you sure you don't want to wait a little longer and add to the drama?" I inquired sarcastically, as I swiped a piece of cubed cheese from the platter on the table in front of them.

"Look who's funny." The governor raised an eyebrow.

"How are you doing on the Trump stuff?" I forged forward.

"What do you mean?" He looked up at me.

"I mean in your speech. You know the Biden people are expecting you to take him to the woodshed on COVID," I reminded him pointedly, as if he didn't know.

"I'm working through it." I sensed his reluctance, which I wasn't thrilled about.

"We can't pull punches here, Governor. It's the Democratic Convention, and you're the nation's most trusted voice on Trump's greatest vulnerability. They're going to assume you'll take him apart."

"Yeah, I hear you. I said I'm working through it. I'll show it to you when I'm ready," he said, his voice testy.

"Okay," I relented. I knew I was annoying him, so I decided to let it go for the time being. I turned to head back to the office.

"How are you doing with Jared?" he asked, before I could leave. Tables turned.

"Fine."

"Just fine?" He asked, skeptically.

"We've had a bunch of calls, but mostly it's just the bureaucrats talking in circles. I spoke with Jared this morning, and he promised to get on the next call to start moving things along," I elaborated.

The governor hated mixing politics and government. He was a diehard believer in working with whomever was in office to deliver real results. It was a trait that had been admirable decades earlier, but in the age of hyper-partisanship, his approach had become an Achilles' heel. Cuomo would often talk about how President Clinton still negotiated and passed legislation with Newt Gingrich while Republicans in the House were impeaching him. Clinton believed government functioning was the only priority and refused to allow for paralysis even while the other side was trying to kick him out of office. He passed that belief down to the governor, who—for better or worse—spent his first two terms in office being criticized for collaborating with Republicans and centrists who were in control of the state senate. His tendency to be bipartisan had become a major liability in his 2018 primary against Cynthia Nixon; I could only imagine what the blowback would be if he appeared to be going easy on Trump.

Now, with the 2020 presidential election less than one hundred days away, our government priorities appeared to be on a collision course with our political ones. The governor had a nonaggression pact with Trump and was determined to see it through. The benefit of jumping on the hyper-partisan bandwagon along with every other Democrat in America had marginal returns, while the cost could be three massive infrastructure projects. Even worse, we didn't know what would happen in the election, and if Trump stayed in office somehow, it would mean at least another four years before we could dream of approvals or federal funding coming through. At the same time, no one in the country had more credibility on COVID than Andrew Cuomo, and the Biden campaign had rightly identified COVID mismanagement as Trump's most significant weakness. There was an anticipation of the role the governor would play, and if he didn't come through at the convention, it could appear that our support for the Democratic ticket was less than wholehearted, which was not an option.

Over the next several days, Janno Lieber, president of MTA Construction and Development, Beth Garvey, special counsel to the New York State Executive Chamber, Rick Cotton, and I participated in a handful of calls with Jared Kushner and his team. The governor wanted the maximum-possible federal funding for the Second Avenue Subway extension to Harlem. A year earlier, California had set the bar when the state received 49 percent for one of its big projects, and Cuomo wanted the same deal for New York.

"I think we can do 33.3 percent and push it through quickly," a federal DOT bureaucrat said during one of our painful group discussions, which were long on excuses and short on results.

"That's not even remotely in the ballpark of what we were thinking; am I right, Janno?" I interrupted.

"That's correct, Melissa," he confirmed. "In fact, based on the scope and merits of the project on its own, we are guaranteed that amount without any special approvals or expediting."

"Okay, so with all due respect, what are we doing here, folks?" I was losing patience quickly.

"The governor and the president have an agreement, and we need to honor that and see it through. How do we raise that percentage up for Governor Cuomo and his team?" Jared questioned his people. He could tell things were about to go sideways.

"Well, we'll have to go back and look," said someone from the DOT.

"How long is that going to take?" Jared cut him off before it turned into another twenty-minute nonanswer.

"Uh, can you give us a week?" another nameless DOT employee piped in.

"Melissa, does that work on your end?" Jared asked.

I sighed, exasperated by the red tape. "Sure, Jared, we can talk again in a week."

We hung up, and within thirty seconds my phone rang again. It was Beth Garvey.

"Melissa, you know they're playing us, right?" she asked rhetorically.

"I do," I acknowledged.

"Good. I wanted to make sure we're all on the same page, because these calls are a massive waste of time." Beth was annoyed, which was completely understandable.

I couldn't put off giving the governor the bad news any longer, even if it meant interrupting his final edit of the convention speech.

He picked up on the first ring. "How did it go with Jared?" he said by way of greeting.

"Can I be perfectly honest with you?" I asked rhetorically.

"I would hope so."

"We are being played—you are being played. The president wants you on the sidelines in this election, and now you're on the sidelines, and they're running out the clock."

"So it didn't go well, huh?" he responded, sarcastically.

"I'm being dead serious. They're basically offering us what we're automatically entitled to on the Second Avenue Subway, and the AirTrain Environmental Impact Study is still going to take months." My voice rose an octave. "They're slow-walking this thing, and it's working!"

"Alright, alright, calm down," he said.

"What I'm saying is, if you're thinking of holding back in your convention speech because of some supposed deal we have with the White House, don't," I urged.

"Melissa, if we go too hard, it will blow everything up," he objected.

"Blow *what* up? There's nothing to blow up! And, by the way, what does this guy expect? That you're not going to be political in a convention speech? Come on!" I couldn't hide my frustration any longer. We were being extorted, plain and simple.

The governor continued to rework his speech, finally landing on a version that he was comfortable with: prosecuting a truthful argument relevant to Americans as they made the decision on whom to cast their vote for, but also not hyperbolic or gratuitous. Tyrants respond to strength, and so my instinct on Trump was always to go hotter and harder, but the governor insisted on trying to thread the needle.

The speech was set to air the Monday of the convention, between Bernie Sanders and Michelle Obama. Most of the event's speeches were pre-recorded because of COVID. I was at the mansion that night, thinking we would pull a small group of staff together to watch, but when I arrived, the governor told me he wasn't interested.

His father, Mario Cuomo, had arguably delivered the most famous keynote address at the Democratic National Convention, in San Francisco on July 16, 1984. "A Tale of Two Cities" masterfully challenged Ronald Reagan's concept of America's shining city on a hill. At age twenty-six, Andrew Cuomo wrote that speech with his father and Tim Russert. They refused to share it with anyone ahead of time for fear that its contents could leak or that party leadership would attempt to edit it. The governor loved to tell the story of the '84 convention and how Mario Cuomo was paranoid that the teleprompter would fail midway through. To account for that possibility, one of their junior staffers spent the speech crouched down inside the podium with a hard copy printed out in a binder so that, in the event of a teleprompter malfunction, he could hand it up to Mario open to the right page.

"This isn't a real convention," the governor explained. "There's no drama, no audience feedback, no energy." While comprehending the necessity, he detested the virtual format.

"I'm going to sleep," he announced. "Let me know how it all goes in the morning."

I knew the speech backward and forward and was there when he'd recorded it, but as I watched it, along with the rest of the country, I was proud of where it had landed—true to his principles, while using his platform to make the case for why the country desperately needed a new president.

I monitored Twitter and cable news for a while after the evening's speeches wrapped up, relieved to see that his remarks were well-received, hailed as powerful and eloquent. No one was saying he didn't go hard enough or that he was over-the-top. He was exactly where he wanted to be.

The next morning, I picked up my iPhone and saw six missed calls, three from our communications director, Peter Ajemian, and three from Rich Azzopardi, trusted senior adviser to the governor. I opened Twitter to see if there was something I'd missed: a fire, a flood, a COVID outbreak?

I had missed something alright, and while it hadn't been a literal natural disaster, a storm was definitely brewing.

It seemed that while Trump didn't appear to watch the convention in real time, he had either seen the post-event coverage or someone had briefed him on it after the fact. Either way, he wasn't happy. The president had launched an overnight Twitter rampage, retweeting eleven posts, quote-tweeting another with his own commentary, and posting one tweet of his own—all targeted at Governor Cuomo. Most of his tweets criticized the governor's own COVID management in New York, focusing on overall death totals, particularly those in nursing homes. Others flagged positive comments the governor had made about the president in the past in which he said to "keep politics out of it." The whole thing was so personal, it was as if he was using social media to speak directly to Cuomo, and his message was simple: You broke our agreement, and now I'm coming for you.

I sank back into bed, pulling the covers over my head, and silently chastised myself. Fuck. This is exactly what the governor wanted to avoid. And it's my fault.

The governor was working from the mansion that day, and this was not going to be a phone conversation. I walked into the living room to find him drafting a PowerPoint presentation while simultaneously dictating a speech to Stephanie.

"Can I talk to you for a minute?"

"Uh-huh," he responded without looking up.

"So the convention speech was incredible, really well-received. I heard from the Biden team that the vice president is very happy."

"Uh-huh," Cuomo replied, again without breaking his concentration on the task at hand.

"But it seems we struck a nerve," I continued.

"Oh yeah, with whom?" he asked, still with minimal engagement.

"Trump. He lost his mind last night. He tweeted at you thirteen different times, and we're starting to get press incoming asking for a response," I said.

"Thirteen times? What about Michelle Obama or Bernie Sanders?" Now I had his attention.

"Bizarrely, he's entirely focused on you. I don't really know how to describe it, but his tweets feel extremely personal."

"What's the reaction?" he wanted to know.

"Based on their comments on Twitter, I think the press is mostly confused as to why it is that, out of everyone in the Democratic Party, you are the one who seems to get under his skin more than anyone else," I ventured. Just then, my iPhone started to ring. I looked down to see Jared Kushner's name flash across my screen.

Fuck, fuck, fuck.

"Who is that?" the governor asked. My attempt to present a poker face seemed to have failed.

"Jared."

"Well, answer it and see what he says."

I nodded and started to walk out of the room to take the call when he added, "Melissa, don't be defensive." He knew me too well.

"Morning, Jared, how are you?" I asked with false cheer, as if I didn't know why he was calling.

"Melissa, are you kidding?"

"With what?" I feigned ignorance.

"The governor's speech last night. It was completely over-the-top and incendiary, and the president is furious."

"Yes, I saw his Twitter feed this morning," I allowed, "but, Jared, the governor only mentioned Trump by name two times in the entire speech, and it was a convention speech. You guys had to know he was going to bring up *something*. Honestly, I think he did a great job of saying the least amount necessary, and . . ."

"Melissa, the deal is off." Jared wasn't buying it.

"What deal?" I knew full well but was going to make him say it.

"I've told my team to stop working on the AirTrain, the Second Avenue Subway, and Gateway. We will not negotiate with you anymore."

"I'm sorry, Jared," I said. "I want to be clear: we don't mix politics and government decisions here. Are you saying that because of the governor's convention speech, the president is pulling his support for these projects?"

"I'm not doing this with you, Melissa. Goodbye." Jared hung up on me.

I couldn't believe it. Donald Trump, the president of the United States, the most notorious bully in all of politics, had lost his mind over four sentences in a convention speech. It was official: Andrew Cuomo lived in his head, rent free. The problem, of course, was this was the exact outcome the governor was actively trying to avoid. I walked back into the living room, where the governor was still sitting as I'd left him.

"What happened?" he asked, this time looking me in the eyes.

"Well, that didn't go well," I said.

"Are they upset?" he wanted to know.

"That's the understatement of the century."

He was as puzzled as I was by Trump's public tantrum. "I went as light as possible in that speech," he said.

"I know, and I pointed that out," I agreed. "Jared said the president is furious and believes we broke our word." I hesitated for a minute, summoning the courage to speak the words I knew Cuomo didn't want to hear. "He said he's dropping negotiations on Gateway, the AirTrain, and the Second Avenue Subway."

The governor leaned forward, pushed his glasses down the bridge of his nose, and exhaled, "Well, we knew that was coming. What did you say?"

"I said we don't mix politics and government."

"And?"

"And then he hung up on me."

"Of course he did—I'm sure you freaked him out," Cuomo mused. "He probably thought you were recording him." I was not.

"Listen, I know this isn't ideal, but the truth is they were screwing us on those projects anyway," I said. "There's no way he was actually going to deliver anything before November. They were just going to continue to dangle the prospect in front of us to keep you quiet." I believed what I was saying, but I was also trying to convince myself and the governor that my pushing on the speech hadn't just cost the state billions of dollars, thousands of jobs, and three major infrastructure projects that he'd worked his ass off to make a reality.

"Yes, I know you feel that way." He also acknowledged my guilt and, to his credit, didn't attempt to rub salt in the wound.

"But now that it's over, we can get in the game a little more. Honestly, what else can they do to us?" I asked innocently enough.

It was less than one week before we would find out.

"Melissa, we need to jump on the phone with Judy Mogul, Dr. Zucker, and Linda Lacewell immediately," Rich Azzopardi's urgent voice came across the line.

"What's the problem?" I asked, relatively unruffled.

"We're under investigation."

"Who's we?" I asked. He had my attention.

"The governor, our office, the Health Department," Rich replied.

"For what, exactly?"

"COVID in nursing homes," he said.

"Wait, what? How do you know?" My heart started beating faster.

"We found out at the same time as the rest of the world—through a press release."

Unbelievable.

On the afternoon of August 26, 2020, the Department of Justice announced a civil inquiry into COVID deaths in nursing homes, as Rich had indicated, by press release. The investigation, according to the release, would review the impact of COVID health policies on deaths in nursing homes, specifically quoting the New York State Department of Health's March 25 guidance. Despite a dozen states—Democrat and Republican—having enacted similar policies, it focused on only four: Pennsylvania, Michigan, New Jersey, and New York. Two swing states, two states with governors who were vocally critical of the president, all Democratic. The press release, which was issued by Department of Justice employees charged with upholding the law, praised the COVID responses of two deep-red states: Florida and Texas.

We had officially entered the twilight zone.

As I tried to map out exactly what to do next, my mind searched my ever-growing cache of Trump files.

Two years earlier in 2018, shortly after the governor had been reelected, we flew down to meet with President Trump to discuss infrastructure funding for the Gateway Tunnel. Economically speaking, it was arguably the most important corridor in the Northeast, and it was literally crumbling. The governor had become fixated on getting the federal funding necessary to stave off any further decay before a looming problem became a crisis, but for years, he couldn't get the federal government to pay attention to it. After months of cajoling, Trump agreed to a meeting to discuss it over lunch. And so the governor, Rick Cotton, and I boarded the state prop plane and headed down to Washington, DC, to make the case.

When we arrived, we were escorted into the Oval Office to find President Trump, his then chief of staff John Kelly, US Secretary of Transportation Elaine Chao, and, oddly, US Trade Representative Robert Lighthizer. Chao later told Rick and me that Lighthizer was there because he happened to be present when Trump was on the phone with the governor and set the meeting. "The president told his assistant to include everyone in the room, and no one wanted to correct him that a US trade representative had no relevance to the conversation," Chao explained and then added with a laugh, "I've ended up in numerous Obamacare meetings the same way." *This is how these people run the White House?* I wondered, in total disbelief.

Donald Trump and Andrew Cuomo had known each other for decades. Two tough guys from Queens, raised by larger-than-life fathers. By all accounts, Trump was unfit, but the governor had respect for the office and conducted himself accordingly.

"Mr. President, good to see you," the governor said, extending his right arm to shake Trump's hand.

"Andrew, so glad you could make it," Trump responded with the formality of a frat brother. The group stood around awkwardly as the president and the governor chatted.

"Mr. President, the dining room is all set. Shall we head in and start our lunch meeting?" General Kelly asked.

"In a minute, in a minute," Trump responded. "Andrew just got here." He turned his full attention back to the governor.

"Oh, Andrew, you know what we should do?" Trump asked excitedly.

"What's that, Mr. President?" the governor played along.

"What's Chris's number?" Trump requested, picking up the phone on the Roosevelt desk.

"I'm sorry, Mr. President?" the governor inquired, rightly confused.

"Your brother. What's his number? It would be hilarious if we prank-called him right now," said the president.

Cuomo reached for his pocket, forgetting that, per White House protocol, he had relinquished his BlackBerry upon arrival. "I think Chris is busy right now, Mr. President, but I'm happy to tell him you asked about him when he and I speak later," the governor responded coolly, not wanting to acknowledge he didn't have Chris's number committed to memory.

"Oh, come on, it would be so funny!" Trump protested.

Cuomo laughed awkwardly, trying to move the conversation along. "I really do think he's tied up at the moment, but I promise I will tell him."

"Okay, fine. But, it would have been fun," Trump looked modestly defeated that his old acquaintance from New York didn't seem interested in palling around.

"Excuse me, Mr. President," his assistant appeared in front of us. "Lunch is ready; shall I bring your guests this way?" She was doing her best to keep her boss on schedule. I both pitied and admired her; you had to have a lot of patience to be in her position.

"What are we having?" he asked, seriously wanting to know.

"Beef, shrimp, and chocolate cake for dessert," she replied dutifully.

"Oh, that's great," Trump turned to the governor. "Andrew, you're gonna love this chocolate cake—it's incredible," he swiveled his head and turned to me. "Bet you've never eaten dessert before, huh?" he remarked, apparently referring to my frame. Jesus Christ. The whole thing felt like I was having an out-of-body experience.

Then, as everyone collectively turned to walk down the corridor off the Oval Office into the president's private dining room, Trump grabbed the governor's forearm, leaned in to whisper, and said, "Hey, Andrew, can you believe this?" He opened his arms wide as he looked around.

"Excuse me, Mr. President?" the governor countered, uncertain what he meant.

"This!" President Trump repeated, again eyeing his surroundings. "Can you believe this?"

The governor nodded, forcing a second awkward laugh, before putting his arm around the president and gesturing toward the dining room in an attempt to end the conversation and sit down for lunch.

On the plane ride back to Albany that afternoon, recounting that very moment, the governor asked me and Rick, "What do you think President Trump meant by that?"

"What do you mean, what did he mean?" I asked. Was this a trick question?

"What do you think Trump meant when he kept repeating, 'Can you believe this?'" the governor reiterated.

"Who the hell knows what Trump ever means, but the way I heard it was, 'Andrew, can you fucking believe this? I'm president of the United States. We're having lunch at the White House. I'm standing behind the Roosevelt desk in the Oval Office!'" I said, my voice rising.

"Yeah, that's what I thought he meant, too," the governor said, putting his earbuds in, a signal that the conversation was over.

"In fairness," I continued, "at least it shows some level of self-awareness. I mean, c'mon, I know I can't believe that man is president."

The governor nodded as if to placate me and closed his eyes.

But Trump was president. And that title, whether he deserved it or not, included all the power that came with it.

And now, two years later, feeling scorned by his "buddy" Andrew's keynote speech at the Democratic National Convention, Donald Trump was using that power and the full weight of the Department of Justice to investigate his political enemies in the middle of a global pandemic, at the height of the most consequential presidential campaign in history. It was an unprecedented and obvious abuse of office. Remarkably, not only wasn't he trying to hide it, he was gleefully trumpeting it by press release.

And no one could do a damn thing to stop it.

CHAPTER 15

Misplaced Priorities

When we arrived in New York City for a COVID briefing the day after Labor Day, the streets that had gone from eerily deserted in March to chaotic and, at times, violent in June, now looked and felt almost normal. A new normal, of course—pedestrians in masks, yellow taxis with plastic partitions separating passengers and drivers—but way closer to normal than the hell we had been through together. Businesses that had shuttered in the spring were gradually bringing their workforces back, and foot traffic, though light, was increasing dramatically. People were returning from the suburban havens they had fled to months earlier seeking shelter from COVID's insidious threat. There were still far too many vacant storefronts, but for the first time in months, I could feel a palpable energy emanating from the city and, with it, the faintest glimmer of hope.

I could start to see signs of normalcy in my own life, too. The immediate crisis at bay, Steph, Larry, and I moved out of the mansion, with Larry returning to his full-time job in New York City, Steph moving back into her actual home in Saratoga, and me relocating to my sister's house in Albany.

New York's COVID numbers continued to lead in terms of the lowest positivity rate in the country, remaining below 1 percent for thirty-two consecutive days, while hospitalizations, intubations, and lives lost were at all-time lows for the pandemic. No other state had been nearly as successful at increasing economic activity while staving off the virus.

Staring at the calendar, we had identified two major challenges to ensuring that our progress continued unabated: ushering hundreds of thousands of kids back into classrooms and onto college campuses in the fall, and the upcoming religious holidays. Schools and religion have always been the third rail of politics; with COVID, that reality was made ten times worse. With the Trump administration—no surprise— providing negligible guidance on how to manage such milestones, we once again made it up as we went along, trusting our guts and experience more than our federal government.

Colleges were mandated to maintain a certain level of testing every two weeks; one hundred cases or more would trigger automatic remote learning. Local school districts had to report any cases in their classrooms to the state, and we, in turn, would publish them weekly so that any incidents were known to the public. With 4,360 public schools in the state, this was going to be a massive undertaking that required striking and maintaining a careful balance between the fears of teachers and administrators who were needed to run the schools, and the desires of parents and their children, who so desperately wanted and needed to be back in classrooms.

The upcoming Jewish holidays would be particularly challenging. We had asked families to forego their usual customs for almost a year, and with the numbers being as low as they were, it was difficult to rationally justify not allowing religious gatherings. In New York, areas downstate, from Brooklyn and Queens to Rockland and Orange counties, were home to concentrated Orthodox communities. They prayed and gathered en masse, with thousands of people singing and dancing and embracing at huge synagogues and, in some instances, in the streets. If one or two sick people attended services, there was a real chance that hundreds, if not thousands, could end up sick in the community, and from there, it would only be a matter of time before the virus would seep out into the surrounding areas. Celebrations of the high holidays could be the ultimate superspreader events. The governor dispatched Dr. Zucker and our intergovernmental team to make a direct appeal to the leadership of the individual congregations, discouraging gatherings once more this year and instead recommending virtual prayer and celebration. We were hopeful that our overtures would make an impact, but, based on the negative reaction they were getting, we were deeply skeptical that we were getting through. Given the incubation period, we wouldn't know the impact for weeks. All we could do was pray.

While scary and unknown, the fact that children were returning to school and we were contemplating in-person holidays fueled hope that we were close to reclaiming "real" life, or at least approaching some form of normalcy. I could see signs of it in my own family, too.

My brother, Joey, and his fiancée, Kathleen, were set to marry the second weekend of September, after what had been a tense few months of canceling caterers and bands before finally accepting the reality that no more than twenty-five people would be present. Even at the height of a once-in-a-century pandemic, the event still maintained all of the traditional drama that accompanies family affairs—for me, anyway.

Matt had driven to Albany in June, but other than that single occasion, we hadn't been in the same physical space since January. The wound was still fresh, and I was very much in denial. While I had confided in my sister and brother about the unraveling of our marriage, I still hadn't told my parents that divorce was inevitable. Jessica's daughters, Alexa and Ashley, often asked where Uncle Matt was, and while COVID presented a convenient built-in set of excuses, there was no way I could explain his absence from Joey's wedding. I called Matt and asked if he would be willing to be there; it was important to me, and he loved my brother. While he was uncomfortable with my parents being in the dark about the true status of our relationship, he was willing to play along.

Personally, I loathe how the Pinterest/Instagram generation has fed the voracious machinery of this country's wedding industry. I can't count the number of events I've been to that were more about performance than intimacy, and I have no fewer than a dozen bridesmaid dresses in my already overstuffed closet to prove it. Joey and Kathleen's

COVID wedding was the opposite. While not the 200-plus-person affair they had originally planned, the day was perfect. An outdoor ceremony at Kathleen's alma mater, Siena College, followed by a candlelit dinner on the terrace at our family's country club. There was no oversized wedding party—no bridesmaids or groomsmen—just eighty-eight-year-old Nonno playing the role of best man opposite Kathleen's closest cousin as maid of honor. Absent were the college roommates, work acquaintances, and friends of our parents that had packed my wedding years earlier. In their place: Kathleen and Joey's immediate families, along with a few aunts and uncles. Everyone at the ceremony could truly see one another and appreciate each other. Their wedding was the happiest of any I had attended.

"You know, I wish this had been our wedding," I said in a quiet moment when Matt and I locked eyes over dinner.

"Oh, come on, Melissa, you didn't want this." Matt was right. Our wedding four years earlier was all pomp, complete with four days of events, two hundred people, boldfaced names, fireworks, and a *New York Times* announcement. I don't remember spending any concentrated time with Matt over those four days, let alone my close family. If it had been up to him, we would have married on a beach somewhere, with twenty-five people, toes in the sand. I was the one who pushed. But that night in the midst of a plague, with my marriage on the brink of dissolution, looking at my brother, truly blissful and content, I was struck with a wave of emotion, cataloging years of misplaced priorities, caring too often about what others thought and too little about genuine happiness. And just then, a single tear began to trickle down my face.

"Hey, hey, what's wrong?" Matt asked tenderly.

"Was this all my fault?" I asked, genuinely looking for an answer.

"Melissa, come on; you know it's not," he said, pulling his chair closer, wrapping his arm around my shoulder. "Honey, it's going to be okay—you are going to be okay. You're beautiful and brilliant and successful. You are a good person." He paused. "The truth is, sometimes, no matter how hard we try, things don't work, but that's okay."

I nodded, trying to pull myself together before anyone else could see that I was obviously upset.

I left that night thinking about the impact COVID had had on families across the globe. It forced everyone to slow down, stay home, and reconnect. And while it was hellish on so many levels, it forced healthy self-assessment, too. There's nothing like the fear of death to make a person realize what truly matters in life, and I hoped that when it was all over, the positive impacts of COVID would carry forward, including the end of the impersonal factory wedding.

As the days ticked by that September, it was clear that the entire state was feeling that it was time to get back to real life, and COVID compliance was beginning to slip. The rules had to be rational in order for people to follow them, and after three straight months of positivity under 1 percent, "better safe than sorry" was not translating to people anxious to get back to their lives. New York City under Bill de Blasio continued to be an unruly mess, with reports of underground raves, packed outdoor bars, and pop-up weddings with hundreds of people. Politically, the mayor was incredibly close with the Orthodox community in the city and had no interest in enforcing size limits on gatherings. We were beginning to get nervous that the state was backsliding and that we would soon see it in the numbers.

At the end of the month, I took my first weekend off since COVID began. In this instance, "off" meant physically away but still working. I arrived in Nantucket for my sister, Jessica's, fortieth birthday with our brother and his new wife and a small group of Jessica's friends. Her husband, Jim, who orchestrated the festivities, had strict instructions: Everyone had to be tested before boarding the ferry. Despite the pandemic, he was hell-bent on making sure his wife was safely, properly celebrated. That Saturday morning, I woke up and fished around for my BlackBerry. The daily COVID report had come in overnight, and it wasn't good. For the first time since June 5, New York registered over 1,000 new COVID cases. What we feared in the abstract was beginning to play itself out in the numbers. *No. No. No.*

I got dressed and went down to the kitchen of the cedar-shingled house we were renting, poured a cup of coffee, cracked open my laptop, and called Dr. Zucker to ask what he thought. In his assessment, there were two possibilities: One, this was an anomaly—we were doing so much testing that we were catching more cases in young, healthy people than we otherwise would—or two, the tide was actually beginning to turn. It had been two and a half weeks since the Jewish high holidays and three weeks since kids had gone back to school. Exactly what we had feared would happen was happening. Suddenly, I could feel a wave of PTSD reverberate through my body. We had just beaten this, and it had almost killed all of us. It can't possibly be that we're going backward. Just then, I looked up to see my sister coming down the stairs.

"Hey, sissy, whatcha doin' down here?" she asked, riffling through the cabinet for a coffee mug.

"Just catching up on some work."

"I thought you were 'off' this weekend," Jessica said, an edge to her voice.

I looked up at her, "Yup, you know me—I'm definitely 'off,'" I said with a half smile. I was always on my phone or laptop or BlackBerry, a bone of contention with my family at holidays or events. I would often attempt to use humor as a way to fend off any real confrontation about my inability to give them all of me.

"Well, is everything okay?" she wondered.

"Honestly, Jess . . ." I hesitated. This was hardly the birthday conversation I wanted to have with my sister, but I couldn't help myself. "It's not. I don't want to sound hysterical, but we're going to report over 1,000 new cases of COVID as of yesterday. It's the first time we've gone over 1,000 since the beginning of June."

"Okay. Well, I know we're doing more testing," she responded. "Could that be part of it?"

I shook my head. "You know this thing—it's exponential. If we found 1,000 cases, that means there's many more than that out there, and that with every passing minute, those people are giving it to other people. Between schools and indoor dining and people breaking the rules on mass gatherings—there's just too many people in confined spaces . . . I just . . ."

"You just what?" she prodded.

"I just have a bad feeling about this," I answered honestly.

"Do you think they'll end up closing schools again? Remote learning is terrible for kids—they can't go back to trying to teach eight-year-olds on computers." My sister was doing the same thing every New Yorker would do when they learned COVID was ticking up: assume the worst-case scenario of what the backslide could mean for their lives and preemptively panic.

"I don't know, J. It's too soon to know anything, and I could be wrong," I admitted, "but I don't think I am."

Three days later, on my thirty-eighth birthday, the governor, Dr. Zucker, Rob, and I were back in our New York City press room to make a startling announcement: COVID numbers were going back up again statewide, with twenty "hot spot" zip codes reporting over 10 percent positivity. Those zip codes directly overlapped with large Orthodox communities. It was exactly what we had dreaded would happen, and as we knew too well, when you see COVID spreading in the numbers, it's already too late. We were going to need a new strategy—fast—and that strategy would have to account for the fact that the public was no longer listening the way they were six months earlier.

CHAPTER 16

The Second Wave

The morning of Sunday, October 4, I headed over to the mansion for a couple of media interviews the governor had scheduled and a meeting to discuss the week ahead. Afterward, I sat on the wraparound porch overlooking the grounds, stealing a few moments of quiet to myself—the crisp autumn air a reminder that we were entering yet another COVID season—and thinking back on all that had happened over the last eight months. We were still at least two months from the potential of a vaccine, but in that moment, I felt genuine calm—a feeling, I should have known, that would not last long.

Just then, I felt my phone vibrate in the pocket of the long black overcoat I had just pulled out of the closet for fall. I glanced down—it was our recently promoted communications director, Peter Ajemian. Thinking it could wait, I side-buttoned the call, slipping the phone back into my pocket. Thirty seconds later, it began vibrating again. Peter was not an alarmist, and if he could get an answer from someone else, he wouldn't bother me. Two consecutive calls meant something was up. I pressed "accept."

"Hey, Peter," I said. "What's going on? All okay there?"

"Melissa, did the city tell you about this plan they submitted?" he wanted to know.

"What plan?"

"Apparently, the mayor just held a press conference and announced that he wants to close schools and all nonessential businesses in nine zip codes."

"Wait, what?"

"Yeah, and he wants to close 'high-risk activities' in eleven other zip codes," Peter added, "and the press is asking us for comment."

"What does he define as 'high risk'?" I wondered.

"It's unclear." Peter responded.

"Well, it would be nice to know what we're commenting on," I said, trying to keep the sarcasm and exasperation in check; this wasn't Peter's fault. "I'll call Emma and then talk to the governor and Dr. Zucker and circle back."

This was a trademark move of the de Blasio administration, to make some major decision over which they had no legal authority, then trot it out in the press—sans discussion with us—inevitably resulting in two outcomes: (1) confusion for the public over what was actually going on and (2) days of stories on the mayor and governor's dysfunctional relationship. It was a maddening pattern, which resulted in hours of wasted time and made everyone look bad. Bill de Blasio's bull-in-a-china-shop style was annoying and counterproductive on a good day; when he engaged in it during COVID, with the stakes as high as they were, it felt selfish and petulant.

Emma claimed they had "tried" to contact us five minutes before the mayor's press conference, adding that it wasn't "up to her" how the information was being communicated. Translation: I agree this was totally dysfunctional, but the mayor wouldn't let me tell you earlier.

"The mayor knows he has no legal authority to do any of this, right?" I asked rhetorically. "He knows it's not logical?"

Silence.

The city's plan made absolutely no sense; it was a one-dimensional solution to a three-dimensional problem, but that was par for the course when dealing with de Blasio. In some ways, he was just as irrational as Trump: with both of them, it was all politics, all the time.

As it had from the beginning, the COVID rate varied widely by region across the state. The governor sought to establish the most data-driven response system possible, setting policy based on the infection rate in different communities. Over time, as we built out our testing capacity, we established a highly accurate and sophisticated system based on specific mapping that could tell us infection rates virtually block by block. The governor would make decisions, as he often said, "on the numbers," correlating policy to the infection rate.

COVID didn't follow postal routes. In New York City, arguably the most densely populated urban area in the country, zip codes do not capture entire neighborhoods, let alone address the issue that once an area was seeing increases in positivity, it was only a matter of time before the surrounding area would see the same spread. Furthermore, New York City residents were not sedentary; they did not live their lives within the zip code that their apartments were in. They traversed across the city's five boroughs and its surrounding suburbs—as well as bedroom communities in Connecticut and New Jersey—for work or to socialize, and they would unwittingly take COVID with them. Making matters more complicated, school enrollment is not based on zip code, meaning children from surrounding areas could be impacted by de Blasio's closure, despite not living in the infected area. Most confounding of all, we already knew where the numbers were spiking: it was mainly in Orthodox Jewish neighborhoods where the COVID rules were not being followed or enforced. Despite this, the mayor did not propose limiting gatherings at religious institutions, even though everyone agreed the outbreaks were being driven almost single-handedly there. Why? The ultra-Orthodox are a homogeneous community and unified. The head rebbes—or grand rebbes, as they are often called—have tremendous power in the community. When a rebbe endorses a candidate, the vote in the community is virtually 100 percent for that candidate. The rebbes are therefore politically powerful because they provide politicians with a significant block of votes. The Orthodox rebbes had long helped prop up de Blasio's career and had been key to his election as mayor. He had no interest in doing anything that could upset them, public health be damned.

The announcement led to mass confusion—de Blasio stated as fact that the closures would go into effect that Wednesday, despite having no legal authority to set the policy. And so, once again, we found ourselves needlessly scrambling. It was an unmitigated and totally avoidable disaster.

At our press conference the next day, the governor addressed the mayor's edict. State health officials believed the source of the current spread was twofold: religious gatherings and schools. The city had too little testing to confirm that schools were the source of the spread, but given the strong likelihood that infected children were going to school and infecting their teachers and all of their classmates, we agreed that schools in the impacted areas should be closed. On general closures, the governor was not as eager as de Blasio to immediately shutter nonessential businesses again. There was no evidence from our contact-tracing program that suggested nonessential businesses were the source of the spread, and our goal was to take a more refined, data-driven approach versus blanket closures. While we knew that we needed to make some difficult decisions about restricting religious gatherings, we would wait to meet with community leaders first in an effort to gain buy-in.

As we boarded the helicopter following Monday's press conference, my phone buzzed with a *New York Times* breaking news alert: "Cuomo Rejects N.Y.C.'s Shutdown Plan for Virus Spike, but May Offer Own: The abrupt announcement caused confusion over the official response to the virus surge in some areas and threatened to deepen tensions with the mayor."

That was a news summary I could not, unfortunately, argue with.

Once back in Albany, the governor called Jim, Rob, Dr. Zucker, and me to his conference room. He quickly instructed us to engage the nation's most-respected epidemiologists to come up with a nuanced strategy to address hot spots, applying the lessons we had learned in the spring. We had twenty-four hours to put together a team, come up with a strategy, consult local community leaders, secure an enforcement mechanism, and announce it to the public. Pizza and coffee were ordered; it was going to be a long night.

I was a proponent of tightening restrictions as much as possible. Looking at the numbers, I felt things were out of control. I feared the worst and didn't want to go back to mass graves on Hart Island or calls to health-care workers' families to notify them that their loved one had died.

"We should just shut it all down again," I said to the governor when the rest of the team left the room. "We know where this is going. Let's just get out in front of it before it's too late."

"Melissa, this isn't March," Cuomo argued. "We know more now. We have the testing capacity. Masks work. We don't need to be as drastic."

"This is a mistake," I insisted, shaking my head.

"Melissa, you aren't being rational; you're being emotional," Cuomo reasoned. "This is your trauma responding, not your head. Recognize it so you can confront it. These are big decisions, and we have to make them based on today, not what was going on eight months ago."

While my inner feminist instinctively bristled at the paternal tone, in retrospect, he was right. I think most New Yorkers, particularly those in New York City, who had lived through the worst of the nightmare, suffered from that same PTSD that I did. That fear drove them to wear masks, get tested, and respect the rules. Others—particularly those upstate who had not experienced that same trauma—did not respond as emotionally to the increase in cases and were against draconian measures on closings.

The following day, we unveiled the Cluster Action Initiative, developed in consultation with national public-health experts, including Dr. Noam Ross of the EcoHealth Alliance, Dr. Michael Osterholm of the University of Minnesota, and former CDC director Dr. Tom Frieden. The theory behind the initiative was that you had to not only address the actual hot spot, but also the areas surrounding it to ensure you were truly stopping the spread. The health team, along with senior members of the COVID task force, developed heat maps identifying the epicenter of an outbreak as red zones, with strict rules and restrictions.

Less-severe restrictions were put in place for surrounding communities—orange and yellow zones that served as buffers to ensure the virus did not spread beyond the central focus area. Within red zones, mass gatherings were prohibited, nonessential businesses were closed, dining was restricted to takeout only, and houses of worship were limited to ten people. Restrictions would stay in place for fourteen days, followed by a data-based reassessment. Within minutes of the announcement, leaders in the Orthodox Jewish communities began expressing outrage. That outrage quickly manifested into scenes of chaos.

Overnight, hundreds of maskless ultra-Orthodox men took to the streets in protest. They burned masks and set fires throughout their neighborhoods. Jacob Kornbluh, a reporter covering the protests for online news publication *Jewish Insider*, was called a Nazi and a *moyser*—a Yiddish word meaning "informer"—before being swarmed by an angry mob, pinned up against a wall, and assaulted.

An elected official representing Borough Park, in Brooklyn, started giving out my cell phone number to protest organizers, who in turn directed people to send me menacing texts from untraceable spoof numbers. The messages addressed me as "you anti-Semitic bitch" and included missives like "Hope you get breast cancer." As the city convulsed, the mayor responded by deflecting blame onto the governor. Cuomo ignored him, intent on holding the line.

President Trump, who had himself gotten COVID two weeks earlier and, according to every reputable poll in the country, was on the brink of losing the White House, seized on the situation. Taking to social media to stoke the chaos, Trump linked to a video of members of the Orthodox community clashing with the NYPD and tweeted: "Wow, what does this grim picture remind you of? I am the only thing in the Radical Left's way! VOTE" followed by a second tweet reposting conservative actor James Woods, who tweeted, "Rounding up the Jews is an optic that I would never have expected to see in my American lifetime. De Blasio is a criminal. No wonder he changed his name from Wilhelm. He is an anti-Semite thug piece of s—."

Less than a month from the election, Trump was continuing his jihad against Democratic states, with his ire trained yet again on his favorite nemesis, Governor Cuomo. Despite New York City's deep blue leanings, the ultra-Orthodox communities were overall avid Trump supporters, and his support served to further embolden them.

Back in my office, I scrolled through my phone, watching Trump do his best to whip his supporters into a frenzy. All of it felt off. Something about the sequence of events struck me as orchestrated. Just then, I received a call from Jake Adler, our Jewish community liaison. Someone in the community had received a robocall blasted out to thousands with instructions for that night's protest, stating unequivocally that the Trump campaign was involved and directing the messaging of the protests. Bizarrely, it wasn't focused on the new COVID restrictions, but instead on nursing homes: "We are in touch with the Trump campaign [the community would later claim this communication was false]. They are urging everyone to come out with signs 'Cuomo killed thousands.' Come to 13th Avenue and hold big signs 'Cuomo killed thousands' as many as possible, as big as possible. The more signs we have the bigger the national outcry will be."

Number-one agitator Heshy Tischer, a prominent Orthodox Jewish community activist, openly tweeted, "Urgent: Who can print 'Cuomo Hates Jews' and 'Cuomo Killed Thousands' on flags?" It was a nakedly political and cynical ploy by the Trump campaign to further damage the governor, using their preferred messaging around deaths in nursing homes. I privately speculated about whether Jared Kushner, whose family was notoriously close with the ultra-Orthodox communities in New York and New Jersey, had a hand in it. Jared and I hadn't spoken since our falling-out after the Democratic Convention, our only communication coming in the form of Trump's Twitter missives and the DOJ investigation we believe Trump directed. The election was weeks away, and it couldn't come soon enough for me. I had had it and didn't have the energy for their petty war anymore, one that was growing increasingly personal and dangerous by the day.

Our most immediate problem was that one of the ultra-Orthodox sects in Brooklyn was planning a wedding for the upcoming weekend. And it was not just any wedding. It was the wedding of the grand rebbe's grandson, with an estimated number of attendees at 10,000 people. The governor was speaking with the rebbe, imploring him to reduce the number of people at the ceremony. It was déjà vu all over again. We were back to another New Rochelle, the first hot spot in the country, when COVID circulated through a series of community and religious events that brought together thousands.

Cuomo had deep relationships with the Jewish community—particularly the Orthodox community—going back to when his father was in office. Since he'd become governor in 2011, any time Israel was under siege, he would travel there to demonstrate solidarity. In 2020, he was the only senior American official to attend the seventy-fifth anniversary, in Poland, of Auschwitz's liberation, placing stones imprinted with the words "New York State Remembers" on the train tracks that led into the death camp. He stood up to antisemitism not just with rhetorical condemnation but by passing sweeping policy initiatives. Cuomo's credibility in the community had been unassailable. As the Orthodox riots raged, the governor spent days personally calling prominent rebbes and other community leaders, appealing to them to bring sobriety and rationality to the situation. The continued mass gatherings and violence were going to both exacerbate the spread of the virus and demonize the Jewish community, he cautioned. The rebbes reluctantly agreed. That outreach, combined with around-the-clock, behind-the-scenes work with our team, began to bring the temperature down. The NYPD began arresting organizers, sending a concrete message that violence would not be tolerated. The protests persisted for several days before finally fizzling out, while the broader community, at the urging of the rebbes, began to adhere to the COVID restrictions.

Two weeks later, undeterred by the backlash, Cuomo formally unveiled and adopted what would become our new approach to

combating COVID: the Microcluster Strategy. He outlined modifica-
tions to previously announced zones, established new ones in areas
where there were recent upticks in cases, and set criteria for areas to
exit a zone. The goal was to detect small outbreaks, take swift action,
and eliminate them.

It was official: the second wave was here.

Polling indicated public attitudes were falling along party lines:
Democrats more cautious and accepting, Republicans opposed. The
growing divide between public-health experts and elected officials
and their constituents was beginning to create a tension that I knew
would not be sustainable for long; constituents elect their representatives, and if their representatives are not making decisions that align
with their desires, they don't get reelected. The pandemic superpow-
ers granted to the governor by the state legislature created a buffer
for local elected officials, who could blame Cuomo for decisions on
closures; up until that point, not many had, since the majority of their
constituents had been on the same page. With the general election
approximately a week away, our goal was to try to keep the public
calm in order to minimize any political pressure on our public-health
response. But no matter how hard we tried to keep our eyes on the
horizon, the president's politics found us.

"Hello?" I looked at the clock on the cable box in the living room of
the mansion—it was just after 8:00 p.m. on October 27, one week from
Election Day. What now?

"Do you see this shit?" It was Rich. "Look at your inbox—there's a
whole chain. Those DOJ fuckers did it again," Rich was not happy.

"Did what?"

"They're investigating us on nursing homes. And the best part is,
I found out from the *New York Post*, who they gave the letter to," Rich
fumed. "The first cut of the story is already up; they didn't bother waiting for a response."

"Didn't they already do this?" I asked. "Am I losing my mind?"

"Yeah, this one goes beyond the public nursing homes, and it just went to New York," Rich said. "Some guy named Jeff Clark sent it, which, according to our lawyers, doesn't make any sense. Anyway, can you jump on a call with the Department of Health people in five minutes? We need to figure out what we're saying here."

"Okay, calm down, buddy," I tried to assure him. "Jesus Christ, the election is in a week. I think it's pretty clear this is Trump directing the DOJ. Don't you think even the *New York Post* will have to acknowledge that?"

I could almost visualize Rich's eyes rolling over the phone.

"You've read the *New York Post*, right? No, I don't think they acknowledge that, and for all I know, this story is going to be on the front page tomorrow!"

The letter "obtained" by the *New York Post* notifying the state of an expanded nursing home investigation led by the Department of Justice was not sent to the Department of Health. In fact, it took us nearly five days to track down a copy. The undated letter was signed by Jeffrey Bossert Clark, the then acting assistant attorney general for the DOJ's Civil Division. At that time, Clark was already known to be a Trump sycophant, actively politicizing the DOJ. The fact that his was the name affixed to the letter confirmed our belief: This was an improper and politically motivated attempt to use the DOJ to punish President Trump's political detractors. It was so obvious, and yet, as forcefully and as loudly as we shouted about it, no one in the media would blow the whistle. None of it made sense at all. Until suddenly, too late, it did.

Three months later, the *New York Times* reported that Trump secretly plotted to replace Acting Attorney General Jeffrey Rosen in the final weeks of the administration to use the power of the DOJ to try to overturn the election results. The person he plotted with and planned to install to do his dirty work? Jeffrey Bossert Clark.

I shook my head.

Of course he did.

CHAPTER 17

Schadenfreude

The morning of November 3, I woke up feeling cautiously optimistic. After four hellacious years, it was finally here: Election Day.

I picked up my phone to see a slew of text messages on my college-friend chain, all with the same general tone—concern. My best friends from college are all incredibly successful in their chosen fields. Lawyers, a nutritionist, psychologist, commercial real estate executive, and interior designer. I was the only one in our group to have gone into government, and they often turned to me to provide informed insight on the political landscape. Four years earlier, I assured them unequivocally that there was no possible way Donald Trump would become president. "The electoral math doesn't work," I had said confidently.

Needless to say, my bona fides were on the line.

"Missy, are you sure this time?" was their overwhelming refrain, and while I believed there was no possible way lightning could strike twice, I hedged. "Look, anything can happen, but if you believe the polls and the early-voting turnout, it just doesn't seem possible. . . . Biden's got this," I'd responded before closing my eyes the night before. It didn't seem my answers were reassuring them, and I understood it. I wasn't really reassured, either.

When Barack Obama was president, the federal government played almost no role in our day-to-day lives in the governor's office. Of course, there were exceptions—after Hurricane Sandy, we relied upon billions of dollars in federal funding to rebuild—but, generally speaking, we had almost no interaction with 1600 Pennsylvania Avenue. To the extent that we needed something, the feds would try to step in to provide it; otherwise, it was more of a congenial coexistence.

Four years of Trump, on the other hand, was a living nightmare. Every single day started with the possibility that precious work hours would be hijacked by having to respond to the president's Twitter feed. Trump and his team actively plotted to undermine and hurt our state at every turn. They repealed the SALT (state and local tax) deduction to effectively increase New Yorkers' overall taxes in order to provide tax cuts to swing states and high-income earners outside of New York. They retaliated against us for allowing undocumented people to obtain driver's licenses, a law that existed in nearly a dozen other states, by temporarily kicking New York (and only New York) out of the trusted-traveler program that expedites customs clearance for pre-vetted passengers upon arrival in the United States. They dangled funding for infrastructure, like the overdue repair of bridges and tunnels, over us, as a way to rein in criticism. Most recently, they had pressured the Department of Justice to investigate their political detractors, from John Kerry to Hillary Clinton, with Andrew Cuomo evidently at the top of the list. The president himself regularly took personal shots at the governor and his family, to which the media would then ask us to respond. Life under Trump's malevolent thumb was not only scary in terms of his foreign and domestic policy decision making or his lack of leadership during COVID. It was exhausting. And it had to end.

Anyone who has ever worked on a campaign will tell you that Election Day is the longest day of their life. When you're an operative whose principal is not on the ballot, the day is even longer: Everything is completely out of your control, and there is nothing left to do but hurry up and wait. Consultants and operatives fill their hours by checking the weather and asking each other what they are hearing about turnout over and over and over again until the polls finally close. This Election Day felt longer. Like, crawling-across-the-Sahara-in-a-dust-storm long.

Hopeful of electoral victory, I asked Cuomo if a group of us could commandeer the mansion's pool house to watch the results roll in. He was happy to oblige, but when I asked if he would join us, the governor demurred: "Joe's got this, I'm going to get a good night's sleep," he said before heading upstairs. In his absence, a group of senior staff gathered in the pool house. To us, it was like watching the Super Bowl. We picked up a few six packs of beer and hunkered down to watch history. Steph arranged to have a giant whiteboard wheeled in so that we could truly dork out with state-by-state predictions, placing bets on the outcome.

Early in the evening, things seemed to be going in the right direction. Biden was quickly picking up steam as Michigan and Wisconsin—two states that had gone for Trump four years earlier—flipped blue. At 264 electoral votes, we only needed one of the uncalled swing states—Georgia, Nevada, North Carolina, or Pennsylvania—to go for Biden. I picked up my iPhone and shot off a text to my college friends: "See, guys—I told you! Nothing to worry about this time :)" before turning back to Steve Kornacki's coverage. Just then, Twitter began reporting that Arizona was going for Biden.

"Is this real? Is it over?" I asked eagerly.

"Pump the brakes, guys." Rich looked up from his iPhone. "It looks like the rest of the states are not going to be called tonight. And only the AP and Fox News are projecting Arizona. None of the other networks are reporting it; they're saying it's too close to call."

"Yeah, but if Fox is saying it, how can it not be true? They aren't exactly incentivized to throw this thing," I reasoned.

"Agree, but the other networks aren't calling it—and it looks like Trump voters are not going to go quietly," Rich countered. "According to Twitter, they're already showing up en masse to protest at election headquarters in Maricopa County."

Even the most amateur political anthropologist will tell you Republican political operatives thrive in chaos. They crave it. While Democrats, for the most part, believe there is honor in playing by the rules,

Republicans have a tendency to flip the table over and play dirty. They believe the ends justify the means, a tactic that successfully won them the presidential election twenty years earlier when they essentially sanctioned fistfights—literally and figuratively—in the Florida recount that put George W. Bush in the Oval Office. Was this going to be a repeat?

"So, wait, we won't know tonight? How is that possible? Shouldn't the margins be big enough to call some of these states? The polling out of Pennsylvania said this wasn't even going to be close," I sputtered.

"I love you, Melissa, but you hear yourself, right?" Jim responded. "What did we learn about public polling in 2016?"

No, no, no!

"Don't panic. I'm sure everything is going to be fine; it's just not going to get called tonight," Jim continued, checking his watch. "And I think I should get home to Jenny; she's had the kids all night." Peter and Rich stood up, ready to head out, too.

"Who wants to go to the Excelsior pub with me?" Rich asked.

The party was officially over.

I looked down to see a barrage of text alerts from my college chain: "Missy! WTAF is going on? Is Arizona called or not?" I sighed and side-buttoned my phone.

"I think we call it a night, lady." Now even Steph was standing up.

"Ugh, not you, too! Come on, we should stay up!" I implored. "One of these states has to go our way."

"I hope you're right, but I don't think it's going to happen tonight," she said, putting on her long red peacoat.

The next three days proceeded in slow motion. While Biden preached patience, Trump stoked conspiracy. With promises of legal challenges and protests breaking out across the South and Midwest, it was beginning to feel like we might be in for Groundhog Day. Until, finally, the morning of November 7.

"Melissa, are you seeing this?" my sister, Jessica, shouted from down the hall to the guest room on the first floor that I was currently living in.

"Hang on! I'll be there in five minutes," I shouted back.

"No five minutes!" Jessica was suddenly standing in my doorway; too excited to wait, she let herself in. "Biden won! Come on! Let's go celebrate!" My sister was always a passive Democrat, left-leaning but not really engaged. Like tens of thousands of other Americans, Trump changed that: After he had won four years earlier, she became an MSNBC junkie, got a Twitter account, and read every national political article written in the *New York Times.* She had been glued to the election coverage until it was called.

I turned on the TV to see it for myself. *Jesus Christ. It's over. They can't hurt us anymore.* Overcome with raw, genuine emotion, I could feel my eyes start to well up with tears. And I wasn't the only one. The images on television were incredible. New Yorkers of all ages and races took to the streets in celebration, strangers embracing and high-fiving, cab drivers honking their horns, people clapping and cheering. The sentiment of Trump's home state was overwhelming and universal: Don't let the door hit you on the way out.

As I picked up my phone to text Steph and Rich to meet me and Jessica downtown to properly celebrate, I was interrupted by an incoming call from Dr. Zucker. He wanted to make sure that I saw the daily COVID numbers. Public-health experts had forewarned that Halloween parties could cause a flare-up, and they were right; the numbers were beginning to spike across the state. I pinged the governor to make sure he was aware, and he asked me to set a meeting with Zucker and the senior team for the following day. We were moving into the holidays, and if we didn't get a firm handle on things, Cuomo feared the situation could really spiral out of control. Time to pivot again.

Over the next twenty-four hours, Rob and I spoke with our counterparts in our neighboring states to get a sense of what others were thinking; whatever decision we had to make would be made easier if done as a coalition.

There were two major concerns with the holidays looming: alcohol and house parties. The later it got, the more people drank, and the more they would let their guard down. And if you were drinking, you weren't wearing a mask. We couldn't rely on restaurants that had been out of business for months to self-police, and local governments had proven themselves totally ineffectual at compliance enforcement. The only airtight way to ensure people weren't drinking and gathering and making bad decisions was to unilaterally close all bars, restaurants, and other State Liquor Authority–licensed establishments. Everyone agreed there would be no public buy-in to close them altogether, so we settled for the next-best (palatable) thing—instituting a 10:00 p.m. curfew.

There was no real way to address the problem we saw spring up from Halloween parties. In the absence of other options, more and more people were having house parties of twenty, thirty, forty people at a time. The issue was no longer massive superspreader events like the ones that had driven the spread of COVID the previous spring; instead, the celebration problem had morphed into what the governor called "living room spread." To address it, Rob and I advocated that we limit indoor and outdoor gatherings at private residences to no more than ten people. There would be no way to enforce it, but we still believed it was worth trying.

Cuomo opposed the idea from the outset; he believed it was a bridge too far and that the public would resent our telling them what to do in their own homes. Rob and I pushed back, arguing that if we wanted a policy that, based on contact-tracing data, actually addressed what was causing spread, this was it. Besides, we pointed out, it was less about the actual policy and more about hammering home the messaging. And we wouldn't be standing alone on this particular hill: Connecticut, Massachusetts, and Rhode Island had already implemented similar policies. Reluctantly, Cuomo agreed to join them.

The following Monday, we announced that, effective that Friday, all bars, restaurants, and any establishment licensed by the State Liquor Authority (casinos, recital halls, etc.) would be required to close from 10:00 p.m. to 5:00 a.m. daily. Restaurants would still be allowed to provide curbside, food-only pickup or delivery after 10:00 p.m. The governor also announced that indoor and outdoor gatherings at private residences would be limited to no more than ten people.

We felt the public backlash almost instantly.

As Cuomo predicted, there was widespread resentment of the ten-person rule, with people outraged that the government would attempt to dictate what they could do in their own homes. At the same time, small-business owners and restaurateurs were furious at the newly enacted curfew, which would cost them much-needed revenue during their most-profitable time of year.

It was the first moment during COVID when a decision we made was truly met with widespread resistance and outcry; we feared we were losing the public, which would have devastating consequences should we need to reenact any of the draconian shutdowns from the spring before. A Siena poll taken following the announcement showed the governor's job-approval rating slip from 61 to 54 percent.

"It doesn't seem that unreasonable to me," Jessica said in an attempt to calm my concerns on the way to our brother's house for dinner.

"Yes, well, what does your Libertarian husband think about it?" I asked, lowering my voice so that Alexa and Ashley, who were in the back seat of the car, couldn't hear me talking about their father.

"C'mon, Missy, Jim's not your target audience," Jessica reminded me. "And anyway, he has been supportive of most of the COVID stuff. He gets it. I think most people do."

My phone rang from its resting place in the cupholder between our seats.

"Saved by the bell," Jessica joked. "Who is it?"

I looked down. "Unknown number," I responded.

Jessica turned to the back seat, "Girls, quiet down. The governor is calling Mimi." After seven years, they knew the "unknown" call drill.

"Hi there," I answered.

"Is this Melissa DeRosa?" Not the governor's voice.

"Yes, it is. Who is this?"

"Melissa, this is Dan Rather calling," the caller replied. I was still puzzled. Why would Dan Rather be calling me? Cuomo had been on Dan's radio show days earlier to talk about his new book. Maybe that had something to do with it?

"Mr. Rather, how are you? What can I do for you?"

"Melissa, your tweets are inappropriate, and you shouldn't post them anymore."

It was not Dan Rather.

"Excuse me?" I asked, but the line was dead.

"Who was that, Mimi?" Alexa asked eagerly from the back seat.

"No one, baby," I said.

"Mimi, who was that?" Jessica was confused.

"I have no idea," I whispered. "It was totally bizarre, J. It was some guy claiming to be Dan Rather and then going on about my Twitter feed." Just then, my phone started to ring again.

"Who is it?" my sister asked.

"No caller ID," I murmured.

"Are you going to answer it?" Jessica sounded more concerned than curious now.

"No, I'm letting it go to voice mail." I stared at the phone, wondering who it was and what was going on.

"Maybe that time it was the governor?" Jess speculated. "Maybe try him and see?"

I picked up the phone and scrolled to "AMC."

"Hello?" the governor answered on the first ring.

"Hey, did you just call me?"

"No, and I'm under the car, working, right now. Do you need something or can I call you later?"

"Yeah, no, that's fine. I had a missed call from an unknown number and thought maybe it was you."

"It was not."

"Okay, call you later."

I looked up at Jessica, "It wasn't him."

The phone started to ring again.

"No caller ID," I quietly reported.

"Mimi, pick it up and figure out what's going on," Jessica urged me. I nodded.

"Hello?"

Suddenly the voice on the other end was as menacing as it was creepy: "ME-LISS-A! ME-LISS-A! ME-LISS-A!" I quickly hung up.

"Jess, this is scaring me," I whispered, hoping the girls wouldn't hear me.

"What did he sound like? What did he say?" she demanded. Before I could answer, it rang again. No caller ID again.

"Okay, Mimi, calm down, it's going to be okay," Jess assured me. "Answer it on speaker so I can hear it, too," she glanced in the back seat. "Girls, please be quiet, we need to hear what this person is saying to Mimi."

I reluctantly answered the phone on speaker. "Hello?"

The voice on the other end sounded possessed, shouting "Melissa DeRosa, you CUNT! I'm going to slice your pussy, you murderer, do you hear me, MELISSA?" My heart jumped into my throat as I fumbled to hang up. I could feel fear creeping through my chest to the tips of my fingers, which started to tingle. I was having a panic attack.

"Mom, who was that man? Is he going to try to hurt Mimi?" Alexa asked. "Is he going to try to find her? Will they come to our house?" I turned around to find both my little nieces in tears.

"It's okay, girls. Everything is fine," Jess interjected. "It was just a very sick man, but he can't get to Mimi. Everything is going to be okay." My sister glanced over at me. "Call the state police. Now," she whispered.

As we pulled into the cul-de-sac and up to my brother's new house, I opened the door and jumped out before the car had even stopped moving. I needed to call the state police but didn't want to have any more conversations in front of my nieces; they had been traumatized enough.

Vinnie Straface had been on governor's details going back to the Pataki administration, rising through the ranks to become the head of the security detail in 2019. He was a detail-oriented, consummate professional who had worked alongside Cuomo through countless crises and emergency situations. When I called him that afternoon, it was the first time he had ever heard me shaken. I told him I was scared and asked if the guy could possibly be in Albany. Did this person know where I was staying? What car I drove? Did I have anything to worry about? Vinnie reassured me that he wouldn't let anything happen to me or my family. Within hours, he was able to trace the call.

"The guy's name is Gary Goldstein. He made the calls from Brooklyn," Vinnie informed me.

"Wait, why do I know that name?" I asked, searching my recollection.

"He's the guy from Twitter over the summer," Vinnie responded. Months earlier, my father had called me in a panic. He closely monitored my Twitter feed and had noticed that a guy named Gary Goldstein had been tweeting increasingly aggressive, harassing attacks. Sometimes he raged about the nursing homes, but other times, his invective was weirdly personal, commenting, for example, on my "sickly, skinny" appearance. Dad had done a Google search and discovered that Gary Goldstein was an ex-con who had been arrested at least eight previous times for drugs, robbery, domestic harassment, and domestic violence.

At that time, I wasn't sure how seriously to take Goldstein's unwanted attention, so I notified the state police. They told me that there was nothing that they could do, given that the tweets didn't explicitly threaten me. They recommended that I block him and not let it bother me, and so I did. But apparently he hadn't gone away, and, given where it escalated to, it appeared he had spent the past several months feeding his anger and obsession. I walked into my brother's house to find that he and Kathleen, my brother's new wife, had been fully briefed by Jessica. As I opened the door, Joey stood up and rushed over to give me a huge bear hug. "Are you okay, MDD?" he asked lovingly.

I burst into tears. "Not really . . . it's just . . . this is all *too* much. I'm so tired. I can't take this anymore." I started to sob into the shoulder of his navy sweater.

"Mimi, is that man going to try to find you?" Ashley was standing next to me.

"No, he's not," Joey said. "You have nothing to worry about, little lady." He offered a reassuring smile to Ashley, whose lip was trembling. Just then, we heard the front door open and a familiar voice ring out. "Hello?" It was my brother-in-law, Jim. He hadn't been expected for dinner, but when Jessica called and told him what had happened, wild horses couldn't keep him away. Jessica and Jim had been married for almost fifteen years, and over time, Jim had truly become my big brother in every sense of the word. He was loyal and loving, and he teased me mercilessly in a way that only siblings can. A college hockey player, he still worked out every single day as if he was going to take the ice any minute, and he looked it. That afternoon, he was as protective as I had ever seen him, and I appreciated it.

"We're in here," Jessica called back.

Jim found us in the living room and immediately wrapped me in a big hug. "Are you okay, Missy?"

"Not really," I answered honestly.

"I always said this was going to happen," Jim said, throwing Jessica a look.

"Jim, not now," she responded tersely.

"No, I always said the longer she was in this job, the more she was on TV, at some point, some nutjob was going to threaten her," Jim went on, as if I wasn't standing right there. The doorbell interrupted his low-key tirade.

"What now?" Jess asked, exasperated.

"Looks like the state police are here," Joey responded, seeing the faint neon red-and-blue glow of lights out the front window.

"Who wants Kim Crawford? Anyone? Anyone? I've also got pizza." Kathleen could sense tension building and jumped in with a bottle of wine to try to bring everything down a notch. It worked.

"Oh, I'll take a glass," my sister responded.

The trooper at the door was there to take an official statement from me. "And, Melissa, I've got Vinnie on the phone. He'd like to talk to you," he said, handing me his cell phone.

"Melissa, I've made the decision," Vinnie announced. "Until this is resolved, and while you continue to maintain this high-profile role, I'm going to assign you a security detail."

"Is that really necessary?" I asked.

"At the moment, yes," Vinnie answered.

Back at Jessica's that night, with an unmarked state police car idling on the street outside, I lay in bed, staring at the ceiling. *When is this going to end?* I took an Ambien, closed my eyes, and hoped that when I woke up, this would all have been a bad dream.

It wasn't. And things were about to get worse.

Local governments that had been eager for the state to step in and create "red" zones and close businesses were beginning to crumble under pressure from their constituents. Compliance was replaced by protests, and while polls suggested a plurality of New Yorkers still supported our COVID restrictions, those who didn't were getting louder and more organized. Their message was simple: we are done. And the public's ire was turning on politicians who they saw as preaching one set of rules while living by another.

"Melissa, do you see this Newsom thing?" Rich asked from my doorway, looking down at his iPhone.

"What Newsom thing?" I answered, distractedly.

"Apparently, he was having dinner at someplace called French something, and he wasn't wearing a mask. I don't really get it, but he's getting absolutely slaughtered on social media, and it looks like it's becoming a thing in California."

I picked up the phone to call one of Newsom's top advisers, Dee Dee Myers.

Dee Dee had been a role model of mine for as long as I could remember. I had met her years earlier at a fundraiser in Los Angeles and was instantly starstruck. As press secretary in the Clinton

White House, she had been smart, savvy, sophisticated, and the most high-profile, and most visible, woman in the administration. She was also the real-life inspiration for C. J. Cregg, the fictional press secretary on my all-time-favorite TV show, *The West Wing*. At the fundraiser, Cuomo acknowledged her as a longtime friend and colleague in his talking points before introducing me to the crowd of well-heeled donors as his communications director turned chief of staff. After he was done speaking, I walked over to introduce myself. She shook my extended hand.

"I can't believe I'm meeting you. You're C. J. Cregg," I gushed in a way that I almost never did.

"Actually, since, according to the governor, you went from communications director to chief of staff, *you're* C. J. Cregg." This interaction didn't just make my day; as a *West Wing* junkie, it made my life. She offered to stay in touch and help in any way that she could, and I took her up on the offer, reaching out from time to time for advice or to vent generally. During COVID, I called her regularly. The press was fixated on comparing California to New York in everything that we did. It was always the same: The New York press held California up as the model of perfection, while the California press gushed about the leadership of Governor Cuomo. Dee Dee and I would compare notes and provide each other with a sounding board for decision making.

Dee Dee picked up her phone with a cheery, "Hey, Melissa, how are you?"

"You know, never a dull moment," I replied, "but I saw the news and wanted to check in to see how you guys are doing out there."

"Ugh, you know, we've had better weeks. It's just the perfect combination of every buzz word: *lobbyist, Michelin star–rated restaurant, Napa, birthday party.* Throw that in with the images of a maskless governor indoor-dining, and well, you have yourself a Fox News field day," Dee Dee responded.

"I'm sorry. If it's any consolation, I'm just seeing it for the first time here," I said.

"Yeah, look, it was absolutely a mistake, but the way the press is acting is so over-the-top."

"I hear you. It's almost like they're enjoying it," I paused. "What's that word? *Schadenfreude.*"

"Yes, that's exactly what it is," she agreed.

When I was growing up, my father taught me to think of politics as a contact sport. You're on a team and almost always playing against another: Democrats vs. Republicans, House vs. Senate, executive vs. legislative. The press, he explained, played the role of referee; it was "their job to keep everyone playing honest; they were there to call fouls, offsides, and out of bounds." Over time, however, the role of the press began to shift. As it became more of a business, the hunt for ratings replaced news value. Rather than relaying to the public what the news of the day was, they chased whatever the public deemed interesting, as dictated by "likes" and "clicks" on social media. It was in that vein that Gavin Newsom, one of the most popular governors in the country, who had demonstrated steady leadership during a once-in-a-century pandemic, was vilified and nearly kicked out of office for attending a birthday party for a well-known lobbyist at a fancy restaurant without a mask on. It became a social media and cable news feeding frenzy, which fueled a recall effort. It was surreal.

"I spoke to Dee Dee today," I said as I walked into the mansion living room, where the governor was sitting, taking notes preparing to go on Alan Chartock's radio show.

"Oh, yeah. How are things in La-La Land?" he responded without looking up.

"Newsom is getting absolutely crushed out there over this French Laundry debacle," I said.

"It's just Fox News; it'll die down in a day or so," he responded, unimpressed.

"She said they've been dealing with it for a week now, and the press won't stop. Apparently, there's now an organized protest effort following them around, and . . ."

"Sorry to interrupt, guys," Steph said, appearing in the doorway, "Governor, you've got two minutes before Chartock."

"Okay, got it," he answered.

"Anyway, it just feels like there's a real anger out there, and . . ."

"Yup, I got it," he responded. "Let me finish up and do this and we'll talk after, okay?" I nodded and walked out of the room to find a quiet spot to listen to his radio interview. The governor didn't like to do radio interviews with me in the room; he said I made him anxious. So instead I would listen from a room or two away, and if I caught any mistakes or had any points I thought he should make, I would write them down on a piece of paper and give them to Steph to hand him. It was an imperfect system but one that had kept both of us mostly sane over the years.

I sat down on the red-velvet sofa in the drawing room and fumbled around on my phone to find the WAMC streaming app and clicked to listen, while opening up my laptop to answer emails at the same time. I hated when the governor went on Chartock without any real hard news to make; the press detested the access we gave Alan and were always critical of the interviews. Nine times out of ten, they either wouldn't cover what Cuomo said on air, or they'd write something overtly snarky and obnoxious. The interview that day had zero news value—the intention was to just go on and chat. On its face, it was a total layup: election results (check), the Emmy the governor had just been awarded for his national leadership at our daily press conferences (check), Biden transition announcements (check). Then Alan asked the most seemingly benign question possible:

> *Alan:* And what are you doing for Thanksgiving? You're gonna sit around, poor Andrew Cuomo, sitting around the table, looking down, a knife and a fork in each hand, looking down at a piece of turkey and no one else there. I mean, what's the story here?
>
> *Governor Cuomo:* The story is my mom is going to come up and two of my girls, is the current plan, but the plans change.

But that's my plan. But I'm going to work, I have a lot of work to do between now and Thanksgiving. I'll tell you what's frightening, the COVID rate over the past three weeks, the hospitalization rate has gone up 122 percent . . .

No, no, no! I couldn't believe my ears. "My mom is going to come up?" "Two of my girls?" The second the words came out of his mouth, I knew the press would kill us. We had just set a policy weeks earlier saying no more than ten people for Thanksgiving and encouraging people to stay within their pods—even though four Cuomos was still six under the limit, the fact that eighty-nine-year-old Matilda Cuomo would be traveling along with two of the governor's daughters was grounds for political execution.

I grabbed a piece of white printer paper and a black Sharpie and began scribbling words furiously: "THANKSGIVING—YOU DIDN'T REALLY MEAN YOUR MOM IS COMING!" By the time I ran into the living room, I could hear the tail end of the interview:

> *Alan:* Anyway, listen, I'm out of time. I hate to do that because it's so much fun to talk to you, and thank you very much for being here. Let's see what the press have to say about this conversation.
> *Governor Cuomo:* Whatever it is, it'll be nasty.
> *Alan:* Right you are. Great to talk to you, Governor.

They had no idea.

As the governor hung up, I was standing in the doorway, out of breath, and holding my useless piece of paper.

"What?" he asked.

I could feel my iPhone vibrate. I looked down. "Peter Ajemian," I relayed.

"Answer it, see what he says."

"Trust me, I know what he's calling to say."

Over the next ninety minutes, the press had a field day—Fox News, CNN, MSNBC, all with variations of chyrons reading: DESPITE THANKSGIVING WARNING, GOV CUOMO TO HAVE 89-YEAR-OLD MOTHER TO DINNER.

"I really think you're overreacting, Melissa," the governor said when I told him about the media response.

"Really? You think?" I responded sarcastically.

"First of all, you know I was never actually going to have my mother here. We just haven't broken that news to her yet. And the kids have been quarantining for two weeks to be able to see me," he protested.

"Yes, I know that, but no one else knows that," I complained.

"Who is even writing?" he wanted to know.

"Oh, let's see: Gannett, the *Daily News*, *Newsday*, the AP, and the *New York Times*."

"The *New York Times*?!"

"Yes, oh, and the *Post*."

"Well, of course the *Post* is writing," he scoffed, rolling his eyes.

"I mean the *Washington Post*," I responded. "We have to issue a clarifying statement, and you should probably call your mother." I sighed. "The press is giddy. They are going to play this as Gavin Newsom all over again."

The media wasn't just reporting on the governor's comments; they were relishing his misstep. We had to stop the bleeding. Shortly after, Rich issued a clarifying statement:

"Given the current circumstances with COVID, the governor will have to work through Thanksgiving and will not be seeing his family. Don't tell his mom—she doesn't know yet."

And just like that, Thanksgiving was officially canceled. I opened the *New York Times* app on my phone and scrolled to see if they actually wrote a story, and there it was: "Cuomo Invited His Mother for Thanksgiving; New Yorkers Noticed. The governor was accused of hypocrisy after he said his mother and two daughters were traveling to Albany for the holiday. He withdrew the invitation."

Maybe this isn't that big of a deal, I thought to myself.

"How bad are the stories?" Rich asked. As I clicked the link on the *Times* home page, I got a text alert.

Ugh, so sorry you're having to deal with this . . . it'll pass. It was Dee Dee. Word had reached California in no time.

"Who is that?" Rich asked.

"Dee Dee Myers—just commiserating," I told him.

"Well, God knows they've been through a lot," Rich said. "You know, Melissa, I've been thinking . . . the Emmy, the book, the President Cuomo stuff . . . I just think this seesaw is at a tipping point," he ventured. "The press is done with the hero-Cuomo narrative, and I just think . . . I don't know—the way they pounced today—what is it called when someone is excited about another person's mistake? I've been trying to remember the word all day, and I can't."

"*Schadenfreude,*" I responded dryly.

"Yes! *Schadenfreude*—how did you know that's what I was thinking?" Rich asked.

"It's been in the air lately," I answered, "and something tells me, it's only the beginning."

CHAPTER 18

Finding Ways to Respond

"THE GOVERNOR HAS NO IDEA THEY'RE COMING," STEPHANIE SAID.

It was early in the afternoon on Saturday, December 5. The governor's birthday was the next day, and I was on the phone with Stephanie, making sure the plan was in place.

For his sixty-third birthday, Stephanie plotted to give the man who had everything the one thing he longed for most: time with his children.

"Okay, great. I'm going to go to the office to get a few hours of work in, and then let's plan to meet for a drink around five before we head over," I suggested to Stephanie.

"Pre-gaming for the governor's socially distanced surprise birthday dinner with his daughters and senior staff? Really, Melissa?" Stephanie couldn't resist yanking my chain.

"I can't tell if you're kidding," I admitted.

"Of course I'm kidding! See you at five."

After we hung up, I stood, thinking about all of the things our already overextended team would need to do in the next several weeks: the vaccine rollout, the annual State of the State address, the budget—all on top of combating a second wave New York was in the midst of enduring with a public that was COVID-fatigued. Even without a once-in-a-century pandemic, the average tenure for a White House chief of staff is a little more than eighteen months. At that point, I had been working for Cuomo for one hundred months—forty of those as secretary. And I was exhausted. I could feel my chest tighten. *Can we continue to go at this pace? Can I?*

Just then, the haze I was in was abruptly interrupted as my wrist started to vibrate, my Apple watch alerting me that Rich Azzopardi was calling.

"Hey, is everything okay?" I asked, conditioned by now to expect the worst.

"I mean, yes and no," Rich responded.

"Now what?" I prodded.

"Lindsey Boylan."

"Lindsey Boylan?" I echoed. "What does *she* want?"

"She went on a Twitter rant saying that our office was the most toxic team environment she had ever worked in, claiming that she tried to quit three times before it stuck," Rich said.

"Well, that's quite the revisionist history."

"Yeah, can you remind me what happened again with her at the very end?" he asked.

"Liz Fine made a formal complaint to the [executive] chamber about her. There were a number of African American women on the staff who said she had bullied and harassed them, and they reported it. One of them even reported that they had to take leave to deal with health effects related to her interactions with Lindsey. Howard Zemsky actually authorized the whole thing," I recounted. Liz Fine was counsel to our Economic Development Agency, and Howard Zemsky was the agency chairman; Lindsey was his former chief of staff before joining our team in the executive chamber. "There were complaints about her from women on our staff as well. She stormed out after Alphonso met with her to discuss the complaints about her toxicity, sent out a blast email announcing she was quitting, and then a few days later, she called Alphonso to ask for her job back," I added. "When Alphonso didn't give in, she actually tried the governor directly through Stephanie, but the governor never responded," I continued. "She actually tweeted something similar before."

In May 2019, shortly after announcing her candidacy against longtime Upper West Side Congressman Jerry Nadler, Lindsey took to Twitter to "speak out" about her "toxic" and "demoralizing" experience working for the state, tweeting:

> I was the only mother of young children on senior staff in my last job in politics. They didn't "get it" even with all the "right" policies. It was a toxic and demoralizing experience. Now I run my own company full of, [sic] especially moms. #LindseyBoylanForCongress #PrimaryNadler

Her tweet struck me as ironic, since she regularly told a young female staffer in the office that, as long as you had money, could afford taxi cabs to ferry you around and pay for a nanny, you could "have it all." The hashtags in her tweet summed it up: She was running for office and thirsty for "likes," followers, and press attention. Up until that point, Lindsey had only ever tweeted positively about working for the governor, even highlighting his work championing women's issues.

"Yeah, I thought it was something like that," Rich said. "Look, I'm just reading what I see on Twitter. It's Lindsey, and the New York press doesn't take her seriously, but you know Fox and the *Post* will pick this up if it gets on their radar."

"Yep, any excuse to take a shot at Cuomo, no matter the source," I concurred.

Rich reminded me that Lindsey had announced twelve days earlier that she was now running for Manhattan borough president, fresh on the heels of her crushing congressional defeat, and was once again actively seeking attention. We decided not to give her ours.

After we hung up, I checked Twitter for myself. There they were: seven back-to-back tweets attacking our office and senior staff, venting about how toxic we all were.

Hours later, Lindsey was at it again. Only this time she wasn't just exaggerating; she was flat out lying:

"Yes, I did not sign whatever they told me to sign when I left. Nope!" she tweeted.

Come again? We didn't ask her to sign a nondisclosure agreement, or anything else, when she left. Her behavior was getting more erratic, but I decided against alerting the governor right away; I wanted to let him enjoy his birthday and the reunion with his daughters.

On the flight down to New York City the following Monday morning, December 7, while the governor was rightly focused on our impending press conference with Dr. Fauci on New York's winter surge and vaccine rollout plan, I was reading clips. As predicted, both Fox News and the *New York Post* had picked up Lindsey's tweets. Rich and I had refrained from commenting because we didn't want to give the story legs, and believed that if it was successfully confined to the far-right media, no mainstreamers would pick it up. I hadn't yet briefed the governor and hoped I wouldn't have to.

As we drove the short distance from the 34th Street helipad to our office on Third Avenue, I filled in the governor about Lindsey's weekend Twitter frenzy on our alleged toxic office and the revisionist history around her departure and advised him: "In the event that we get a question, just let me take it. I don't want you to give sound on this. She is running for office and looking for attention. I don't want to elevate the issue." He nodded in agreement.

At our press briefing that morning, not a single reporter brought it up. Rich was validated; the New York press corps knew Lindsey and that she was running for office. They didn't consider her a credible source. Maybe I was overreacting.

It turned out she had only just begun.

Every few hours, like clockwork, Lindsey's tweets kept coming and grew sharper, vacillating between absurd and menacing, taking aim at senior staff in our office with whom she had personal grievances, in addition to the governor himself. In between tweets about how terrible our office was, she would post a link to donate to her campaign, attempting to capitalize politically on the newfound attention she was getting. Judging by the comments, it appeared her strategy was working. Lindsey served as a convenient political vehicle for the Far

Right, who feared the governor nationally, as well as for far-left interest groups, who often battled with the governor locally.

"MDR, you gotta minute?" I looked up to see Rich standing in my doorway.

I motioned him inside.

"Bernadette called." Bernadette Hogan was an Albany reporter for the *New York Post*. "She said that she had heard that Lindsey left on bad terms—something about bullying subordinates and creating a toxic work environment herself."

"Interesting," I replied. "Where'd she hear that?"

"Unclear, but it's obviously true, so I wanted to flag it," Rich said.

"What did you say?" I asked.

"I said I wasn't playing that game and shooed her off the phone."

"Okay, that sounds right." Where was this going?

"Melissa, she said if it were true, she'd be interested in that story, given Boylan's continued tweets," Rich elaborated. "But I don't like getting into a back-and-forth with Lindsey. Plus, it would be our word against hers, right?"

"What do you mean?"

"I mean, Lindsey would probably just deny it," he said.

"Rich, the whole thing was documented," I responded, genuinely surprised that he didn't know that.

"It was?" he asked, his interest piqued.

"Yes. It was a thing at the time. Liz Fine formally requested she be removed from her agency line and from her office on their floor at ESD [Empire State Development, the economic development agency for New York State]. Zemsky actually authorized the whole thing. And then Alphonso had to formally counsel her. When stuff like that happens, the whole thing gets documented."

Rich and I locked eyes for a few seconds as this revelation set in.

"What do you think?" I asked.

"I think the same thing I've thought since this started—do nothing," Rich answered. "It will backfire. I really believe that."

"Even if it proves that what she's saying is bullshit?" I pressed.

"You weren't with the administration at the time, but [our state operations director Howard] Glaser went on the radio and read some agency guy's personnel file to prove that he had been a disgruntled bad actor on some random issue, and it completely boomeranged; it generated stories about how we were bullies, and the guy in question became a hero. Let's not do that again," Rich continued. "It costs us nothing to keep it in our back pocket, but you can't unshoot that gun. Once the bullet is out of the chamber, there's no taking it back, so let's just let this play out. I still think she'll punch herself out, and that'll be that."

"Okay, that makes sense," I conceded. Rich seemed confident in the wait-and-see approach, but I wasn't completely sold on it.

Every politician has a kitchen cabinet of advisers, generally made up of former government and political staff. Ours changed a bit over the years but had remained almost fully intact; it consisted of the core of our first-term team as well as our most-trusted legal advisers.

Over the course of the week, with every passing Lindsey tweet, one of the members of that kitchen cabinet got a call from me; I became obsessed with soliciting advice on what to do, but unlike almost any other time that I can remember in my life, I remained paralyzed, the proverbial deer caught in the headlights.

One former adviser believed it was important to prove to reporters early on that she was lying. "Cut it off at the knees, DeRosa" he said, urging me to get the story out.

"I don't do press, but I believe this will be viewed as a heavy-handed overreaction," countered another adviser.

The conversations volleyed back and forth for days, with every tweet prompting me to spark another round of solicitations from the group.

By that Friday, I was resigned to the fact that there was nothing we could do to stop Lindsey from spewing her version of reality on the internet. I muted her feed, determined to let it go and focus on what really mattered: The vaccine rollout was slated to start the following Monday.

I got back to my sister's house earlier than expected, had dinner and a glass of wine with her, then climbed into bed around 7:00 p.m. to watch some TV and get some sleep.

I had barely settled in to watch an old episode of *The West Wing* when a Bloomberg breaking-news alert hit the wires: "Biden Considering New York Governor Andrew Cuomo for Attorney General."

The Bloomberg bulletin was a strategic leak engineered by the Biden team to enrage the Republicans who viewed Cuomo as their greatest political threat and steer them into confirming someone else— likely Merrick Garland—whom they would otherwise find objectionable, but less objectionable than Andrew Cuomo.

Within seconds of the Bloomberg story going live, my phones started to light up. Every national and New York reporter wanted to independently confirm the story. Given that we believed that it was a strategy being executed by the governor's friends Ron Klain and Steve Ricchetti, we decided to let the story ride. We wouldn't confirm anything, but we wouldn't knock it down, either.

That was our mistake, and it proved to be a big one.

The forest we missed through the trees was that, in that moment, Biden's strategic float was poking the bear, and we were the ones about to get mauled.

At 9:12 that night, Rich called.

"Melissa, are you seeing this?"

"Seeing what?" I asked, turning on the light on the bedside table.

"Look at Boylan's Twitter feed."

I opened my laptop: "@JoeBiden, if you make this man Attorney General, some women like me will be bringing the receipts. We do not need a sexual harasser and abuser as 'the law' of the land."

"What the actual fuck? Is she kidding with this?" I asked in total disbelief. "What do we do? Have we gotten any incoming?"

"No. Again, look, the New York press corps knows Lindsey; they know that she's erratic and is running for office," Rich said. "I don't think they would pick something like this up. It's too serious an allegation to screw around with. And these guys—they don't love the boss, obviously—they get that he's rough and tumble, and, yeah, there's the bully narrative out there, but they've covered him for forty years, and never once has anyone come close to making a sexual-harassment claim—not even a whisper."

"So you think we do nothing?" I clarified.

"I think we watch it, but yeah, we do nothing," he replied.

I hung up the phone and closed my eyes, but didn't sleep for one minute the entire night. I felt out of control and anxious. I knew this wouldn't be the end of Lindsey's rants. Why should it be? She was getting the attention and affirmation she was seeking on Twitter. Her outrageous claims over the previous six days had gone unchallenged. She was more and more emboldened with every passing hour. No, this was going somewhere very bad: I could feel it.

That Sunday morning, the first call I got was from Rich: "Did you see Lindsey's tweet?"

"Jesus Christ, what now?"

"She's claiming the boss lied about eagle feathers," Rich responded. "I'll tap something out in case the North Country newspapers call, but mostly I was just flagging for you because I thought you'd find it funny."

"Um, Rich?"

"Yeah?"

I was looking at her feed and couldn't believe my eyes.

> @LindseyBoylan: Yes, @NYGovCuomo sexually harassed me for years. Many saw it, and watched. I could never anticipate what to expect: would I be grilled on my work (which was very good) or harassed about my looks. Or would it be both in the same conversation? This was the way for years.

What I didn't know at the time was that on December 8, three days after Lindsey first began tweeting about a "toxic" work environment, Charlotte Bennett DM'd her. The two didn't overlap in our office and had never met, but connected over social media.

According to text messages made public later, Charlotte thanked Lindsey for speaking out about the toxic work environment and went on to say that Cuomo "came onto" her.

"This is exactly what he does to every woman," Lindsey responded.

Charlotte was officially on Team Boylan, responding that "we need women like you in leadership positions" and offering to help in Boylan's political "campaign in any way."

It was only after this exchange that Lindsey changed her line of attack. And suddenly, that Sunday morning, she had a new narrative, graduating from "toxic work environment" to vague claims of sexual harassment.

I raced to the capitol, where Rich and Linda met me in my office. Minutes felt like hours that day, and no one knew what to do. I convened conference call after conference call with our kitchen cabinet, taking everyone's temperature and obsessively scrolling through Twitter.

We begged reporters to hold off on posting stories until we could craft a response, but our overtures fell on deaf ears. In the world of online media, press no longer operated on deadlines and took the attitude that they could update their copy later when we had a response; the obvious problem with that was that once the story is up and a narrative begins to harden, our response would be irrelevant, falling to the next-to-last paragraph of the copy.

I asked Rich and Linda to step out of my office, closed the door, and called the governor, putting the question to him directly.

"We need to have a serious conversation," I began.

"Okay," he answered.

"Is there any truth to what Boylan is saying on Twitter whatsoever?" I asked.

"No, Melissa. Isn't it obvious? She is running for office. This is about her campaign. And she's still angry that we wouldn't rehire her all those years ago," he said. "I harassed her about her looks? And I harassed her about her work, which in her words was 'very good'?" he continued.

"That's what she says," I confirmed.

"And she says it went on for years and everyone saw it?" he continued.

"Mmm-hmm."

"Well, let me ask you, Melissa. You've been here for the last, what, seven years."

"Yes," I answered.

"Did you ever see me 'harass Lindsey about her looks'?" he asked.

"I mean, of course not, and you know how I feel personally about Lindsey, but I have to ask these questions," I pressed.

"No, Melissa, absolutely not. Ask everyone if they ever saw me harassing Lindsey in any way," he responded. "Don't you think someone would tell you?"

I paused for a moment to think. "Yes," I answered truthfully.

"Okay."

"Okay. So I'm going to advise we go with a flat denial from the press office," I said. "That's the way Joe Biden's team handled it when first confronted with allegations."

Just as COVID was heating up in March, Joe Biden had been accused of sexually assaulting former Senate staffer Tara Reade nearly twenty years earlier. It had led to a cascade of seven other women making allegations against him. The hypocrisy of how it was handled by the press and the Democratic and Republican parties demonstrated the politicization of the #MeToo movement.

Republicans—who historically belittled #MeToo, dismissing and defending allegations of rape made against Trump and Supreme Court Justice Brett Kavanaugh—attempted to capitalize on the claims to damage Biden electorally. But with the White House on the line, the same

Democrats who were quick to call for Al Franken's resignation and purported to subscribe to the "believe all women" mantra went quiet. As a result, Biden had been one of the only high-profile men to withstand otherwise career-ending #MeToo allegations. Other than far-right outlets, the press was not invested in furthering a storyline that would benefit Donald Trump at that point in the calendar, and over a few weeks, the allegations about Biden seemed to disappear.

Cuomo gave me the green light to follow the Biden approach: "Okay, if that's the way you think we should handle it, I'm okay with it. It's the truth," he said.

I jumped off the phone and reconvened with the kitchen cabinet, letting them know that we were okay to make the flat denial. But as the stories began to pop, they were all landing the same way: The media wasn't confining their reporting to Boylan's vague allegations, instead folding in her prior week of tweets about a hostile and toxic work environment and hints of being asked to sign a nondisclosure agreement as context, trying to create a bigger picture out of three blurry dots.

Because we hadn't engaged up until that point, refuting Lindsey's false allegations was proving impossible. When we spelled out the actual, provable facts—that Lindsey left when confronted with accusations of bullying African American colleagues and creating a hostile work environment, then turned around and wanted her job back, and was never asked to sign an NDA—reporters all wanted to know why we hadn't said so at the outset five days ago. The press was happy to include a denial, but that would only be spun as a "he said, she said," without the fact-checking that would have vindicated us.

Confronted with this reality, after a long and tortured back-and-forth, the team settled on a strategy: We would give a simple statement on the record from our press secretary that directly responded to the allegations of sexual harassment—"There is simply no truth to these claims"—and, after further legal vetting and sign-off from the lawyers, we would separately release the documented evidence of the terms of Lindsey's departure that proved unequivocally that what she was saying was false.

As the team fanned out to execute, I leaned back in my chair and tried to think about what else I could be missing. Just then, my phone rang, and I was surprised to hear Roberta Kaplan on the other end.

The world knew Robbie from her history-making win in front of the United States Supreme Court when she successfully argued on behalf of LGBTQ activist Edith Windsor, a decision that invalidated the 1996 Defense of Marriage Act and required the federal government to recognize same-sex marriage. In the years since, she had branded herself as a champion for protected classes and founded a successful practice based in New York City. Following the Harvey Weinstein scandal, she teamed up with Michelle Obama's former chief of staff, Tina Tchen, and a number of high-profile Hollywood actresses to form Time's Up, an advocacy group that fought to change sexual-harassment policies across the country and established a legal fund for women who could not afford to bring sexual violence or workplace claims on their own.

The governor and Robbie had known each other for years and, through her role at Time's Up, partnered to change New York's sexual-harassment laws and extend the statute of limitations for rape. As chairwoman of the Council of Women and Girls, I spearheaded the effort and negotiations with the legislature and worked closely with Robbie, getting to know her in the process. The two of us bonded after a particularly contentious closed-door meeting with the steering committee of the council, when the head of the New York Civil Liberties Union and I exchanged harsh words over our administration's proposal to extend the statute of limitations on rape, with Robbie squarely on my side.

The legislative victories were a watershed moment for Time's Up. Subsequently, an internal power struggle played out, with several of the most senior women in leadership jockeying over who would be point person with the governor and me.

Little did I know, in the hours following Boylan's tweet, that the women at Time's Up were circling the wagons, too. Fox News had reached out to the organization, preemptively attempting to paint them as hypocrites if they didn't take a hard line on the vague allegations against Cuomo. The idea being floated was that we do an internal investigation. Time's Up board member and political commentator Hilary Rosen thought that I should run it, an idea so preposterous as to never pass the smell test. Robbie quickly shot it down, rightly taking the position that if I were in charge, it would not be independent.

"Hi, Robbie. Sorry, things are crazy over here. What can I help you with?" I asked, wary of her answer.

"I just wanted to check in on these Lindsey Boylan tweets," Robbie said. "Time's Up is getting pressure to weigh in and call for an independent investigation."

"Seriously, Robbie?" I couldn't believe it. "Lindsey is running for office. This is very clearly a political ploy on her part to get attention and smear the governor. Did you see her tweets all week long attacking the office and our current and former staff? She is a disgruntled ex-employee with an ax to grind, and the press knows it. If Time's Up weighs in, this goes to an entirely different level and gives her credibility that, quite frankly, a vague tweet doesn't deserve."

"I know, I know, I hear you," Robbie continued. Calling for a review is how Time's Up handled the Biden allegations—same playbook. Their position was indicative of a nascent movement gone awry. #MeToo twisted itself into a pretzel with a one-size-fits-all approach to allegations, despite their degree of severity. Joe Biden had been accused of pinning Tara Reade up against a wall in a Senate building, reaching under her clothing, and penetrating her with his fingers. Putting aside where you fall on the validity of that claim, it did not fit in the same category of Lindsey's "harassing me about my looks" allegation, but both the media and Time's Up reacted as if they were no different.

"Robbie, I fight just as hard as anyone on this particular topic, but if Time's Up is going set a standard that they have to weigh in anytime anyone makes a vague allegation on Twitter, the #MeToo movement is in trouble," I said. "You'll set up a dynamic where allegations become used as a standard campaign tactic."

She paused for a moment. "I hear you, Meliss. Let me talk to the group and come back to you" she said before hanging up.

Hours later, Time's Up privately confirmed to me that they would take a wait-and-see approach, agreeing that a nonspecific allegation on Twitter did not warrant a call for investigation. And while all the major national and local outlets did cover Lindsey's claim, it wasn't front-page news.

"I asked you about this Boylan stuff days ago," I could hear Bernadette Hogan from the *New York Post* lecturing Rich on speaker after her story was filed. "You guys don't listen."

With the exception of the *New York Times*, every single news outlet—from the *New York Post* and the *Daily News* to the Albany *Times Union, BuzzFeed*, and the Associated Press—that had been provided documentation about the actual circumstances of why Lindsey left the administration believed it was incredibly relevant context to the story and included the information in their copy.

All in all, it seemed the story was contained for the moment. We weren't sure what was going to happen next, but we also didn't have time to focus on it. There was something far more important about to happen.

The next morning, Stephanie, our IT guru Harold Moore, deputy director of operations Reid Sims, the governor, and I gathered in the conference room as Sandra Lindsay, an ICU nurse in Queens, prepared to receive the nation's first COVID vaccine. (We had decided to have the governor participate virtually so as not to co-opt or distract from the moment.)

I felt something poetic in the fact that the first person in the nation to receive the vaccine was a Black female ICU nurse from New York, whose frontline workers had endured such horrific suffering as the epicenter of the crisis. That morning was one of the few bright spots on the horizon for a divided nation still reeling from the trauma and uncertainty of a once-in-a-century pandemic, coupled with a bitterly contested presidential election. The only word to describe what the moment of that first vaccination represented was *hope*. After the press conference was over, the governor walked around and hugged each person in the conference room one by one. We all shared the silent sense of accomplishment that we had made it that far, and the belief that we would reach the other side.

The moment, sadly, did not last long. Cuomo was set to host another press conference a few hours later, and we needed to be ready for questions on Lindsey's tweets from the day before. Since the governor himself had not yet addressed them, anything he said would make news and prolong the press cycle. He needed to answer the questions honestly and concisely, making as little news as possible, while not saying something that could be insensitive, misinterpreted, or provocative. While the goal was simple, the execution would be tricky. The stakes in the press conference were high, and I needed a gut check. I picked up the phone to ask for advice from the person I believed was best situated to give it. Robbie answered on the first ring.

"Meliss—everything okay?" she asked.

"Yes, I think so," I replied. "The governor is about to do a press conference where he'll get asked about Boylan's tweets. My plan is to advise him to stick as closely as possible to the statement from yesterday and avoid saying anything that could be perceived as new."

"That makes sense," she agreed.

"But from your perspective, is there anything that he needs to or should say in addition to the flat denial?" I wanted to know.

"Yes, he needs to be emphatic that women have a right to come forward and be heard. He could even point out that he personally fought for and won the right to make that easier legally here in New

York," Robbie began. "But whatever he does, he has to reinforce a woman's right to speak up."

I jotted Robbie's thoughts down furiously, hung up, and headed back into the governor's office, where I found him sitting at his desk reviewing the day's PowerPoint.

"Governor?" I asked anxiously.

"Mmm-hmm," he responded, still studying his PowerPoint.

"I'm sorry to interrupt. The press conference is about to start, and I want to go through your responses on the Lindsey tweets," I said.

"Okay," he said, looking up. I had his undivided attention.

"From a PR perspective, the most important thing you can do is not to make news; that means sticking as close to the statement we put out yesterday as possible. Any new sound on the topic could give it legs and make it a bigger story," I said, handing him an index card with the previous day's statement written down.

"Okay, and the group thinks that's enough?" he said, glancing at the card in front of him.

"Well, I spoke to the Time's Up crew, and their view is that it is vitally important that you communicate unequivocally that women have the right to speak out and that, if given the chance, you point to the laws you passed making it easier to bring claims."

"Okay," he responded, flatly. I could tell he was unconcerned and still believed this was just a fleeting publicity stunt for Boylan's campaign and that people would see right through it. The only thing he was focused on was getting vaccines in New Yorker's arms.

The temperature of the Red Room was 65 degrees that afternoon, but as I sat there, I could feel myself sweating. When the question-and-answer portion of the briefing started, the question was simple and across the plate: Were her tweets true? I tensed up as Cuomo began to answer.

> I heard about the tweet and what it said about comments that
> I had made, and it's not true. Look, I fought for and I believe

a woman has a right to come forward and express her opinion and express issues and concerns that she has, but it's just
not true.

When pressed if he ever commented on Boylan's appearance, the
governor reiterated once again that her tweets were untrue.

I totally respect a woman's right, fought for a woman's right, to
express any concern, any issue she has in the workplace. . . . I
support that. But the tweets were simply *not true.*

And that was that. We were on to the next topic.

The exchange felt almost forced and pro forma. While the press had
to ask the question, it didn't feel like they believed the premise. In the
forty years that they had been covering him, Andrew Cuomo had been
accused of everything under the sun—being a bully, a manipulator, in
league with Republicans, hiring corrupt aides—but about the only thing
there was never so much of a hint of was sexual harassment. If Boylan's
tweets were true—that he had harassed her for years and everyone saw
it—the press corps that had covered Andrew Cuomo for decades would
have had to have been incompetent or asleep at the wheel.

Afterward, while the governor, Larry, and our health team turned
their attention back to where it belonged—on vaccine distribution—I
was distracted by incoming calls that had nothing to do with COVID.
Various members of our team were starting to get unsettling reports
from former staff. Lindsey was working with Wigdor, a plaintiff's law
firm accused of using the press to strong-arm settlements. She and one
of the lawyers there had begun spamming, through LinkedIn, women
who had worked for the state government over the past ten years with
the same verbatim text, claiming that they had heard that individuals
might have information to share, and asking to speak.

Unsure of what to do, a small group of senior staff and alumni huddled to begin reaching out to see who was hearing from Lindsey, what

she was saying, and if anyone she targeted had had any experience working for the governor we should know about. Everyone responded the same way with some version of "absolutely not." As was later testified to, Lindsey had a terrible reputation with many of her former colleagues, and they certainly hadn't witnessed any kind of harassment. I picked up the phone and dialed Liz Fine, Empire State Development's counsel, who had reported the initial complaints made against Lindsey years earlier, to ask for her thoughts.

Fine lamented about Boylan's behavior in the workplace, reminding me that people at the agency were afraid to report her out of fear that she would retaliate against them. Liz agreed to call a former employee who had made a recent donation to Boylan's political campaign to see if there was any information she could glean, but that came up short.

Just then, I heard a knock at my door, "Melissa, do you have a minute?" It was our budget director, Robert Mujica.

"Of course, Rob. Sorry, it's been a crazy few days," I said, apologizing for being distracted.

Rob stepped in, closed the door behind him, and began walking toward my desk, his voice hushed, "Melissa, obviously I see what's going on, and, well . . ." he paused, pulling his iPhone out of his pocket and unlocking the screen. "I just thought you needed to see this." Rob handed his phone to me with a text from Lindsey on it. The same day she had texted Dani back in March about the governor's executive order to change the congressional petitioning deadline, she had simultaneously texted Rob—except his message had a much more pointed ending:

> Absolutely not helpful please relay that while we are
> ok, I see what the point is here and I will find ways to
> respond. Life is long. And so is my memory. And so
> are my resources.

Staring at the texts, my eyes widened, "Why didn't you tell me about this sooner?"

"Honestly, Melissa, when she sent this, I just ignored it. I mean, it's Lindsey. She says stuff all the time," he continued, "but when I saw what she tweeted about the governor over the weekend, I remembered these texts, and just thought you needed to know about them."

My mind was reeling. *What the hell is she up to?* I had to find out.

I picked up the phone and called the one person I thought might know what was going on. I braced myself for an uncomfortable conversation.

Howard Zemsky was the chairman of Empire State Development and Lindsey's former boss. The two of them were incredibly close . . . until they weren't.

In December 2017, at the height of #MeToo, a member of the staff had reported that they had seen Lindsey and Howard (who were both married to other people) kissing in a bar. Our counsel was forced to confront them with the claim, which both flatly denied. Howard was Lindsey's boss, and whatever the actual truth, the situation felt fraught—a ticking time bomb. Shortly after, a job opened up in the governor's office that Lindsey was well qualified for, and she accepted it when it was offered to her. Distance here was a good thing. For the moment at least, her relocation felt like a bullet dodged.

"Melissa, what can I help you with?" Howard asked me now.

"I'm sorry to bother you with this, but it's Lindsey," I said.

"Uh-huh, I saw the press," Howard replied vaguely.

"Yes, so I'm trying to figure out what's going on here," I went on. "Have you spoken to her at all?"

"No, Melissa, I really haven't spoken to her for well over a year," Howard responded cautiously.

"*Can* you speak to her?" I inquired, expecting the answer I got.

Howard sighed audibly. "Melissa, I really can't do that, and you don't want me to," he said. "Listen, something happened with Lindsey at some point."

"Meaning?" I urged him to continue.

"I don't know how to explain it. She has really changed." He referenced the personnel issues with the people at Empire State Development and the terms of her departure from state government. "And, I don't know . . ."

"Howard, you're trying to tell me something. What is it?" I asked, trying to pull it from him.

"I don't know what I'm saying, but I really don't think it's a good idea for me or anyone else to reach out to her. I think it will just make whatever this is worse," he answered, sounding both nervous and resolute. "In fact, I'm sure of it."

I hung up the phone but couldn't get Howard's voice out of my head. I couldn't quite put my finger on what was going on, but I was only getting half the story—that much I was sure of. But I didn't have any time to spend psychoanalyzing it, either.

CHAPTER 19

Fanning Out

THE PRESS BEGAN TO FAN OUT.

The *New York Post* and the *Times Union* were turning over every possible rock to see what they could find on Cuomo. And after a solid week and dozens of calls, both papers had come up short. Rich reported back that neither publication could find anyone who would corroborate Lindsey's claims, and while many said the work environment was highly demanding, difficult, and at times all-consuming, none characterized it as toxic. Neither paper planned to move ahead with their stories.

After being briefed on the swirl happening around us, the governor—never one to be comfortable when he was in an out-of-control situation—pitched an idea: What if we drafted an op-ed clearly laying out the true story of Lindsey's departure and the nonexistent NDA?

While everything was documented, I still thought the op-ed was a colossally bad idea.

"No, no, no," I told the governor.

"Why no?" he asked, perplexed.

I quickly ticked off my reasons. "Number one: you will take a story that is completely contained and blow it up way out of proportion. And two: it will look like we are bullying her or somehow shaming her," I asserted.

"Okay, well, maybe you're right," Cuomo reluctantly conceded, "but why don't you ask some people and see what they think?"

A proposed piece was drafted, which I dutifully shared with Robbie Kaplan. Much to my surprise, she read the op-ed and thought it was mostly fine.

"I think if, as long as you take out any reference to anything about her being inappropriate with male staff at a work event—anything that could be perceived as 'shaming' her—then this is okay," she responded. Lindsey was running for office, after all, and if we were solid on the facts, the office had the right to correct the public record. "I'll run it by Tina to get a second opinion," she said, referring to Tina Tchen, the president and CEO of Time's Up.

Really? Had I been overreacting to the idea? This second-guessing of my once-solid convictions was becoming a worrisome habit. I reverted to form and pushed through my doubts.

I reported back on my conversation with Robbie while still advising heavily against the strategy; I strongly believed that it would be viewed as a gross overreaction and backfire on us. The governor wanted to hear from more people and told me to ask the kitchen cabinet for their view.

I knew this drill. When Cuomo had something in his head, he would need to work through his own process to get to a place of acknowledging that it was actually a bad idea. The number of scathing letters to legislators or open letters to the press that were written in response to a negative article but never sent had reached the hundreds by year eleven of the administration. The inner circle had gotten used to the drill—a version of President Lincoln's "Write a letter, stick it in a drawer"—even if it took days to close the drawer and keep it shut.

This time, after several versions of the draft—each time tamping it down more and more—and a number of "come to Jesus" phone calls, everyone was on the same page: This was a bad idea, and we needed to collectively move on.

But I was the one who secretly couldn't let this drop.

I was still dogged by my hunch that the Lindsey jigsaw puzzle had more pieces than we realized, and we were missing some. Without them in sight, I convinced myself, we would never see the bigger picture. My conspiracy theory feasted on a tidbit in the *Daily News* that week, confirming second-hand information that was ping-ponging around Albany: One of Lindsey's consultants had quit over her tweeted allegations against the governor. Lupe Todd Medina had been frustrated working with Lindsey in the weeks leading up to the incident, and when Lindsey told her campaign that she was making the claim against Cuomo, Medina supposedly asked: "What are your allegations based on?" Lindsey allegedly replied, "While I don't have anything specific, I know in my heart that it's true." According to the *Daily News*, Lindsey's Twitter allegations were "the last straw" for Medina, and she promptly quit.

I kept racking my brain for more angles and sleuthing online for clues. That's when I discovered that Lindsey's campaign manager was a guy named Trip Yang. I recognized Yang as a lefty operative who had worked for another one of our chief political agitators, then New York City councilman Jumaane Williams, years earlier. Williams had since become the city's public advocate, an elected post that served New Yorkers as a type of ombudsman with the city government. He had succeeded Tish James in that position and had made a full-time job out of criticizing the Cuomo administration. Tish had also recently employed Yang as a consultant to her campaign for attorney general.

Until that point in December 2020, Tish had been an uneasy political ally. A Brooklyn-born African American lawyer, Tish had been on my radar for a while, and she was one of the possible running mates I had in mind when I pushed the governor to drop then Lieutenant Governor Kathy Hochul when he sought a third term in 2018. I hadn't been senior enough to be involved in Hochul's selection back in 2014, and she wasn't Cuomo's original first choice. At the time, our then lieutenant governor, Bob Duffy, had made the decision to go into the private sector, setting off an intense search for his replacement. Being from Queens, Cuomo believed strongly that governing the entire state meant having regional balance represented in its statewide elected officials and was single-mindedly focused on Buffalo. His sights were set on Byron Brown, a working-class, African American mayor of the Queen City, known for his pragmatism and operational fortitude, whom Cuomo got along with very well personally. But, in our vetting, we found out that, while not public, Brown's name came up in a wide-ranging US Attorney's Office investigation into some of western New York's most influential power players. While we didn't believe Brown was involved or that he would do anything unethical (he was ultimately cleared), the unknowns around the nascent case were fraught, and, wanting to avoid even the hint of a scandal, Cuomo was forced to move on from his first choice. He settled for Hochul, a one-term white Congresswoman from Buffalo's suburbs who sounded Canadian when she spoke. She would supposedly help "shore up the moderates" and solidify the western New York vote for Cuomo. Back then, I vehemently believed the state was, in fact, moving more and more left, and selecting Hochul would anger our downstate progressive base. It was no secret within the administration that I was never a Hochul fan. She was an A-rated member of the NRA who was best known for pandering to white Republican voters by threatening to arrest undocumented New Yorkers attempting to obtain driver's licenses, and I felt she lacked policy chops and hurt the ticket more than she helped.

Four years later, then a trusted member of the governor's "inner circle," I got the green light from Cuomo to start looking for Hochul's replacement ahead of the November election. Over the next several weeks, I flirted heavily with the notion of advocating Tish James, who was widely known to be eyeing a run for New York City mayor.

It didn't matter: We never got far enough to have any direct conversation with Tish James about the prospect of joining the 2018 ticket.

The conversation between our campaign chairman, Bill Mulrow, Kathy's chief of staff, Hochul, and I had been dragging on for almost thirty minutes, and it was time to address the elephant in the room. "You're out, Kathy," I said, sitting across from the lieutenant governor at a long mahogany conference table in our Third Avenue campaign conference room. It was March 2018, and the decision had been made. Kathy Hochul was off the ticket.

"Melissa, I can win this thing," Hochul pushed back as her chief of staff and Mulrow looked on in silence.

"I appreciate that you think that, Kathy," I responded coolly, "but if you're really going to pull this off, the governor is going to have to divert millions of dollars to get you over the finish line. And, frankly, we want to go in another direction." We wanted someone more progressive who we thought could play more of a substantive role on the team. Her predecessor, Bob Duffy, had been a real partner to Cuomo and was often dispatched to deal with complex political and policy issues, whereas Hochul mostly cut ribbons and spoke at second- and third-tier events. While her folksy "aw shucks" approach earned Hochul some political friends upstate, she lacked connectivity when it came to actual voters.

After a prolonged back-and-forth, we devised a face-saving exit strategy: We would help Kathy find another job—a promotion—and she would quietly leave the ticket. Unfortunately, the job she eventually identified as being suitable proved to be way beyond reach: president of Planned Parenthood. The governor dispatched me to make some calls to see if there was any shot, but all I got were awkward pauses and "Don't call us, we'll call you."

Hochul reacted by starting an aggressive shadow campaign in the press through her upstate surrogates—basically her own personal Upstate Lives Matter protest. It worked. The governor had no interest in angering upstate politicians and decided to give her another chance. Cuomo went on to spend over $5 million of his campaign money to ensure Hochul won her primary, which she did by just six points, twenty-four points behind Cuomo at the top of the ticket.

As for Tish James, fate intervened. She ended up being elected attorney general in the upended 2018 race after incumbent Eric Schneiderman was forced to resign in the aftermath of Ronan Farrow's *New Yorker* piece alleging he had physically and emotionally abused several women he had been dating.

Of course, we had had a couple of minor bumps along the way, but overall Tish's team and our office maintained a decent political and working relationship. I didn't think twice about picking up the phone and dialing her office to further my Lindsey research.

"Hey, Melissa—long time. How are you?" Ibrahim Khan, Tish's chief of staff asked.

"Crazy times, Ibrahim," I responded. "So, listen, I have something to talk to you about."

"Fire away," he urged.

"Trip Yang," I said.

"Our consultant? What about him?" he asked.

"Well, apparently he's now serving as Lindsey Boylan's campaign manager."

"He's working on her campaign for Manhattan borough president?" Ibrahim said he didn't know that.

"Yes," I confirmed. "And I'm sure you saw her tweets this weekend."

"Yes, of course, but she didn't say anything more, right? Refused to speak to the press? Feels like it was a pretty contained story," he said.

"It has been so far, but word has come back that she's been DM'ing dozens of former staff members, trying to find other people to say negative things about the governor," I continued. "And I don't want to put you in an awkward situation, but I was hoping you could call Trip and find out what the hell is going on. Her comms person quit as a result of her tweets, and having known and worked with her for as long as I did, I can just feel this isn't on the up-and-up."

A few hours later, Ibrahim circled back. He told me that Trip thought something about the situation didn't feel right, either, but that, as a male campaign staffer, he didn't think he could walk out on her after she'd made #MeToo claims, however specious. He reported that Lindsey had engaged a lawyer and believed she had one or two people lined up with her.

Nothing about the situation felt right, and as the days went on, the same question kept reverberating in my head: *What am I missing?*

My question was partially answered that Thursday afternoon when a former staffer flagged a tweet from a woman named Kaitlin: "Keep going, Lindsey—men like him [Cuomo] shouldn't be in power." Kaitlin only had a couple dozen followers, but something stuck out: A constant agitator against the administration, Alessandra Biaggi, had "liked" her tweet.

Who was Kaitlin? How did she know Biaggi? And how did she fit into this?

A quick search and several phone calls later, I ascertained that Kaitlin had worked in the governor's office five years earlier. Cuomo had met her at a fundraiser held by the lobbying firm where she worked at the time, and her former boss, Queens Congressman Joe Crowley (who would later be defeated by Alexandria Ocasio-Cortez), raved that she was a brilliant up-and-comer. At the time, Stephanie's assistant had just left for a job in the private sector. The open position was entry-level—answer phones, get coffee, keep the governor's schedule moving—but required someone with political savvy and impeccable organizational skills. The congressman's recommendation was all the governor needed to hear; Kaitlin sounded well suited for the job.

Or so he thought.

As it turned out, Kaitlin did not respond well to pressure, did not have an appetite for the long hours the position required, or the necessary skill set—which was not shocking, as very few people did. But as a result, she lasted for approximately three months before Cuomo instructed Jill to let her know it wasn't a good fit; she should find Kaitlin a job that would better suit her elsewhere. She eventually landed at NYSERDA, the state's energy and research development agency. No one on our team had been in contact with her since.

Now I found myself analyzing the tweet of a junior assistant I hardly knew as if it were the DaVinci Code. She had worked with the governor for such a short period of time so many years ago. Was she angry because he had transferred her from working with him? Had he yelled at her? What was her relationship to Lindsey? How did she know Biaggi? Nothing was adding up, and my need to know was becoming all-consuming. I decided we needed to have someone contact her and try to find out what was going on. This was my modus operandi—not to sit back and wait, but to use my contacts and connections to identify a problem before it grew.

It turned out that our former press secretary, who currently worked as the director of communications at the MTA, had once briefly shared an office with Kaitlin during her tenure on Cuomo's staff, and while they were never close, they had had rapport at the time. Because of Kaitlin's mysterious connection to Biaggi and engagement with Boylan, I didn't trust that the call wouldn't somehow be twisted. I picked up the phone to conference with a former counsel, whom I asked to weigh in.

"Is this okay?" I asked.

"Yes," the lawyer assured me.

I asked what the former office-mate should say to draw Kaitlin out.

"Don't put words in Kaitlin's mouth. You can be open-ended in your own statements and questions, but make sure that you aren't speaking for her," he advised.

"Is it okay to record the conversation?" I wondered, worried that if Kaitlin was working with Lindsey and Biaggi and this was an attempted political hit job, the call could somehow be twisted.

"Yes, and assume she is recording you, too," he counseled.

To say Operation Call Kaitlin was a disaster is an understatement. The exchange was short and curt. Kaitlin was guarded and didn't provide any insight into the motivation of her tweet and, if anything, sounded skeptical.

The minute the call was relayed back to me, I knew it had been a mistake. I had been acting like an operative when the situation demanded a lawyer. What did I think was going to come from the call? If Kaitlin was working with Lindsey for political purposes, she was never going to disclose that. And if it was something more, the outreach should have come from our counsel's office, not under a false pretense.

I looped in the lawyers and discussed what had happened.

Twenty-four hours later, Kaitlin came back to us.

I was pacing around the first floor of my sister's house that Saturday morning before the next shoe was about to drop.

The head of NYSERDA had called. Kaitlin had apparently reached out the night before, reporting the strange phone call she had received two days prior about her tweet. Kaitlin went on to disclose what we already knew: Lindsey was trying to put together a group with the goal of assembling ten to twelve women to make a claim against the governor. At that point, I understood it was just Lindsey, but she was in touch with Kaitlin about potentially joining the group. Kaitlin apparently felt she had had a bad experience working in the executive chamber, that she had been yelled at, that she was under tremendous pressure, and that she had been very unhappy, and that it took her a long time to get past it. At Judy's instruction, NYSERDA assured Kaitlin that whatever was going on, she was free to do as she wished. It was unclear whether Kaitlin was claiming she was sexually harassed or complaining about a "toxic" work environment—two claims Boylan had successfully woven together.

My head was spinning. What would this group of ten to twelve be?

The next several days were impossible.

To the outside world, I must have looked fine. I had reason to be happy. While the vaccine rollout was bumpy, at least there was a vaccine to roll out. Plus Trump was just mere weeks from leaving the White House for good and closing the book on the most chaotic and polarizing presidency in history. But inside I could feel myself beginning to break down.

Eleven months of sheer exhaustion, coupled with the trauma we were all processing over navigating COVID, compounded by the stress of the unknown of Lindsey and now Kaitlin—it was all too much to handle. I could feel that I was starting to reach my breaking point, but there wasn't a way out.

My office had begun to feel more and more like a casino where time was irrelevant. Every day was the same. Wake up around 4:30, be at the office by 5:30, work until 8:00 or 9:00, go back to Jess's house, sleep if I could, and repeat.

As I lay on the red leather sofa in my Albany office on the evening of December 23, I decided it was time to go home. I had been negotiating with the legislature on the last batch of bills for the year and had spent the day troubleshooting the state's vaccine-scheduling website, which was constantly crashing. At that moment, there was nothing left to do. But just before I reached the door, I hesitated. There was one last call to make before I left.

"Hi, Ibrahim. Merry Christmas," I said.

"Same to you. What can I help you with?" Ibrahim asked.

"Have you heard anything from Trip about what Lindsey's up to?" I fished.

"You know, last I spoke to him, it sounded like things were kind of off the rails. Lindsey was still trying to put together a group and some 'legal strategy,' but it doesn't sound like she was gaining any traction. I'd honestly put this out of your mind, Melissa. It doesn't feel like it's going anywhere," he replied.

"Got it. Thanks, Ibrahim," I said.

"Anytime. Enjoy the holiday," he replied.

"You, too. Happy holidays," I wished him before hanging up.

A few weeks later, Ibrahim's words appeared to be playing out.

Judy received word from NYSERDA that Kaitlin wanted to speak directly with her. Judy agreed on the condition that there were other witnesses present. On that call, Kaitlin made clear that she was not sexually harassed by the governor and that she had never said she was; she wanted that point communicated unequivocally. And she said that she was not joining the group Lindsey was attempting to put together. This had all been a misunderstanding.

What?

None of it made sense. Everything felt off-kilter. Kaitlin's about-face should have been good news, but it felt like foreshadowing.

Despite my ominous feeling, there was in fact no way I could have known just how quickly my world was about to spiral out of control.

CHAPTER 20

Must Come Down

IT WAS A NEW YEAR—IN THEORY, A HOPE FOR A NEW BEGINNING. Having just been appointed to serve on President-elect Biden's transition committee to advise the incoming administration on its COVID response, I was at the apex of my career. It should have made me fulfilled or excited, but, honestly, it didn't. The past year had been exhausting, and like the rest of the country, I yearned for the dark cloud of COVID hovering over us to finally move on. And I was hoping that the year ahead would bring us all happier times.

But 2021 was foreboding from the start, and it was destined to shape my life in a far different way.

The kumbaya sense of solidarity that COVID had initially created—that we were all in this together—had begun to sour months earlier, and during that cold winter, even what should have been cause for optimism devolved instead into contentious politics.

Any hope that the new COVID vaccine would return life to some sense of normalcy was supplanted by the chaos of the rollout. With too little vaccine to go around, we were in the position of making impossible decisions about who would get priority to get the shot, pitting categories of people—essential workers, teachers, the immunocompromised, the elderly—against one another, while local governments grumbled about not having a bigger role in the decisions around distribution. Meanwhile, the computer program used to schedule appointments was constantly crashing.

Then, less than one week into the new year, what should have been a pro forma transfer of power morphed into an attempted insurrection when a violent mob of Trump extremists stormed the capitol in Washington. I was sitting in my office in the capitol in Albany when Rich appeared in the doorway, "MDR, are you seeing this?" he asked, ignoring the fact that I was clearly on a conference call and not seeing whatever he was referencing.

"What's up?" I mouthed, covering the receiver of the phone.

Rich picked up the remote to my television and flipped to MSNBC.

"*This!*" he exclaimed, pointing at the TV. "It's insane!"

Surreal images of chaos and bloodshed in Washington, DC, the fitting culmination of the Trump era, splashed across the screen. Anger, fear, and ugly divisiveness brewing across the country had been steadily building and building. There's only so much pressure any person, any society, any system can take before something finally blows. That day, it did.

In Albany, I had spent the morning on the phone.

Nursing home deaths had become politicized and weaponized to the point of no return. Since the start of the pandemic, we released death numbers at our daily briefings based on where people had died: hospital deaths, nursing home deaths, total deaths. Those numbers were reported to DOH daily by the state's 261 hospitals and 613 nursing homes through surveys asking for statistics on COVID patients. But nothing about COVID had been simple or straightforward, and collecting data proved to be challenging, to say the least.

When COVID first began, the federal government did not issue guidance on how death numbers should be tallied, leading states across the country to count deaths differently and unevenly. In April, for example, the CDC introduced the concept of a presumed COVID death: someone you believed died from COVID based on their symptoms or circumstance, without actually having tested the person. Labeling someone *presumed* was just that—a presumption on the part of the person making the determination, and far from accurate, a lesson we learned after a former member of the New York State Assembly,

Richard Brodsky, died the second week of April. His death was initially deemed presumed COVID, but his family insisted he be tested to be sure and as it turned out, he didn't have COVID at all. But in the interest of being overly cautious in an attempt to be accurate and transparent, we adopted the approach of reporting presumed COVID deaths in addition to confirmed COVID deaths, making New York one of only nine states in the entire country to do so. When we made the change, Trump accused New York of inflating our COVID death numbers to make him look bad. (His adopted state of Florida, by comparison, not only didn't include presumed deaths in their overall COVID fatalities, but reportedly presumed elderly deaths that spring as being the result of pneumonia or influenza.)

Beginning in the late spring and metastasizing over the summer, the Far Right—with Trump leading the way—was spreading conspiracy theories blaming Democratic state governments for nursing home deaths. Around that time, the press started asking for a different accounting: the number of people who were in nursing homes but left the nursing home and subsequently died. At the height of the pandemic, this was a forensic nightmare that required nursing homes to track where residents went after leaving the nursing home and what happened to them. If a person went to a hospital and died, they would already be counted in hospital deaths. So the nursing home would need to trace the former resident, find out if they lived or died, and then coordinate with the hospital over who would report the death to ensure there was no double-counting. The exercise did not change the number of total deaths, which was always accurate and not in dispute, but reallocated deaths that had occurred in hospitals to where the patient came from as opposed to where they died.

As the press began to raise questions about nursing home patients who died outside of nursing homes, DOH revised its survey in the middle of the spring, requesting data about all previously reported deaths, the location of each death, and the patient's COVID-19 status. In the early months of the pandemic, DOH revised its survey more than a dozen times in an attempt to get accurate information. Initial results were a mess, comprising wildly confusing, incomplete, and inaccurate responses from facilities overwhelmed by the first throes of a pandemic. Some nursing homes reported presumed COVID deaths going back to the prior December, before COVID existed in the United States, while others reported that every single death that occurred in their facility since March 1 was a presumed COVID death. Patients had been doubled-counted as deaths in nursing homes and in the hospitals they had been admitted to, or by hospitals and the nursing homes they were sent to. Some facilities recorded presumed COVID deaths, while others reported only confirmed. Many nursing homes reported "presumed" patient deaths in hospitals that hospitals did not report as COVID at all. Some patients who had COVID, but were still alive, had been given dates of death in the future.

To accurately reconcile the data, in August 2020, administration officials began auditing COVID deaths among nursing home patients.

Due, in part, to the compliance requirements of the Health Insurance Portability and Accountability Act (HIPAA), nursing homes initially didn't even report patient names to DOH, instead listing only their initials. Part of the verification process required identifying the actual person attached to the initials. In an attempt to ensure accuracy of the data, a team at the Department of Health called every single nursing home to match up the initials of patients they had reported as having died in hospitals against hospital databases to make sure they did actually die there. When all was said and done, the out-of-facility nursing home deaths initially provided to us through surveys were flagged as wrong by roughly six hundred, or nearly 20 percent of the reported out-of-facility deaths being analyzed. As the auditing process was underway, at the end of August, the legislature had sent us a letter asking for, among many other things, a full accounting of nursing home numbers. We received it at almost the exact same moment the DOJ had directed their political nursing home investigation into New Jersey, Michigan, Pennsylvania, and New York.

We were preparing to release the results of the audit to coincide with the upcoming legislative health committee hearing; the numbers were to be given to members the day before Dr. Zucker was supposed to testify, allowing them time to prepare their questions for him.

That had been the plan, anyway.

But one week before, that plan went out the window.

"Melissa, I just heard from the AG's office."

It was Dana Carotenuto, our head of legislative affairs and policy. Dana had joined our team in 2018 after nearly a decade in the legislature and had seen it all. She was as seasoned, steady, and politically savvy as the come. "They're about to release a nursing home report, and they're claiming that we—that the March 25 health order—could have had a role in increased deaths. They're also saying that we undercounted the deaths by up to 50 percent," she announced.

"Wait, what?" I couldn't believe Tish was blindsiding us with this. And how were they even reaching that conclusion? Zucker's analysis lined up with what other states—which didn't have the March 25 order—found that staff and visitors were unwittingly bringing the virus into the facilities before we could even test for COVID or mandate safety measures like masks or no visitors.

"Their position is, like—well, it could have, it could not have," Dana relayed.

"By putting that in the headline, they're going to have reporters say that the AG's office is saying that the March 25 order impacted deaths," I predicted.

I'd heard enough. Furious, I dialed the AG's chief of staff.

"Ibrahim, how are you guys blindsiding us with this?" I demanded. "We need an opportunity to look at what you guys did. This is going to be highly politicized. . . . We need to make sure what you guys are saying is true and correct, and we need to make sure the Health Department goes through the numbers with you and that everyone's on the same page. You can't just drop this from the sky!"

"It's too late," Ibrahim told me. "I'm sorry, it's too late."

"How is it too late? It hasn't gone out yet. Set up a call with Dr. Zucker and his team this afternoon. You can release it tomorrow, but it's more important that it's right!"

As Ibrahim and I kept going around in circles, I finally understood what had happened: the AG had already given some favored reporter or reporters an embargoed copy of their report to run *before* their office called to tell us about it.

"How did you not give us a heads-up?" I asked, remembering my friendly conversation with Ibrahim at Christmastime. Now he was nonchalant.

"Oh, like we did with the NYPD–de Blasio investigation?"

"Huh?" I asked, genuinely confused. Two weeks earlier, Tish had filed a lawsuit against the NYPD and de Blasio for excessive force used against civilians during the height of the George Floyd protests. Ibrahim had called to give our office a heads-up the day before. Overnight news of the lawsuit had leaked to a reporter at NY1. The AG's office believed it was us. It wasn't.

"Ibrahim, we had nothing to do with that!" I argued. "Releasing a report on a topic this sensitive that includes false information does not somehow make us even for something we didn't do in the first place!"

They wanted to extract maximum pain from our office and not give us an opportunity to either review their work or to respond. Like the governor, Tish's term expired in 2022. Now I had reason to wonder which office she was actually eyeing.

I had our health team quickly review one of the major points Tish was pushing. The AG's office was going to announce that 323 nursing homes didn't have COVID in their facilities until a COVID patient was admitted *after* the March 25 admissions policy had been issued, arguably undermining DOH's finding that staff introduced COVID into nursing homes.

The AG's office was wrong. The actual number wasn't 323. It was 6. And it was the exact opposite conclusion of what Zucker's team had determined by contacting *all* of the nursing homes.

I called the AG's office back, got both Tish and Ibrahim on the line, and put it on speakerphone with an office full of senior staff quietly looking on.

"Guys, you cannot put this out," I reiterated. "One of your major conclusions is based on a false assumption, and we have the numbers to back it up."

Once again, this time in stereo, I was told it was too late.

"Melissa, I hear you. I can put out a statement later in the day clearing that point up," Tish offered. I came undone. How could someone who the public entrusted to pursue, present, and preserve the truth so blithely shrug off releasing information to the public, knowing that information was wrong.

"You're politicizing this entire thing," I said. "You're doing this to try to hurt the governor. This isn't about honestly releasing numbers. You need to pull this back, go to the *New York Times* or whoever you gave it to and tell them that the numbers aren't correct, and that you need to take a beat and something needs to get fixed."

While I was still on the phone with them, a *New York Times* exclusive on the report popped, and the AG's press office released the report to the media at large.

The news cycle was immediately flooded with stories about how Cuomo's March 25 order could have led to increased deaths, and that we had dramatically undercounted the nursing home fatalities by 50 percent. (Their own report actually acknowledged that our overall death number was reported accurately.)

The narrative spread like fire through dry grass.

No one took note that the overall death total was always the same. Or that we had always been transparent about the fact that we were counting nursing home deaths as "in nursing home" and hospital deaths as "in hospital."

I called LouAnn and Shontell, the assembly and senate's top aides, and explained that we couldn't wait for our previously scheduled meeting with their members the following week. We needed to publicly release our audit immediately, in the same news cycle as the AG's "investigation." We needed to get the actual correct numbers out there. We would make it up to them.

Ten days after Tish's report dropped, Dr. Zucker and our senior team sat down for a closed-door meeting with the members of the legislative health committee, the senate, and the assembly together to answer any questions they had. When the question of why we hadn't released the audit information earlier, when they had asked for it back in August, I jumped in.

> The letter [from the legislature requesting nursing home data] comes in at the end of August, and right around the same time, President Trump turns this into a giant political football. He starts tweeting that we killed everyone in nursing homes, he starts going after (Phil) Murphy, starts going after (Gavin) Newsom, starts going after Gretchen Whitmer.
>
> He directs the Department of Justice to do an investigation into us. He finds one person at DOJ—who since has been fired because this person is now known to be a political hack—who sends letters out to all of these different governors. And, basically, we froze, because then we were in a position where we weren't sure if what we were going to give to the Department of Justice, or what we give to you guys, what we start saying, was going to be used against us while we weren't sure if there was going to be an investigation.
>
> That played a very large role in this. We went to the [legislative] leaders, and we said to the leaders, "Can we please pause on getting back to everybody until we get through this period and we know what's what with the DOJ?" We since have come through that period. All signs point to, they are not looking at this. They dropped it. They never formally opened an investigation. They sent a letter asking a number of questions, and then we satisfied those questions.

While the meeting had started off as highly contentious, over two hours the ice thawed, and the discussion became productive. By the end, the tone had shifted entirely to downright collegial. We were joking around with members, and everyone promised a more open dialogue moving forward.

When the meeting wrapped up, I was riding high. I got a call from the senate's top aide, who had sat in on the meeting: "You killed it, DeRosa! Seriously, the members are thrilled. They are happy about the access and the honesty, and by the end, I felt like we had all gotten to a new, more productive place. Great job!"

The assembly speaker's top staffer hadn't been in the meeting, so I shot her off a note: "Any feedback from your members?"

The next morning she responded, "Kim reported back that he thought for the most part the meeting was productive." Ron Kim, an assemblyman from Queens, had been a longtime adversary of the administration. Years earlier, after the *New York Times* released a huge exposé on worker abuses in nail salons, we had teamed up with him to pass the strongest worker protections for nail salons in the country. But shortly after, Kim reversed course, saying we had gone too far and calling for a repeal of broad swaths of the law. As the *New York Times* reported,

> As it turns out, while Mr. Kim's position on the law was evolving, nail salon owners, previously a largely disconnected group, were rapidly organizing. They started a sophisticated effort to fight the law. And, behind the scenes, they funneled tens of thousands of dollars in political donations to Mr. Kim.

In the same article, our counsel questioned the motivation behind Kim's reversal, insinuating it could have been because of pay-to-play. Shortly after the story ran, the US Attorney's Office was circling Kim, and he believed we were to blame. Ever since, he had been one of our most vocal critics and had aggressively taken up the nursing home issue. I had told LouAnn that I was concerned he would be disruptive in the meeting, but her text indicated he actually thought it went well.

For a moment, I felt a sense of relief. The legislature was satisfied with the meeting. The audit was out. It was time to refocus on reopening New York and getting vaccine shots in arms.

I had no idea what was coming.

As it turned out, someone secretly recorded the meeting and leaked it to the *New York Post*. There was one person in that room who had an ax to grind and who was suddenly appearing on national television, from CNN to *The View*, blasting the governor and calling for my resignation. That person? Ron Kim.

The next day, the tabloid trumpeted an "exclusive" and ran my picture under the headline: CUOMO AIDE MELISSA DEROSA ADMITS THEY HID NURSING HOME DATA SO FEDS WOULDN'T FIND OUT. It was the exact opposite of what I had said.

Whereas I had told lawmakers, "DOJ sent a letter asking a number of questions, and then we satisfied those questions," the *Post* was driving a narrative that I said we *hid* the information from the feds, rather than what I actually said—which is that we answered the DOJ fully, but while we went through that process, delayed responding to the legislature. Taking my quotes completely out of context, the story went on to say that I made a stunning admission of a coverup by telling lawmakers "we froze" out of fear that the true numbers would "be used against us" by federal prosecutors. In fact, we were comprehensive and transparent in our responses to the DOJ. Precedent was given to the DOJ request, while other requests were placed on pause, resulting in a delay in producing data for the legislature. I had used the words "froze" and "pause" interchangeably with lawmakers when explaining the reason for our delay in responding to the legislature while we were answering the highly politicized DOJ: "Can we please pause on getting back to everybody until we get through this period and we know what's what with the DOJ?"

And despite telling the assembly's top staffer that he thought the meeting was "mostly productive" and not raising any red flags, Ron Kim was front and center in the *Post* article:

> Assemblyman Ron Kim (D-Queens), who took part in the call, told the *Post* on Thursday that DeRosa's remarks sounded "like they admitted that they were trying to dodge having any incriminating evidence that might put the administration or the [Health Department] in further trouble with the Department of Justice."

Since only the *Post* had the full (leaked) transcript, the broader media didn't have the full context of my comments. And in the race to match the *Post*'s "exclusive," they didn't care. The feeding frenzy was on, and this time, the blood in the water was mine. I was being treated like a "principal" and not a staffer, and I know from experience the dangers of that.

As the story broke, I started getting outreach from legislators who had been in the meeting, all with the same message: We know that's not what you were saying. Are you okay? But rather than speak up in the press and risk the media tsunami turning on them, they put their heads down and hid.

The governor was in his office, two doors down from mine, when the story broke. I struggled not to break down as I went to tell him what the *Post* was saying. As I stood there, this false narrative was becoming national news, on every major network, in every major newspaper, streaming across social media.

Five months later, with Trump no longer calling the shots at the Department of Justice, we would receive a letter from the DOJ verifying that not only had we truthfully submitted the data they requested, but that the death statistics provided did not warrant an investigation into the Department of Health's March 25 admissions policy. But that was five months too late for me.

The next day, I was supposed to accompany Cuomo to the White House for a meeting that President Biden was hosting. It would have been a chance to see old friends and talk about the future. But as I rode with the governor to the airport, I could feel my panic building. As soon as we arrived at the terminal, I turned to him.

"I can't get on that plane," I blurted. "I can't go look those people in the eye. I'm so horrified." Never in my life had I felt like such a failure.

"Melissa," the governor tried to assure me, "it's going to be okay."

I stayed in Albany that day, my retreat the first step down a dark, seemingly endless abyss.

The daily briefings that had made Cuomo the nation's de facto COVID commander in chief—winning him an Emmy, putting him on the cover of *Rolling Stone*—also meant that I was no longer some random woman in state government. The months I'd spent in living rooms across the country had turned me into a nationally recognized political figure. I'd flown close to the sun, right alongside Andrew Cuomo, appearing on magazine covers. Suddenly, absolute strangers felt like they knew me, when the reality was, they didn't know the real me at all. Now, with a single story in a notoriously sensationalist tabloid, the spotlight turned into a blinding searchlight.

The governor was being pilloried by the media and his political enemies as well, which made it all the worse for me. Republicans, including my old friend Elise Stefanik, were demanding his impeachment and the resignation of top staffers (including me, of course).

I had been trying to smooth ruffled feathers in the legislature over their preempted audit review and briefing when I held that private session to explain the situation and take questions. But I had made the situation far worse, and I had hurt the governor. I was the one who was supposed to make sure the administration was okay, and now it was my fault that Cuomo was getting hurt and the administration was being criticized.

Stephanie, Larry, and I had moved out of the mansion back in September when the COVID crisis was easing, but I was still based out of Albany and working around the clock. I was temporarily living at my sister's house, our old family home. In that safe and familiar place, I ended the day literally curled up in a ball. *Oh my God, oh my God, oh my God. How am I going to fix this?*

By the third day, there was no coverage of my alleged attempt to obstruct justice. I thought maybe things were calming down. But they were only just beginning. The *Post*, clearly keen to keep the story alive, decided to take a new tack and reached out to me: Did I have a comment on the fact that people thought there should be an investigation into what I said but the Southern District's US Attorney's Office couldn't do it because my mother-in-law was the US Attorney for the Southern District?

I hadn't told anyone outside of close family and friends that Matt and I weren't together anymore, letting the chaos of COVID and remote work and lockdowns provide a smokescreen for the pain I wasn't ready to share. I loved and revered his mother, and now her good name was going to get dragged through this "scandal" of my own making. I called Matt.

"Your mother," I sobbed. "She's going to be dragged into this. I'm so sorry, Matt. I'm so, so sorry."

Days after the *Post* story broke, our office released a full transcript of my meeting with the legislature. After reading the entire thing, *Politico* published a story, contradicting the narrative spun by the *New York Post*:

> Nothing in the transcript furthers the allegation that
> top Cuomo staffer Melissa DeRosa told legislators that
> data on nursing home deaths was withheld to obstruct
> a US Department of Justice probe. DeRosa said the
> administration had in fact cooperated with the DOJ.

It didn't matter. It was too late. In the world of the nonstop media cycle, fueled by clicks and "likes," the race to be first overtakes the integrity of being right. And once a false narrative hardens, it is nearly impossible to undo—a lesson I would learn over and over again throughout the following year.

Any semblance of a routine fell by the wayside. I stopped running. I didn't have the physical strength. I was still going to the office but felt the combination of a year's worth of fatigue, stress, and pressure, all of it pushing down on me with a weight I knew I could no longer bear.

I could tell everyone was worried by the way they checked in on me, but I didn't have a drop of resilience left. I couldn't lie and say I would be okay when I literally felt like I was dying inside. In addition to Steph, Rich, and my family, there was a small group of outside advisers who I relied heavily on to get through those dark days, who remained supportive and loving through it all, never folding under pressure or in the face of the social media mob—people anyone would want in their foxhole. Jef Pollock, one of the nation's leading pollsters and most astute political minds in democratic politics; Charlie King, chief ally to Reverend Sharpton, informal adviser to countless prominent elected officials, and longtime Cuomo friend, who I coopted as my own along the way; and one other person. I picked up the phone and started dialing. Steve Cohen, one of the A-team, who had been the first secretary to the governor in 2011, was as reliable and unflappable as they came.

"Steve, can you please come up?" I asked. "I need you."

Without question or hesitation, Steve got in the car, left New York City, and temporarily relocated to the mansion. He and the whole team rallied around me, trying their best to rebuild my shattered sense of self: You have brought us through all these things; you work so hard; you always have everyone's back; you always protect us. We're going to protect you.

The governor and Steve came up with a plan for Steve to hold a press conference, clearly explaining to all the reporters what I actually had said to the legislators and what actually had happened with the nursing homes. The press regarded Steve as a type of elder states- man and respected him. I was sitting alone in the living room of the mansion as the rest of the team huddled in the dining room nearby, preparing for Steve's presentation, when I felt my phone buzz. This time, it wasn't about me. I looked down to see a text from a reporter: "Do you have a comment on Lindsey Boylan's *Medium* piece? On immediate deadline."

CHAPTER 21

#MeToo Much

I OPENED TWITTER AND BEGAN TO SCROLL.

It had only posted minutes earlier, but already it was everywhere.

I stood up and walked the few short steps to the dining room, "Guys," I interrupted. "It's Lindsey . . . she's back."

I began reading out loud from the op-ed Boylan had posted on the self-publishing website *Medium*, recounting the details of her alleged sexual harassment. Lindsey began by claiming that in October 2017, she was sitting across from the governor on "his taxpayer-funded jet," their knees so close they were "almost touching," when Cuomo suddenly suggested, "Let's play strip poker."

We all exchanged incredulous looks.

First off, as everyone in that room knew all too well, the governor of New York doesn't have a "taxpayer-funded jet." The state-police plane the governor uses for official business is a thirty-year-old prop plane dating back to when Mario Cuomo served as governor and closely resembles the one that went down in the movie *La Bamba*. But it was par for the course with Lindsey: the continuation in a series of exaggerations and provable distortions.

But that wasn't all. Lindsey went on to label our office's decision to provide portions of her file that correctly described the true circumstances under which she left—allegations of her own bullying and toxicity—as attempts to "smear" her, a common refrain she tactically and successfully deployed from that moment on to shut down any legitimate questions about her story or credibility.

Her piece, full of conjecture and innuendo, culminated with a single concrete allegation: Cuomo had kissed her on the lips in his New York City office once in 2018.

Andrew Cuomo had a rule, dating back to his tenure as HUD secretary—a product of the Monica Lewinsky–Clinton days—that the door to his office always be open, the exception being during sensitive discussions with select, trusted senior staff. It's safe to say that Lindsey Boylan was not on that list. For Boylan's claim to be true, the governor would have had to give her a peck on the lips with Stephanie—whose office was directly connected to his—approximately ten feet away, looking on, a reality Lindsey herself acknowledged, writing, "I left past the desk of Stephanie Benton. I was scared she had seen the kiss."

"Oh, *come on*," Stephanie responded.

"What is she talking about?" the governor interrupted, dismissively.

The group's reaction can best be described as unmoved. Collectively, they turned back to the task at hand: preparing for Steve's nursing home presentation. The press hadn't taken Lindsey seriously back in December when she first made her vague Twitter comments. But that was then, and this was now. And one after another, stories began to pop.

I interjected, "Guys! This is serious!"

I quieted the room and began to tick through Lindsey's claims one at a time.

By her account, the salacious "strip poker" comment was made within earshot of a press aide sitting to her right. I opened my laptop and went into sleuth mode: Our schedules were always posted and saved. I clicked back to October 2017 and found that Lindsey had taken a handful of flights that month. I asked my assistant to get the four people who had been passengers on one or more of those flights on the phone and took the call.

"I just need a yes or no answer," I explained, once we were all connected. "Did the governor ever ask Lindsey Boylan if she wanted to play strip poker on the plane?"

One by one, each of the four staffers responded with the same answer: absolutely not.

We hung up, and I turned back to the team.

"Okay, in terms of a response, I think we should issue a blanket denial on everything she wrote," I said. "And separately release a statement from these four people saying, 'We were on the plane with Lindsey, and this never happened.'"

I went back to the four fellow travelers to ask them if they'd be willing to go on the record in a press statement. The first three agreed, but when I got to Lindsey's old boss, he paused.

"Melissa, can I talk to you alone?" Howard Zemsky asked.

"Sure," I said, ending the conference call. Howard called me right back.

"Lindsey is very aggressive. I'm just nervous about doing anything to provoke her," Howard confided.

"Look, Howard, you absolutely do not have to be on this if you don't want to," I assured him. "If you're not on it, it might look a little bit strange. But if what you're saying is that the governor *did* say something and you just don't want to tell me . . ."

"No, no, no, no, no," Howard cut me off. "That never happened. I just worry about provoking Lindsey."

"Okay, well, think about it, and let me know," I said. I hung up the phone, thinking back to the conversation Howard and I had had two months earlier. If he had sounded unnerved then, he sounded petrified now. Five minutes later, my phone rang again.

"Put my name on it," Howard said. "The governor didn't say it. This is ridiculous. I'll put my name on the statement."

With the release of Lindsey's *Medium* piece, the national press corps was now going full-bore covering "twin scandals"—nursing homes and sexual harassment/toxic work environment. Even though I knew better than to think on-the-record denials from the purported witnesses to Lindsey's claims, in combination with previously provided proof about her lying about the terms of her own departure, would put out one of those fires, a Pollyannish part of me still hoped it would at least slow that track down.

But there was blood in the water, and the sharks smelled it.

Suddenly, you had a bizarre coalition calling for the governor's resignation: Democratic Socialist AOC on the same side as MAGA Elise Stefanik in Congress, locking arms with the Democratic and Republican extremists in the state legislature.

They were bonded by a common interest. It wasn't about whether nursing home patients who passed away in hospitals were counted in a hospital or a nursing home. And it wasn't about alleged sexual harassment. It was about getting Andrew Cuomo out of office.

Little did we know that, behind the scenes, Lindsey had been busy quietly puppeteering two stories, framing her narrative and feeding the reporters validators. In the process, she made a request, it was later disclosed, to Charlotte Bennett, whom she had secretly been in communication with since December. At 7:29 p.m. that Friday, Lindsey shot off a text message (which was later made public):

> TY for amplifying my story. Two updates: I know
> both Ronan Farrow and Rebecca Traister are
> writing about it. It would really help if you were
> comfortable talking to one. Would certainly help
> me. On your own terms . . . he (Cuomo) is very
> wounded . . . bigger problems . . . which is why
> I did it this week.

Thirty minutes later, around 8:00 that night, unaware of all of this, I left the office and got in my car to drive back to my sister's house and the bed in the guest room I wanted so badly to crawl into. I was still driving when the phone rang. It was Rich Azzopardi.

"The *New York Times* just called," he informed me. "They said that they've done an interview with Charlotte Bennett, and they're gonna publish it as soon as tonight. They are saying she is coming forward with allegations of sexual harassment. They are framing her as 'Cuomo's Second Accuser.'" It was official. With two allegations, the governor had a #MeToo scandal on his hands.

"Who called? Who called you with that?" Rich's words knocked me sideways. The car swerved, and I almost drove off the road. I jerked the wheel back and tried to sound calm. "We need to get the kitchen cabinet; we need to get everyone on the phone."

"Okay, I'm on it. Oh, and Melissa?" Rich continued. "The reporter doing the story . . . is Jesse McKinley."

Of course it was.

By the time I got to the house, the *Times* had sent us a list of questions. What had gone from Charlotte telling colleagues in June 2020 that "the governor hit on me" had become "I believed he could hit on me in the future, but I removed myself from the situation first," and then became "I understood that the governor wanted to sleep with me" in the *New York Times* in February 2021, which would subsequently morph into "the governor 'propositioned' me for sex" in a CBS News interview in March 2021.

At the height of the swirl, questions began popping up on social media about Charlotte's history as a "survivor." Tweets began to appear out of thin air, claiming Charlotte had been cited in a lawsuit from 2017 for allegedly teaming up with three other classmates at Hamilton College to make false allegations of sexual assault against a student there. Charlotte had also previously tweeted that when she told Hamilton College president David Wippman—a recognized authority in international law, who had taught public international law, international criminal law, international human rights, and ethnic conflict—about her sexual assault, he "laughed in my face." Our office wouldn't touch this narrative thread with a ten-foot pole. If the lawsuit is real, the press will report it, we told ourselves. They never did.

We debated endlessly about how to handle the incoming. There was no easy answer. According to Judy's interview notes, some of what Charlotte was saying to the *Times* was an exaggerated version of what she previously said. Other parts matched up but lacked critical context. Others were wildly out of step with anything she had said previously.

It was one thing to dispute Lindsey, a political candidate and disgruntled former employee with an ax to grind whose claims were provably false. It was another to respond to Charlotte, a twenty-five-year-old sexual assault victim. There was no right way to engage in the press, and after a long debate, we decided we wouldn't try. The only way to handle it was through a high-level statement from the governor himself—one that could in no way be perceived as attacking or undermining Charlotte—and appointing an independent investigator to lead a review of her claims. Everyone in the office, including the governor, would cooperate.

> Ms. Bennett was a hardworking and valued member of our team during COVID. She has every right to speak out. When she came to me and opened up about being a sexual assault survivor and how it shaped her and her ongoing efforts to create an organization that empowered her voice to help other survivors, I tried to be supportive and helpful. Ms. Bennett's initial impression was right: I was trying to be a mentor to her. I never made advances toward Ms. Bennett, nor did I ever intend to act in any way that was inappropriate. The last thing I would ever have wanted was to make her feel any of the things that are being reported. This situation cannot and should not be resolved in the press; I believe the best way to get to the truth is through a full and thorough outside review, and I am directing all state employees to comply with that effort. I ask all New Yorkers to await the findings of the review so that they know the facts before making any judgments. I will have no further comment until the review has concluded.

We tapped Barbara Jones, a former district judge of the US District Court for the Southern District of New York, whose credentials and reputation were unimpeachable, to lead the review. The rest would play out on the merits, and we would go back to getting vaccines in arms.

We had a plan.

Or so we thought.

Almost immediately after we announced Judge Jones's appointment, one by one, members of the legislature took to social media to reject her. She wasn't credible, they maintained, because years earlier she had worked for the same law firm as Steve Cohen, Cuomo's first secretary. They claimed the overlap in employment created a conflict of interest that disqualified Jones. It's worth noting that, despite Judge Jones not being good enough for the august New York State legislature, Merrick Garland would later propose her to serve as special master for DOJ's Mar-a-Lago/Trump probe. Tish James herself would select Jones to serve as monitor of the Trump Organization during her civil investigation into the president and his children. The legislature's position wasn't rooted in principle; it was a political maneuver to ensure Tish James would be in charge.

At the same time, we received word that Tish James and her staff were busy organizing and executing. Tish wanted to be in charge of the investigation, and she was going to make sure that was how it ended up. I picked up the phone and called the assembly and senate chiefs of staff with one message: we will literally take any lawyer in New York to oversee this investigation except for Tish James.

Even before the nursing home report, the governor never trusted Tish. While I had believed there were benefits to linking arms with her, he was wary of her political alignments and history.

"Go slowly, Melissa," Cuomo had cautioned when I first floated the idea of possibly recruiting her to our ticket. "We don't really know Tish, and she's a product of the Working Families Party and the Clarence Norman Brooklyn machine. Don't get out over your skis until we really vet this and think it through."

Tish was known for her close ties to Clarence Norman, then the Democrats' Brooklyn party boss, who ruled Kings County politics with an iron fist—that is, until he went to jail for accepting illegal campaign contributions. According to an article published in the *Brooklyn Paper*, "James had earned Norman's loyalty as an election attorney specializing in getting insurgent Democratic candidates kicked off the ballot." Since then, she had cozied up to the far-left Working Families Party, winning her first election to City Council with their exclusive backing. Politically, it appeared, she had been beholden to them ever since.

There were other bizarre things about her, too. While she was a councilwoman, Tish walked into a trailer hitch attached to the back of a parked car. She responded by suing the owner of the car, a day laborer, claiming the incident caused "serious, severe, and permanent [injuries] to her limbs and body." The laborer made one-tenth of Tish's salary, and the trailer hitch was legal. The suit was dropped.

Tish was also caught lying with abandon about easily provable things—big and small. For example, in 2013, she told the *Wall Street Journal* she was fifty years old when she was, in fact, fifty-four. In 2014, after the *New York Times* ran a five-part feature on an eleven-year-old homeless girl, Tish claimed she had brought the child to the paper's attention. The *New York Times* publicly refuted her. When asked, in her debate when she ran for Attorney General in 2018, about when she was last in court, she said September, "When I argued before the federal court on behalf of residents of public housing." She didn't argue the case. Despite having reported on all of this, in 2021 the press looked the other way, instead reconstructing a narrative around Tish James "the crusader" who took on powerful interests in the face of adversity. There was one reason why: Donald Trump. As Tish pursued a civil case against Donald Trump, in the eyes of the liberal media—particularly MSNBC and the *New York Times*—she could do no wrong. She was doing their bidding and was sainted in the process. Now that she was going after Cuomo, that principle extended to the far-right *New York Post* and Fox News as well.

More than anything, though, Cuomo always reminded me that Tish couldn't be trusted because of how she had come into our orbit. In 2018, when Cuomo was running in a primary against actress Cynthia Nixon, the far-left Working Families Party—Cuomo's political nemesis—endorsed Nixon's campaign. We were confident that we would easily defeat Nixon (which we later did by more than thirty points), but Cuomo and I were concerned about the possibility that the Working Families Party, a minor third party with outsized sway, would keep Nixon on their ballot line. Doing so could potentially create a situation where Nixon got a small piece of the Democratic vote, inadvertently helping the Republican candidate and possibly even electing a Republican governor. Faced with this possibility, we decided to approach Tish James.

Eric Schneiderman had just resigned as Attorney General, creating an open seat just six months before Election Day. Five candidates threw their hats into the ring, including Tish. The race was wide open, and Tish, while popular among the far-left wing in certain parts of the city, was not known statewide and was certainly not revered for her legal background. But we saw a political opportunity in her. The governor picked up the phone and called Tish's top political consultant, Luis Miranda, father of famed Broadway actor Lin-Manuel Miranda. The two discussed the possibility of an alliance: Cuomo would personally work at the upcoming convention to ensure Tish got the Democratic Party endorsement for attorney general, and Tish would refuse to take the Working Families Party line until *after* the primary and only when they endorsed Cuomo.

"There's no way she'll take that deal," I said to Cuomo when he raised the notion to me. "The WFP brought her to the dance. They are her political benefactors. There's no way she would do that to them."

Two days later, Tish, her chief of staff, Ibrahim Khan, Cuomo, and I were in the back room at Docks, having lunch and sealing the deal.

When we got back up to the governor's office on the thirty-ninth floor, Cuomo looked at me across the desk, "And that is why you can't trust anyone in this business," he said in a teachable moment.

Two years later, with that conversation reverberating through my mind, I was convinced. "Ibrahim was involved!" I said on a call with the governor and some of our legal team. "He was talking to Lindsey's campaign manager since she started making her claims on Twitter. The same campaign manager that was Tish's own consultant in her campaign last year! I'm sure they've been talking all along. How do they not have to recuse on this?"

While I was fixated on the ethics of Tish being involved, Cuomo was focused on the politics. Tish had refused to publicly or privately disavow her own rumored intentions to run against Cuomo for governor the following year. But that didn't matter. She had rallied her allies in the legislature.

"Huh?" The governor asked when I relayed the pushback I was getting. "I don't want Tish because of *what*?" he asked in disbelief.

"She has them saying that you are not choosing her because she's a Black woman." They were leaning into identity politics to get us to back down from picking someone other than Tish to do the investigation, and it was working.

We were boxed in. In a last-ditch effort, we tried to figure out a way to circle the square. Cuomo got Tish on the phone with a new proposal: the chief judge of the Court of Appeals would partner with Tish to oversee the investigation. At least, that way, there would be a neutral check on the process. On the spot, Tish agreed. Within minutes, I had a statement drafted announcing the arrangement and out the door. Five minutes later, Ibrahim told Rob Mujica they were backing out of the agreement. I pushed back, telling Rob that if Ibrahim had something to say to me, he should call me himself. Five minutes after that, my phone rang.

"I'm sorry, Melissa, this construct doesn't work for us," he said flatly.

"Ibrahim, it's too late. Tish gave the governor her word, and the statement is already out the door to the press," I countered.

"Tish hadn't spoken to her staff yet, and now that we've discussed, she agrees that it needs to be her and her alone doing the investigation. We are about to issue our own statement to the press saying what you just announced is untenable."

"I'm sorry, Ibrahim, who is the attorney general here, Tish James or Luis Miranda?" I said, believing this change of heart had been the influence of her outside consultants, who we thought were pushing her to run for governor.

"Ibrahim, I'm going to ask this question again: Is Tish going to say publicly she is not running for governor? Because I don't trust you," I said pointedly.

More silence.

I hung up the phone and called back the top aides for the assembly and senate. If they were okay with the arrangement with the chief judge, we wouldn't back down. But when I called, it was too late: they were in the tank. Both the senate leader and the assembly speaker publicly agreed that the investigation had to be led by Tish and Tish alone. And if we wouldn't do it, the assembly would immediately move to take up impeachment proceedings against the governor. With a gun to our head, we caved. The governor called James back, and the two agreed to two conditions: one, given her obvious conflict, Tish would not be involved in the investigation, and two, she would appoint truly independent reviewers to lead it, specifically stipulating there would be no plaintiff's attorneys chosen. Cuomo was opposed to a plaintiff's attorney for an obvious reason: someone whose business depended on fighting for accusers would approach a complaint from that perspective, and seek to build a one-sided case rather than objectively reviewing facts to reach a fair-minded conclusion. James agreed.

Minutes later, standing in the living room of the mansion with the governor, Stephanie, and the governor's brother-in-law Brian

O'Donoghue looking on, my phone rang. It was Tish. I didn't know what to expect.

"Hello?"

"Melissa, you have to calm down and trust people," Tish dove in, her voice almost maternal.

"Madam Attorney General, I'm sorry, but this entire thing is crazy," I interjected. "And, no, I don't trust you."

"Melissa, I was at an event yesterday. So many people came up to me and said Lindsey Boylan is not credible," she responded. "She is not credible. On the Charlotte Bennett thing, it is just words. Listen, I will talk to you on the side. I will be engaged with you back and forth," she attempted to reassure me.

I paused in stunned silence.

"Melissa, I'm worried about you. You are not sleeping. That's how you made that mistake in the meeting on nursing homes. It's not like you to misspeak. You misspoke because you haven't slept in a year. And I am worried about you. You have to find a way to trust people."

I reflexively launched back, "First of all, that's *not* what I said in the room on nursing homes. The *Post* took half of one sentence out of context and ruined my life. And everyone in that room knows that's not what I said," I continued. "And, yes, I agree, Lindsey Boylan isn't credible, and I think this entire thing is crazy."

"It's going to be okay," Tish promised, "and I need you to trust that it's going to be okay."

I offered a noncommittal "Okay" before we hung up.

"What was that?" Cuomo wanted to know.

"I need to call Elkan and Judy," I said, naming two of our lawyers. "That conversation. It almost feels like that was a setup. Like she was recording me. There was something fucked up about that."

I recounted exactly what had happened and what Tish James had said. Repeating it out loud made it seem even more absurd that an attorney general would be calling and unambiguously reassuring the very office whose actions she was supposed to now be leading an independent review into. *Barbara Jones was conflicted out, but Tish James was the ethical, nonconflicted answer?*

"They're involved in this," I said. I couldn't prove it. But I believed it to my core.

In 2019, pre-pandemic, Tish and I had met for drinks at a restaurant near the attorney general's office in lower Manhattan. I had an agenda, and she was happy to entertain what was on my mind.

"Madam Attorney General, I really think you should consider throwing your hat in the ring for mayor next year," I said, after taking a sip of my Sancerre. Tish's eyes lit up. I could tell she was flattered.

"I appreciate that, Melissa, but I've barely been attorney general for a year. How would it look if I started running for a new job already?"

"I get it," I responded. "It would be a gamble. But you could keep your current job while running for mayor. If you lose, you're still AG. It's a win-win proposition," I said, pushing back.

"I appreciate that, Melissa. Really. But I'm going to sit tight for the time being," she responded, taking a sip of the ice water in front of her.

"Well, can't blame a girl for trying," I joked, ready to move on to the next topic. "Besides, with Eric Adams in the race, it would make winning difficult for you anyway." Adams and James were both from vote-rich Kings County, and it was a common belief that, if they both ran, they would split the Brooklyn vote, likely helping to elect someone else altogether. As the words fell out of my mouth, Tish's face turned sour. I had hit a competitive nerve.

"Oh, Melissa, Eric Adams wouldn't be a concern," she said with a half smirk.

"Alright, you've got my attention," I said. "What do you know that I don't?"

"Let's just say Eric Adams has baggage. The female kind," she said, proud of herself. There have never been any allegations made against Adams, and I have no reason to believe what Tish was intimating was true, then or now. But what Tish James did know is that claims of any kind involving women are explosive. After Harvey Weinstein, there was rightly no tolerance for any abuse. The Democratic political establishment did not tolerate even an accusation. The political pressure was too intense. This allowed sexual-harassment allegations to be used as political weapons, an effective tactic to kill a political opponent. And Tish James knew that, on that day in 2019.

And she knew it now.

CHAPTER 22

Media Circus

BEFORE THE TRAIN EVEN BEGAN TO LEAVE THE STATION, IT WAS off the tracks. The governor and Tish had agreed that the investigation would be overseen by truly independent lawyers, experts in their field—and specifically no plaintiff's attorneys, whom we felt would be inclined to approach it like a trial and build a case rather than conduct an impartial probe. We wanted an honest review, a fact-driven report. Days later, we learned we would get anything but. Tish named her choices: Anne Clark, the head of a plaintiff's firm in New York City that specializes in representing women against employers in sexual-harassment cases, and Joon Kim, a former Southern District US attorney who spent years unsuccessfully trying to tie Cuomo to a bid-rigging and bribery case against one of his former top aides (in May 2023, the US Supreme Court voided the conviction in a unanimous decision).

That night, we contemplated our next move. An outside adviser we consulted with urged us to pull the plug: "This is going to be a hit job. Pull back the investigative authority. Do it now," he urged. But after a lengthy internal debate, we determined it would be legally murky, would create a wave of negative press, and would provoke the legislature into expediting impeachment. The better path forward, we decided, was to rebuild our political standing with individual legislators and the public. If we had their support, we reasoned, we could withstand whatever Tish threw at us in the report.

Andrew Cuomo approaches challenges and threats tactically instead of emotionally, seeing three moves down the chessboard, calmly thinking in terms of what to do next, and then next, and then next. He remained singularly focused on the demands of his job—keep managing COVID, get vaccine shots in arms, focus on infrastructure projects, make sure the government was functioning—and just kept moving steadfastly forward.

At that point, there were two allegations against the governor: Lindsey and Charlotte. That number was about to explode. In the race to be next, the media ran with every allegation being thrown around, no matter how thin, each time notching another number of "accusers" against the governor and painting him to the public as a serial sexual harasser.

"Melissa, the *Times* is calling. They say they have a third accuser," Rich said, his voice panicked.

"What? Who?" I asked, my heart beating faster.

"I don't know. Some guest at a wedding he officiated? When he was working the room, he touched her face and then lower back when they posed for a photo and kissed her on the cheek?"

"I'm sorry, what?" I responded, my vitals normalizing. "Jesus Christ, Rich, I thought you were saying this is sexual harassment or something. I was at that wedding. So were three hundred other people. Including reporters. This is Joe Biden stuff. Shark jumping," I continued. "And you can't possibly mean the *Times*; you meant the *Post* right?"

"No, Melissa, the *New York Times*—and they are going big with it. They're framing it like it's a third accuser," he responded.

The next morning, March 1, the *New York Times* ran that story. On the front page. (They would later hire that woman, Anna Ruch, as a photo editor.)

Next up, we were on to Howard Glaser's wife, Karen Hinton. Karen worked as Cuomo's press secretary in the late '90s when he was serving as HUD secretary; her husband, Howard Glaser, also worked for Cuomo then. To say the three had a complicated relationship would be a gross understatement.

When Cuomo became New York's attorney general and threatened to sue oil giant Chevron for financial fraud, the *New York Times* published an email from Karen Hinton, then a lobbyist for the impacted Ecuadorian villagers, taking credit for the governor's action. "Andrew has no interest in doing this," Karen boasted to her client. "He is doing this for me. Because I asked."

When Cuomo was elected governor, he hired Glaser to serve as state operations director but demurred over the years when Hinton expressed interest in coming on board.

Glaser left the administration in 2014, and the wheels officially fell off the wagon. Cuomo was hypersensitive to optics and the press, and Howard was auditioning for jobs in the private sector for industries that did a tremendous amount of business before the state. Cuomo let it be known through intermediaries that he thought it was a bad idea. Glaser believed Cuomo was trying to sabotage his financial success. The two stopped talking altogether. Karen ended up working as press secretary for de Blasio, relishing taking personal and professional shots at Cuomo in the media, making an already tense relationship between the mayor and the governor worse. Cuomo would vent to de Blasio about her behavior. Howard perceived it as threatening, sending me text missives to that effect. At one point, none of us were talking to each other.

All of that changed in November 2017 after Karen suffered a severe brain injury from falling off of a treadmill. It was then that Howard reached back out, desperate to get his wife the best possible medical care. Cuomo readily helped. It had been an uneasy truce since. Just before COVID, Karen penned a personal letter to Cuomo: "I want to thank you once again for helping Howard with my medical needs and supporting me through my recovery." She went on to say, "You created a more than useful bar for me to jump over when I worked for you in the '90s. I always have wanted to adhere to the lessons learned. Sometimes I have done that, and sometimes I haven't."

I had heard from Karen steadily throughout the pandemic, receiving emails from her asking for Cuomo's help to prop up a client of hers, Mike Espy, who was running for US Senate from Mississippi. Karen also volunteered to aid in our COVID response; we passed on the offer.

Never a shrinking violet, Hinton had previously publicly accused Bill Clinton of hitting on her back in the '90s when he was president and she was a press aide at HUD. In 2018, at the height of the #MeToo era, unprovoked and unprompted, Hinton had published an op-ed in the *Daily News* saying, "I've been fortunate to have male bosses, like Andrew Cuomo and Bill de Blasio, who know how to be respectful of women even while being no-nonsense managers." But that was then, and this was now, and now she was peddling a book. This time, she didn't go back to the *Daily News*, but instead dialed a reporter at the *Washington Post*. Her complaint? A hug that was "very long, too long, too tight, too intimate" from twenty years earlier. Finding out that Karen Hinton was involved further fueled my theory that there was a political setup underway. *Fourth accuser.*

That same night, the next to come forward was Howard Glaser's assistant, Ana Liss, in the *Wall Street Journal*: six years earlier, Cuomo had allegedly called her "sweetheart" and "darling" and put his arm around her waist, while posing for a photo at a staff reception. The photo was framed and still displayed on her desk when the *Journal* interviewed her for the article. She hadn't worked for the state government since 2015. She also said she wasn't harassed. Liss and Hinton would appear on a radio show together. Reporters did not question or find it odd that Glaser's wife *and* his former assistant were simultaneously making claims the same night in the press. *Fifth accuser.*

On Monday morning, March 8, I was making my usual staff calls to get up to speed before heading to the capitol, which at that point bizarrely included checking in with a host of lawyers. But neither Beth Garvey nor Judy Mogul was answering. I decided to try another one of our lawyers before hopping in the shower, and dialed our trusted long-time outside counsel, Elkan Abramowitz.

"Hey, Elkan, just checking in. I can't get anyone. What's going on?" I asked tentatively.

"Oh, well, you heard about the other accuser . . ."

"Wait, what?"

"Yeah, apparently it's a sexual *assault* accuser."

"*What?*"

Elkan suddenly realized I hadn't heard. "Okay, let me hang up. Judy Mogul should really be the one to tell you this," he said.

I disconnected the call and heard my phone clatter to the floor. My hands were shaking. I fought to catch my breath as a panic attack took hold. My sister hurried in to check on me.

My phone started ringing on the bathroom counter; Judy was calling me back.

"Judy, what is going on?" I asked.

Judy resisted; the sensitive nature of the allegations meant the matter needed to be managed away from me. But I wasn't taking no for an answer.

"Judy, I am secretary to the governor. What the fuck is going on?"

As eventually would become public, an aide named Brittany Commisso had confided in my assistant, Farrah, over cocktails at a birthday party the Saturday night before, that the governor had assaulted her. What Farrah described to Judy was violent. The governor had allegedly thrown Brittany up against the wall in the office on the second floor of the mansion, kissed her, and reached under her blouse, groping her breast. The following day, together with Farrah and our other assistant, Tracy, Brittany hired an attorney, a personal injury attorney.

My mind was reeling. Just before Christmas, Brittany had confided in Stephanie that she was going through a divorce and would need more flexibility in her work schedule in order to care for her child, whom she had custody of. Days later, she asked Stephanie and me for a raise to help make ends meet. In the same conversation, she said working with the governor was her "dream job" and she "couldn't wait to get out of bed and come to work every morning." None of it made sense.

"Judy, I'm sorry, I don't believe this," I said. "I know him."

As was later made public, the incident would be reported to the police and to the attorney general's office.

After not returning calls for a day, the lawyer for Brittany Commisso quickly walked back crucial parts of the story. She claimed she "didn't tell Farrah and Tracy" that the governor had kissed her or thrown her up against the wall, but continued to maintain that, in the middle of the afternoon, with a house full of mansion staff on-site, for the first time in his life, Andrew Cuomo forcibly groped someone. Commisso was not interested in talking to the police, but instead sought to preserve her ability to bring a civil suit against the governor at some point.

On March 9, the *Times Union* ran a brief piece about a young aide allegedly being groped by the governor. Cuomo vehemently denied the allegation. No details were provided, and the aide was not identified.

So now there were six.

On March 12, an op-ed ran in *New York* magazine from journalist Jessica Bakeman, who alleged Cuomo grabbed her hand during a holiday party at the executive mansion in 2014 and put his hand around her waist for a photograph. *Seventh accuser.*

But my attention that day was more riveted by a piece in *Politico*: Three far-left New York State legislators, including Alessandra Biaggi, had been caught convening in an open chat room on the social media platform Clubhouse. "How do we make it impossible for our governor to ever run again?" One asked.

Alessandra Biaggi had an answer: they would need "a motherfucking army."

From the looks of it, the infantry was still in the process of mustering, but it felt like an undeclared war was well underway regardless. Like children on a sugar high, the legislature reacted to any press story, regardless of its merits or severity, and threw it into the pile for investigation for potential impeachment.

The *Times Union* ran a story about broken bolts on the Mario M. Cuomo Bridge a whistle blower had reported in 2016. The issue had been addressed and settled, and the bridge was tested by state and federal authorities repeatedly for years before it was open to the public. The bridge is and always has been safe. *Impeach him!*

The *Washington Post* reported that members of the Cuomo family had received priority COVID testing during the spring of 2020. Members of the legislature, their staff, and their family members had received the same treatment. So had members of the press. *Impeach him!*

Accusers were being blatantly recruited, and everyday interactions were being weaponized. But how it played out was baffling: Boylan's political campaign and Charlotte's conversations with the governor were intertwined improbably with the single serious assault allegation—Brittany Commisso's—while truth vanished in the haze. There was no longer any distinction between comments or complaints or claims or crimes. Each "accuser" was given a number regardless of the magnitude of their assertion, and with no proof.

At the same time, Lindsey Boylan was running an aggressive offensive strategy, labeling the governor "Andrew 'rape culture king' Cuomo" on Twitter and working overtime to silence skeptics. Boylan took to social media and email, issuing threats to some questioning her story and, in certain instances, identifying and calling their employers in an attempt to get them fired. I know because one of the people whose jobs she threatened—a prominent photographer—DM'd me directly on Twitter, pleading for help. Current and former staff weren't spared Boylan's wrath. When she wasn't publicly attacking them on Twitter, she was sending email missives about their character and integrity, including texting a former colleague who ignored one of her overtures: "I hope your lack of courage was worth it. You had a friend in me for life, but now you don't, bitch. Good luck." While some of this played out privately, plenty of it was on full display on Boylan's public Twitter feed. Neither investigators nor a single reporter questioned or covered it. Instead she was treated as a wronged truth-teller.

The *Times Union* deleted a story on its website from December in which they had originally reported on the truth behind Lindsey's departure from the office, and reporters who had, just months ago, agreed it was important context had changed their tune. No one could be questioned. To scrutinize was to victimize or smear.

Since the initial and long-overdue reckoning in 2017, the #MeToo movement had evolved. What had started with Harvey Weinstein raping and coercing women into having sex in exchange for starring roles on the silver screen became about Aziz Ansari's date that had gone wrong. It took all interactions—big and small—and put them in the same category. There was no difference between a crude or off-color comment and assault or rape; the single penalty was evenly applied, regardless of the severity of the claim: execution. Reporters' careers had been made off unearthing a complaint and putting heads on walls; it had become a blood sport for them. An allegation was as good as a guilty verdict in the court of public opinion and, when weaponized properly, destroyed the lives, livelihoods, and reputations of anyone in its path, along with their families. In the quest for the moral high ground, politicians—Democratic ones anyway—did not have patience for due process or nuance. And this was politics. In New York, our congressional delegation was headed by Chuck Schumer and Kirsten Gillibrand, two Democrats largely responsible for the offing of their colleague Al Franken on a handful of claims in 2017 that went uninvestigated.

I knew how it could play out all too well—I had, after all, taken a hard line and personally intervened to advise the governor to call for Attorney General Eric Schneiderman's resignation in the wake of his own #MeToo scandal two years earlier. While the governor was reluctant to call for his removal before a proper investigation could take place, I was insistent.

It was at that moment, staring down a primary against celebrity newcomer Cynthia Nixon, that I advised my current boss to stab my former boss in the front.

"Governor, you are in a primary—a primary against a woke female candidate," I exclaimed. "You can't wait for her to say it. You need to say it first, and you have to say it with force."

"Melissa, we don't even know the facts. At this point, all we have is a *New Yorker* story that is thirty minutes old," he responded, uneasy with my counsel.

"Governor, you have a Ronan Farrow story; it claims four women were physically assaulted by the sitting attorney general of the state of New York. And he's not denying it. He's attempting to contextualize it. You are a champion for women. You have no choice but to call for his resignation."

"Melissa, he was your boss. What do you think about all of this?" the governor asked, honestly wanting to know. I had worked as Eric's acting chief of staff before the governor persuaded me to leave the attorney general's office to join the Cuomo administration back in 2013.

"It doesn't matter what I think," I responded without hesitation. "The best thing I can advise you to do is to act quickly and decisively. Otherwise, you'll be playing catch-up with a woman on a women's issue in the middle of a primary," I responded, sure of myself.

Within three hours of the story's publication, Schneiderman resigned, ultimately ending his career and inadvertently elevating the current attorney general, Tish James, to the position. Years later, I would find out that Ronan Farrow had given Eric only a few hours to respond to his litany of career-ending claims and that, according to Schneiderman, there had been at least some exculpatory evidence and important context that hadn't seen the light of day in his story. Whether it fully mitigated the circumstances or not, the world will never know. Eric, and those who voted for him, weren't afforded that due process.

The claims being made against the governor weren't in the same stratosphere as the ones lodged against Schneiderman or Weinstein, but to the press it was all the same. And I was about to break the cardinal rule of the #MeToo era.

When asked about the allegations trickling out at a televised press conference, I requested that the public withhold judgment until the investigation was concluded and further expressed how proud I was to be part of an administration that had worked tirelessly to expand protections and strengthen rights for women in and outside of the workplace. I wasn't toeing the #MeToo party line, and I was about to become the subject of its ire. Their message was clear: If you defend him, we are coming after you, too. First it came in the form of an electronic billboard that popped up in Albany the next day on the interstate off-ramp nearest the capitol. The garish fuchsia sign featured my name in giant block letters: MELISSA DEROSA, ARE YOU PROUD OF CUOMO'S WORK + ACTION?

My young nieces drove past it, nearly every day.

The circus didn't stop there.

The *Daily Mail* called with photos of the governor and me from 2016 at a restaurant in Greenwich village. The photos, they claimed, showed the governor with his hand on my thigh, "working all the way up." I knew about the photos they were referencing. They were the same ones someone tried, unsuccessfully, to sell to the *Daily News* during the height of the governor's 2018 reelection campaign. I knew because a reporter there told me about them at the time. What they actually showed was the two of us sitting three feet apart in a booth, his hand nowhere near my thigh.

The *New York Post*'s Page Six ran a piece littered with vague allegations of inappropriate relationships between the governor and women on the senior staff. Based on the rumors she pushed to investigators in her testimony, it's clear that Lindsey Boylan's fingerprints were all over it. "A female staffer spent the night at Cuomo and [his partner] Sandra Lee's home in Mount Kisco." Never happened. "Cuomo and a female aide had connecting rooms for an overnight trip to Israel." It was a day trip, and the rooms were across the hall from each other. "Senior women would sleep at the mansion after 'female movie nights.'" They were coed senior staff movie and dinner nights when everyone was stuck in Albany, and no one slept over. In the article, Ana Liss, Howard Glaser's assistant—a junior staffer in her mid-twenties who rarely interacted with the governor—was presented by the *New York Post* as an expert on the governor's relationship with his former live-in girlfriend; she was quoted throughout the piece, discussing how often the two were together, as if she would have had any insight whatsoever into their personal lives.

Sexual misconduct wasn't the only show on the media circus. The whole "toxic workplace" theme had shared billing. And I was in the spotlight as well as the governor.

"Ugh, Missy, this *New York* magazine story." It was Sam Katze, one of my closest friends from college, on the phone.

"How bad is it?" I asked, admitting I couldn't stomach looking at it myself.

In a 9,000-word cover story, self-described feminist Rebecca Traister focused on the "cruelty and casualties" of the governor's office, railing about "toxic masculinity," the "brute white patriarchy," and "hierarchical power."

"Well, the upshot is you're a mean girl, but at least you're a mean girl with nice legs," Sam relayed, trying to make light of the situation.

"Wait . . . she talks about *my legs*?" So now self-described feminist journalists railing against Cuomo's alleged objectification of women were objectifying me? What the actual fuck was going on?

"Yeah, there's a comment in there from this woman Ana Liss, who says that you had legs everywhere," Sam verified. This was the same Ana Liss who had admitted to the *Wall Street Journal* weeks earlier that, when she worked for Cuomo, "She didn't have many dealings with Ms. DeRosa, who at the time was Mr. Cuomo's director of communications."

I was furious. "I'm secretary to the governor! I have two degrees from Cornell University. I manage the state government. And Rebecca fucking Traister is quoting some junior staffer I never met talking about my legs! Are you fucking kidding me?"

She wasn't. The full quote from Liss was actually worse: "Melissa DeRosa had Louboutins, and there were legs everywhere, and I just felt stupid."

Traister's story was a well-orchestrated hit piece, giving carte blanche to a litany of far-left, longtime political adversaries, including Alessandra Biaggi, her allies associated with the Working Families Party, and a handful of former employees steered to her by Lindsey Boylan. (One of Boylan's campaign workers was featured prominently by Traister without being identified as working on Boylan's campaign at the same time, while both Kaitlin and Ana Liss testified that Lindsey had sent them to Traister.)

It was clear that Traister had not made any attempt to vet or verify the claims made by those she interviewed, as evidenced by the fact that they were the same people she said commented on the "extreme pressure applied by both the governor and his top female aides to dress well and expensively; some were told explicitly by senior staff that they had to wear heels whenever he was around." It was the *only* claim the attorney general's report definitively knocked down months later, saying, "We found that expectations for women related to wearing dresses or high heels were not at the direction of the Governor or his senior staff." Traister relied heavily on Ana Liss, who made sweeping statements, some she was not in a position to verify and others contradicted in Traister's own story, including when she said, "His [Cuomo's] briefers were always beautiful, leggy young women right out of college." Bizarrely, Traister included this claim in the same article, which begins with a quote from a former male Cuomo briefer, who was identified as taking the job "straight from his position in Barack Obama's White House."

It was disgusting. Traister took at face value the assertion of her dubious, mostly anonymous sources that Cuomo and our staff put a premium on hiring only attractive, preferably young, women. When, in fact, virtually all of our senior staff was made up of some of the most accomplished, hardest-working, and most effective women in government in the country. These were positions they had earned, not because of their gender or appearance, but because they were the most qualified. All day long, my phone pinged with texts from former and current staff—male and female—venting their indignation: This is such horseshit.

The theme of Cuomo as a hot-tempered bully had surfaced for years in profiles of him by political rivals, but now it was intertwined with the sexual-harassment allegations. Boylan was out to make Cuomo

Albany's Harvey Weinstein, and thanks to the lack of rigor, nuance, or journalistic integrity in the media's reporting, it was working. At one point, Boylan had actually given Jesse McKinley at the *New York Times* a quote he planned to publish making the direct comparison—that is, until I got on the phone with his female editor.

"Harvey Weinstein *raped* women. Do you understand how insane this is?" I implored, my voice rising. She did, and the quote was never published, but Boylan's press squad had found their stenographer in Rebecca Traister and succeeded in landing their punch.

The subtheme, per *New York* magazine, was that I was an office bully, too. What had been the name of a text thread ("Mean Girls"), given by a junior male staffer as a joke for a few months in 2016, suddenly defined me in the press. Nicknames that are not literal sometimes exist in offices. For example, the man overseeing the investigation into Cuomo, Joon Kim, and his best friend, Preet Bharara, were referred to as Harold and Kumar when they worked together in the Southern District of New York's US Attorney's Office, a nickname I'm sure the two would contend was a joke, unless, of course, they were prosecuting people stoned (alternatively, maybe it explained why so many of their high-profile convictions were later overturned on appeal).

But that didn't matter. I was Cuomo's chief "mean girl," the second-in-command, overseeing what Traister presented to readers as a political sweatshop. Never mind that I was the architect of our administration's campaigns to pass the $15 minimum wage, the nation's strongest paid-family-leave policy, and the first-ever, four-year free public college tuition program. Forget that I unabashedly and unapologetically used my position to take on issues that matter to me and women like me, not writing about but actually delivering on a wide range of policy priorities, including maternal health, insurance coverage of in vitro fertilization, the Child Victims Act, and seed money for female-run venture capital funds. Nope. Traister took the assessment of a handful of low- to mid-level employees who hadn't worked in our office in years and used it to take careful aim as she assassinated my character and my motivations on behalf of women. And it worked.

I had been reduced to a caricature—looking past and not acknowledging a female coworker in the bathroom. Being vilified for firing off emails to a junior staffer from 6:00 a.m. until 11:00 p.m. and then reintroducing myself to that person the next day. Being defined by the shoes I wore. Traister reduced the blood, sweat, and tears of my twenty-two years in politics and government to a sexist trope, while simultaneously feigning outrage about sexism and toxicity. She did this without ever once requesting an interview with me. The truth, I realized, is that, as it turns out, women can be just as sexist as men.

Like many professional women who rise through the ranks of male-dominated industries, I have been labeled all my life. I've been called a bitch, referred to as having "queen bee syndrome," and been whispered about for having an affair with almost every male boss I have ever worked for. As Cuomo's communications director, I was labeled "Mario Jr.'s PR whore" on social media. Since the first story was written about me, I was labeled "daughter of" an Albany lobbyist. When I got married, it shifted to "wife of" an Uber executive. Now, at the pinnacle of my career, after the world had witnessed firsthand my ability to quote the state constitution chapter and verse, recall arcane facts and statistics, and manage the state government through a pandemic, I had a new label: mean girl. My top qualification: my shoes and legs.

It's true. I am not made of candy glass. Politics ain't beanbag, and if people believe they can push you around, they will. I have gone toe-to-toe with elected officials, union leaders, reporters, CEOs, and advocates. For years, I slept with not one, but two phones on my bedside table and was available to anyone who called, day or night. I worked every minute my eyes were open, and my personal relationships suffered as a result. I wasn't particularly great with names and faces; while I worked in politics, I wasn't a politician, and I was there to do a job. I picked plenty of fights and didn't back down from them. I have taken every job I ever had seriously. And I did those jobs wearing whatever shoes or clothes I chose (which often included jeans and white Converse sneakers), and not because I'm influenced by or insecure about what other women or men are wearing.

Was our office a demanding work environment? Absolutely. Was I a demanding boss? You bet your ass. But I never pushed anyone harder than I pushed myself. And just like the senior staff did, just like I did, just like the governor did, young staffers worked around the clock. Our team was most definitely not a good career choice if you prized work-life balance. The state of New York doesn't grind to a halt at 5:00 p.m. then fire back up again at 9:00 a.m.; natural disasters don't care about your vacation schedule. Neither do terrorists planting bombs in the New York City subway or once-in-a-lifetime pandemics. And round-the-clock budget negotiations are just that. What nobody wrote, because nobody sought out the other side, was that many of us found the work fulfilling and the sense of duty honorable. I felt—and knew, from my friendships with many coworkers, that they also felt—wholly committed to getting the job done, even knowing that came at the expense of sacrificing certain parts of my personal life.

But now, in the midst of the media circus that was unfolding, all that I had worked for, all that I had accomplished, all that I had given up—my identity—was being taken from me.

On March 19, a tweet from another reporter, Valerie Bauman, was posted. In 2007, Cuomo made "unwavering eye contact" during a press conference before he "beelined" for her, "took [her] hand, entered [her] personal space, and looked into [her] eyes as he said, "Hello, I'm Andrew Cuomo." *Eighth accuser.*

On the same day, an aide named Alyssa McGrath (Brittany Commisso's best friend) told the *New York Times* that the governor ogled her from across a desk, said something to her in Italian that she didn't understand but believed referenced her looks, and called her and Commisso "mingle mamas." *Ninth accuser.*

On March 29, a press conference was held by Sherry Vill, a woman from Rochester, New York, and her lawyer, Gloria Allred, to speak out against an incident when Cuomo kissed her on both cheeks while touring her house assessing flood damage and meeting affected residents. Her son took a picture of the interaction, which Vill herself posted on Facebook years earlier. *Tenth accuser.*

In the midst of the insanity, I sought out a friend. Nick Confessore knew I needed to see a friendly face and invited me to his apartment for dinner. He cared about *me*. Wanted to make sure I was okay. We talked about Matt and COVID. How hard the last year had been, the toll it had taken on me. And we talked about what was going on around my administration. The nursing homes, the *New York* magazine piece, the harassment allegations.

That's when I turned to Nick and said, "It's not lost on me that the *Times* has Jesse McKinley driving the train on all of this." There was plenty of buzz in Albany about the irony that McKinley had become the "go-to" reporter for sexual-harassment claims. Stories abounded about how he comported himself with reporters, elected officials, and junior staffers. I kept thinking back to my own encounter with him the previous May and was offended at the hypocrisy of the *Times* when they had him take the lead on the coverage.

"You know, Melissa," Nick said, "when you told me what happened with Jesse, I told Carolyn Ryan about it at the time."

My mind was officially blown.

"Wait, are you kidding me?" Carolyn Ryan, the managing editor at the *New York Times*, the senior-most female at the paper, had known about what happened with Jesse for *ten months*? "What did you say? What did she say?" I asked in disbelief.

"I told her that Jesse had been very aggressive with you," he responded.

"And?"

"And she said, 'That's terrible for Melissa,'" Nick recounted.

I was dumbfounded.

The *New York Times*, the paper that had been driving the coverage on the sexual-harassment allegations—and that had deemed Andrew Cuomo touching a woman's face while posing for a photo at a wedding

reception front-page news—had not only been told about the aggressive and inappropriate interaction between their Albany bureau chief
and the top female aide to the governor in real time, but did absolutely
nothing about it. While allowing him to cover the administration. For
ten months. And now he was their lead reporter covering a sexual-
harassment story.

Nick had told Carolyn about something I had confided in him
about without asking my permission. But I understood why he felt
compelled to—it spoke to his character. He was told something he
knew was both wrong and consistent with what he had previously
heard about Jesse, and he acted.

The next morning, I called my lawyers.

A few days went by before the New York Times counsel called back.
In that call, the Times's general counsel confirmed the sequence of
events: Nick had told Carolyn Ryan about what had happened with
Jesse ten months earlier. The reason they didn't take any action? Because
it hadn't been reported through official channels.

"The Times is taking the position that because Nick conveyed the
information and not you, that they weren't obligated to do anything
about it," my lawyer relayed, incredulously.

There was a clear conflict of interest—one that was known at the
highest levels at the Times. I also believed I wasn't alone in experiencing his behavior. And it wasn't going to be ignored any longer.

My lawyers responded with a simple letter: "Melissa DeRosa is
making an official complaint against Jesse McKinley for his inappropriate behavior toward her and the New York Times for how they
handled it."

Within days, without explanation, Jesse McKinley quietly disap-
peared from the Albany beat.

CHAPTER 23

Time's Up

WHILE THE MEDIA CIRCUS DIDN'T FOLD ITS TENT, AFTER RELENTLESS coverage for months, the cacophony at least somewhat subsided.

Spring came, and we concentrated on vaccine distribution and reopening New York's badly weakened economy. Announced milestones on major infrastructure projects, like the long-stalled East Side Access at Grand Central Station. Made appointments to the Court of Appeals. A sense of normalcy resumed, while Tish James's investigation rippled beneath the surface of our lives and workdays. But really, the five months between when the investigation started and the beginning of August was just buying time, delaying the inevitable, a protracted and tortured death march. Andrew Cuomo's governorship was over the day we were forced to make the referral to Tish James to oversee the investigation.

I was alone in the big red-brick house where my parents had raised us and where Jessica was now raising her own family; that noisy, safe place, where my once-pink bedroom now belonged to my beloved goddaughter, was silent in the growing heat of a summer morning. Jessica, Jim, and the girls had left weeks earlier to vacation on Cape Cod. It was August 3, a Tuesday. I woke up to a frantic phone call from Rich: The attorney general's office had released a press advisory stating they would be making a major announcement, but they hadn't tipped their hand as to the subject.

I could feel my heart start to beat faster and faster.

"Okay, Rich, don't panic. Let me make some calls," I said, trying my best to exude confidence. "But it's more likely this is something about Trump rather than about us. The governor had just testified two weeks ago, and any investigation worth a damn would have to consider that testimony before issuing a report," I reasoned.

Our legal team maintained that, during an eleven-hour session, the governor had testified to a number of facts and circumstances that would require investigators to follow up and check before reaching any definitive conclusions. Particularly when the stakes are this high, the lawyers assured us. It had been five months since Tish James had launched her probe into three instances of alleged sexual harassment made by Lindsey Boylan, Charlotte Bennett, and Brittany Commisso.

My first call was to our outside counsel. I asked that we attempt to determine whether the AG's announcement had anything to do with us. Standard protocol for state inspector generals and AG investigations on the federal level dictated that our office would be briefed about the report before it was issued. The practice allows the subject the opportunity to raise objections before the issuing of a public report, which always carries the potential to do irreversible damage. Our situation was anything but standard or professional. Over the course of the "investigation," the AG's office had been leaking to the press the entire time, asking questions well outside the scope of the investigation, and were actively fixated on rumor and innuendo. They had an agenda that was clear from the start.

I was warned, "I think we need to prepare ourselves that they won't follow the normal protocol here."

We knew the report was coming, and we knew it was going to be unflattering. Despite threatening anyone who testified with a misdemeanor if we discussed anything we were asked about, Tish's office spent months leaking the contours of the report to the press, damaging the governor's public standing and framing the press's impression of what the report would look like.

My second call was to the governor. "Tish advised a press conference for today," I told him. "The reporters are buzzing that it could be our report, but no one knows anything for sure."

He absorbed this for a moment. "Okay. Why don't you come over here just in case we have to manage the press and issue our response," he said, his voice betraying no emotion. Since the legislature had forced us into picking Tish James and she, in turn, chose Joon Kim, the governor believed it was all a setup.

We had spent weeks prior coming up with a rebuttal strategy. Cuomo had prerecorded a video giving his side of the Charlotte Bennett conversations and vehemently denying Brittany Commisso's claims that he had groped her. He went further, attempting to provide context for the litany of reports that he had touched people's faces, put his arm around their waist, and hugged and kissed people at events. He absolutely did. Young, old, Black, white, male, female. And there were thousands of pictures to prove it. The governor had been convinced that if people saw the photos, they would understand how ridiculous the hysteria around the entire scandal had become. There wasn't anything sexual about it; this was the weaponization of everyday interactions politicians all across America engage in on a daily basis. Plain-vanilla meet and greet. We made the concerted decision not to address Lindsey Boylan at all. Most on our team believed that no matter how much he personally disdained Andrew Cuomo, there was no way that Joon Kim—a former US attorney himself—would stake his own reputation on Lindsey Boylan. In our view, she had no credibility, and we weren't going to give her any more oxygen.

I was concerned about the damage the report would seek to do to the administration, but didn't believe I personally would factor in much of it, if at all. Yes, I had authorized the response to Lindsey Boylan's claims, but nearly half a dozen lawyers were involved in and signed off on the initial decision, and the nearly dozen lawyers now involved in the case said unequivocally that it did not constitute retaliation. You are legally allowed to correct the record, and Boylan publicly misrepresented the terms on which she had left our office, they all concurred. As far as Charlotte was concerned, when I first heard that she had said something to colleagues in the bar about thinking the governor had "hit on" her, I immediately instructed Jill to report it to our special counsel, who made the legal determination from there.

I arrived at the mansion to find Stephanie sitting with the governor in the living room, closely monitoring Twitter on her laptop.

"You hear anything?" the governor asked.

"Nothing new, Governor," I reported. "The lawyers have calls into the AG's office, and Rich is making the rounds with the reporters. We should know something soon."

"But, really, even if it is the report, how bad can it be?" he asked, rhetorically. "They're lawyers—they can't lie," he said emphatically.

Cuomo truly believed that, once the public understood the context for his conversations with Charlotte Bennett—that he had a family member that had been sexually assaulted and that, to the extent he was talking to Charlotte, it was through that prism—the entire thing would be over. The single accusation of groping, which came from Brittany Commisso, had zero corroboration, contemporaneous or otherwise, and lacked a pattern. It was a classic he said/she said. Except in this situation, you were asking people to believe that, at age sixty-three, a man notorious for being paranoid, who had lived his entire life in a fishbowl, for the first time ever not only groped a woman's breast but did it in a house full of staff in the middle of the afternoon. Given those circumstances, how could the AG's office find the claim credible to the point that they would say so in a public report?

All of a sudden, my phone started to buzz. It was Rich. I raised my index finger. "I'll be right back, guys," I said, turning to walk out of the room and onto the back patio of the mansion.

"Hey, I'm over with the gov and Steph. Hear anything?" I answered.

"It's the report, Melissa. I've got it from three different reporters. They're going to release the report," Rich said, his words fast and tense. Question answered. The AG's office was telling the press it was the report before they even let our lawyers know it was coming, a blatant blindside.

Before I had a chance to respond to Rich, my call waiting began to beep. It was Shontell Smith, the majority leader's counsel.

"Rich, I have to take this," I said, my voice hurried. "Find out whatever you can, and I'll call you back," I said, clicking over.

"Hey lady," I said, once again trying to exude calm. "What's going on?" I asked.

"Melissa, she's releasing the report. Tish's office just briefed the leaders. They're going to say that the governor violated state and federal law as it relates to sexual harassment and that your office unlawfully retaliated against Lindsey Boylan," she said, matter of fact.

"Wait, what? Sexually harassed *who*?" I asked, my heart sinking.

"It's unclear. You're my friend," Shontell continued. "I wanted to make sure you weren't blindsided. This feels like it's going to get bad. I love you. Please take care of yourself."

I hung up; my hands began to tingle, and I felt my chest begin to tighten. I was having an anxiety attack. I looked up to see Steph coming toward me.

"Hey, hey, hey," she said gently. "What's going on out here?"

"It's bad, Steph," I said, trying to process what was about to envelop us.

I turned to walk back into the house. The governor was sitting exactly where I had left him on the couch. I recounted what Shontell had just reported.

"Sexually harassed *who*?" he demanded angrily. "On what theory?"

"I don't know, Governor, but the report should be out any minute," I said robotically, turning to walk away.

"Where are you going?" he asked.

"I need air." I could barely get the words out before making a beeline for the back door. Text messages were shooting across my phone like pinballs in an arcade game. Reporters, insiders, family members, all looking for insight into what was happening with the governor.

My phone began to ring. It was Rich again. "Hi," I answered vacantly.

"Melissa, they are saying it's eleven women," Rich responded.

As the words fell out of Rich's mouth, my mind wandered back to December 2020, after Lindsey first made her allegations on Twitter. She had told Kaitlin that her goal was to get ten to twelve people to make claims against Cuomo. Seven months later, with the fate of the New York State government hanging in the balance, Tish James was releasing a report with the magic number: eleven.

"Eleven? How? Who?" I was shocked to the core.

"I don't know. Honestly, Melissa, I've never heard of these people," Rich said. "It looks like they are including that random wedding guest whose face he touched. Two random people who he took pictures with at public events." My mind was reeling.

"You can't sexually harass nonemployees," I responded, searching for rationality in an irrational situation. "I helped write the law myself. Sexual harassment is workplace- and gender-based discrimination. How can she include those people? That's three—who are the other eight?"

"It doesn't make any sense, Melissa," Rich readily agreed. "I'm just telling you what it says. She also included that Kaitlin woman who worked for us for five minutes five years ago, who affirmatively said she wasn't sexually harassed in that *New York* magazine piece; Ana Liss, who was Howard Glaser's assistant in 2013, who said he called her 'sweetheart' and put his hand on her waist when they posed for a photo; Alyssa McGrath. Oh, and my personal favorite: The doctor who gave him a COVID test on national television."

"*Huh?*"

"Yeah, apparently, he made a comment on TV referencing her PPE and saying, "You make that gown look good."

We had entered the twilight zone.

Sexual harassment is a gender-based workplace discrimination law and only covers actions that a reasonable person would find to be more than "petty slights" and "trivial inconveniences." In what Rich had just described, the AG had included three nonemployees (a wedding guest and two people attending public events), three employees who themselves said they were not sexually harassed (Kaitlin, the DOH doctor, and Ana Liss), and Alyssa McGrath, Commisso's best friend, who claimed the governor commented on her looks in Italian (even though she didn't speak the language or know what he said), ogled her from across the room, and called her and Brittany "mingle mamas" when they said they were going on vacation after they described *themselves* as being "single and ready to mingle."

"Okay, that's seven—who else?" I asked.

Mixed in with the nonemployees posing for photos at public events and the women who themselves said they weren't sexually harassed was a trooper from the governor's security details—her appearance in the report a complete surprise. Amid ongoing tensions with the state police about unrelated matters, someone else from the state police responded to Tish's public tip line and reported the trooper. "Trooper #1," as she came to be known, hadn't filed a complaint or approached the attorney general's investigators; instead, they went to her. Once engaged, Trooper #1 alleged that over the course of four years, the governor had once kissed her on the cheek, once touched her back in an elevator (another trooper, present during the alleged incident, testified he didn't see anything out of the ordinary), once touched her belly while walking past her as she held a door open at a public event with others present, and once made a single off-color comment about marriage in the company of her and other detail members. She also retained Gloria Allred.

The state police is, and always has been, an old boys club made up almost entirely of white men. Cuomo believed the organization was inherently sexist and racist in their hiring practices. Of the sixty-five troopers on his security detail, only six of them were women and nine were Black. It was an ongoing battle. The old boys club liked the way it was and resisted change. But Cuomo was insistent that the detail—very much part of the governor's public face—have more women and minorities. While the head of the detail himself testified extensively about this, the report ignored that this female trooper's hiring was part of an ongoing push to diversify. In fact, she was recruited and hired to the security detail at the exact same time as another highly qualified Black trooper. The two had the exact same amount of experience. Instead, the report painted a picture that the governor had recruited this particular woman to the detail because he was attracted to her and wanted to be physically near her. What the report didn't disclose (but which would later come out when testimony was released) was that other evidence undermined the AG's theory.

After a period of time on the detail, Trooper #1's supervisor promoted her to be the governor's driver, putting him and Trooper #1 in direct, consistent contact. But after a few "close calls" and what the governor and the head of the security detail deemed to be risky driving that could "get into an accident," the governor requested she be moved to another position, and the state police ultimately decided she would no longer be driving him. The governor's request was that she be moved *away from him*, a change that meant he would rarely come into contact with her. That fact defied the picture the AG's office was trying to paint, but rather than acknowledge it, they hid it from the press and the public.

Gender-based discrimination assumes a woman was treated differently than a man. The report also left out the fact that male troopers testified that the governor kissed them on the cheek or gripped their arm and/or patted their back as he greeted them. As the governor would later explain in his resignation speech, "at public events, troopers will often hold doors open or guard the doorways. When I walk past them, I often will give them a grip of the arm, a pat on the face, a touch on the stomach, a slap on the back. It's my way of saying, 'I see you. I appreciate you, and I thank you.' I'm not comfortable just walking past and ignoring them. Of course, usually they are male troopers. In this case, I don't remember doing it at all. I didn't do it consciously with the female trooper. I did not mean any sexual connotation. I did not mean any intimacy by it."

In the end, essentially, you were left with the original three—Lindsey Boylan, Charlotte Bennett, and Brittany Commisso. But if you shoot the bear, you better kill the bear. Tish was shooting to kill. And, when you don't have quality, you go with quantity.

"Reporters are already moving stories, and the number eleven is in every headline," Rich said. "She stamped Boylan credible, and it doesn't sound like they included any of the governor's context for his conversations with Charlotte or considered his denials on some key details . . . oh and she's claiming the Commisso allegation is true and it happened on November 16, so I'll flag that for the lawyers."

The press didn't scrutinize a word or question why some of these seemingly frivolous accusations would be included in the report and characterized as sexual harassment. Instead, they swallowed it, hook, line, and sinker. Worse, they threw around the phrase "sexual assault" with reckless abandon. The *New York Times* ran a headline declaring Cuomo a serial sexual assaulter, proclaiming it's been "concluded" that he physically victimized at least eleven separate women: THE FALLOUT FROM THE BOMBSHELL REPORT THAT CONCLUDED GOV. ANDREW CUOMO SEXUALLY ASSAULTED 11 WOMEN WAS SWIFTER THAN EVEN HIS CLOSEST ALLIES EXPECTED.

"I don't get it—aren't any of the reporters questioning this? Parsing it? Have they all devolved into being stenographers?" I fumed. "Did they push back on any of this at the press conference?"

"Come on, Melissa. The *New York Times* put that wedding guest on the front page of their paper," Rich remembered. "They're all invested in this. They aren't going to question something that undermines a narrative they helped create." He paused before continuing. "What's more bizarre is Tish isn't saying which laws were allegedly broken, and she isn't referring any case to prosecutors or the Ethics Committee."

"Of course not!" I snapped. "Because touching a wedding guest's face or putting your arm around someone's waist isn't against the law, and law enforcement or a civil body would actually have to do a real investigation!"

Steph was standing in front of me again, "He's asking for you," she mouthed apologetically. I nodded.

"Rich, I gotta go. Call around to the reporters. Try to see if someone, *anyone* is questioning any of this," I directed before hanging up.

I returned to the living room and told the governor what was going on. "She's going too far," he said. "It's going to backfire."

"It's not, Governor," I said firmly. "She knows exactly what she's doing. The press is running with it. You can dispute one or two or even three claims, but eleven is too many. People will think where there's smoke there's fire."

Cuomo's outrage was turning into sheer disbelief. "Melissa, a doctor on national television? A wedding guest? Interactions at public events? Saying 'sweetheart'? Not to mention the credibility issues around Boylan and the truth about the Charlotte conversations. The press isn't stupid! They have to see through this and know it's about Tish wanting me out so she can run for governor!"

Tish James had successfully made herself investigator, prosecutor, judge, and jury to produce a due process–less conclusion, which was sure to lead to calls for a political death sentence.

Lyndon Johnson once said, "The difference between liberals and cannibals is that cannibals only eat their enemies." Andrew Cuomo was about to learn that lesson the hard way. Just then, my phone buzzed.

Jen Psaki, Biden's press secretary, was about to address the attorney general's report on national television. Obviously the president, who himself had been accused months earlier of sexually assaulting staffer Tara Reade, couldn't afford to waste any time in responding or be at the risk of having his own #MeToo allegations resurface.

> The president's message, the vice president's message, my message is all women who have lived through sexual—this type of experience, whether it is harassment or abuse or, in the worst case, assault—deserve to have their voices heard, deserve to be treated with respect and with dignity.
>
> I don't know that anyone could have watched this morning and not found the allegations to be abhorrent. I know I certainly did. And again, the president will speak to this later this afternoon.

It had been mere hours since the AG's press conference. There was no way Jen Psaki or anyone in the Biden press or counsel's office had the chance to read, let alone consider the political nature of the report. But that was exactly what Tish James was counting on. This wasn't about substance; it was about politics. No one would read the report; they all ran with James's statement, written to create sensational headlines and a rush to judgment.

I reached for my phone and dialed Steve Ricchetti, counselor to the president and a longtime close friend of the governor. Two years earlier, as Cuomo was privately considering a presidential run, I flew with him down to Virginia for a meeting convened by Steve between himself, the governor, and Biden at the former vice president's Georgian mansion near the Potomac. It was there that Ricchetti and Biden appealed to Cuomo to sit out the 2020 presidential primary.

"They said I was still young," he recounted to me in the car after the meeting wrapped. "That if I ran this time, he and I would cannibalize the middle, and a Far Lefty would get the nomination." Cuomo, who had been personal friends with Joe's son Beau before he died and was first in line at his wake, was swayed by their reasoning and gave Biden his word that day that he would stand down and support him—a word he kept every day after.

Ricchetti had known the governor for decades. Their families were friends. If anyone could bring rationality to this moment, it was him. Two rings went by before he sent me to voice mail. I had momentarily forgotten the age-old rule my father taught me as a child. *In politics, there are no friends.*

As soon as one politician calls for resignation in these situations, it pressures others to do the same, and this wasn't just any politician. When Joe Biden turned his back on his longtime friend Andrew Cuomo without so much as even a cursory glance at the report, it created a stampede. Within hours, every member of the New York congressional delegation, along with Democratic governors Ned Lamont of Connecticut and Phil Murphy of New Jersey, plus US senators Chuck

Schumer and Kirsten Gillibrand, both Democrats from New York, all called for Cuomo to resign.

None of them had read the report, and none of them asked any questions, a point underscored by the president of the United States himself when calling for his longtime friend and ally's resignation, "Look, what I said was: If the investigation of the attorney general concluded that the allegations were correct, that—back in March—that [sic] I would recommend he resign. That's what I'm doing today. I've not read the report. I don't know the details of it. All I know is the end result," Biden said.

Unlike at the federal level, in New York there are no legal guidelines for the impeachment process. New York's constitution sets no standard or basis for impeachment. There is no threshold of high crimes and misdemeanors to consider; it is purely a political process. And, in this instance, it was a fait accompli—the speaker of the assembly said so.

Shortly after Biden spoke, New York State Assembly Speaker Carl Heastie released a statement saying, "After our conference this afternoon to discuss the attorney general's report concerning sexual-harassment allegations against Governor Cuomo, it is abundantly clear to me that the governor has lost the confidence of the assembly Democratic majority and that he can no longer remain in office." The speaker, a longtime champion of due process, then went further, saying that if the governor didn't resign, the legislature, blindly accepting the report at face value, would impeach him.

Game. Set. Match.

Trial by press conference.

As the cavalcade continued with members of the state senate and the majority leader herself, the state's Democratic Party chairman, Jay Jacobs, continued to hold out hope.

"Melissa, he has to get out there," Jay urged me. "The video rebuttal he released is not enough. He needs to be more forceful and tell his side of the story."

Jay believed the governor had to go out and respond to the allegations on each of the eleven women individually. The problem was that we didn't even know a handful of who the eleven women were. Tish James had solicited complaints from the general public, resulting in a hodgepodge of random people, half of whom either never worked for us or specifically said themselves they were not sexually harassed. Making matters worse, we couldn't properly respond because we didn't even know what they had said since James refused to turn over the interview transcripts from the investigation or any underlying evidence the report was based on.

I hastily convened the remaining members of our kitchen cabinet—the ones who, in the aftermath of the report, weren't currently fighting for their professional lives. I quickly surveyed the group. No one believed Cuomo should go out and address the report.

Comments and questions flew around the room. *It's a trap. If you look like you're attacking the women, you'll get pounded harder. Have we even read the report? Do we know what we're responding to?*

Cowed by the press and the politicians, our outside counsel, former US Attorney Paul Fishman, appeared afraid to respond at risk of getting canceled himself.

Three days went by before we addressed the public. The narrative had hardened. By then, nothing would change it.

Swarms of paparazzi camped out in front of the mansion. Photographers scaled nearby buildings for photos of the governor and his children walking the grounds. Television news crews flew drones with cameras overhead. The press smelled blood, and they were happy to draw even more. And it wasn't enough to go after the governor; they wanted to take down anyone associated with him, too. Longtime public servants who were involved in damage control when Boylan first made her allegations on Twitter were treated as bull's-eyes in target practice. No one was spared. Our former counsel, Alphonso David, who had since been hired to serve as executive director of the Human Rights Campaign, was suspended and subsequently fired. Our former communications director and chief of staff were pushed out of their lucrative consulting jobs. Robbie Kaplan, the chairwoman and founder of Time's Up, whose firm was representing me in the matter, was forced to resign from both roles. Suddenly stripped of counsel at the height of the frenzy, I was left more vulnerable and alone than ever.

And while everyone involved took incoming, it felt like no one got it worse than I did in the press. It began with the *Washington Post*, who called to say they were writing a story about the number of times my name appeared in the report, second only to the governor's.

"So?" I asked Rich Azzopardi in the backyard of the mansion as he delivered the news that the piece was coming. "There are eleven women mentioned in the report. I'm brought up in the context of two of them, and in Charlotte's case, I directed that a secondhand rumor I heard about be taken to counsel for review! Despite what Rebecca Traister or the *New York Post* have been saying for months, it doesn't say I fostered a toxic work environment. It actually says flat out that there was no evidence of an alleged dress code! Why are they focused on me?"

"Melissa, after him, you're the most visible person in the administration," Rich replied. "And it's not just you. They're shooting at everyone the report touched."

In my case, the people being swept up in the wake of the tsunami included those closest to me. CNBC reported that my father, a New York lobbyist for thirty years, was lobbying the administration as the scandals unfolded, while the *New York Post* recycled a story about Matt's mother being the US attorney. How was any of that news? The press would double down with each passing day that the governor refused to resign.

One day, a story about how I, newly proclaimed enemy of women, had served as the chairwoman of the Counsel on Women and Girls devolved into the next day's news quoting a handful of blind sources calling me "ruthless" and "soulless" and saying I would "rip your throat out to get what I want." A lawyer for one of the eleven accusers in the report, Virginia Limmiatis, a random woman I had never met and whose shoulder the governor briefly touched at a public event, issued a statement calling me "Cuomo's enabler in chief." I had a target on my back, and no one, not our lawyers or press office, could do anything to stop it.

Basking in the attention the report got, Lindsey Boylan started making public threats to sue everyone involved based on the AG's findings, and Brittany Commisso, who until that point had remained anonymous, filed a criminal complaint with the Albany sheriff and sat for a national television interview. Alessandra Biaggi took to the airwaves and, despite being a mid-level attorney in counsel's office whom neither the governor nor I had met while she worked for us, railed freely about the "toxic work environment" she witnessed under Cuomo firsthand. Lawyers for the eleven were having their day in the sun, issuing statements of their own. All the while, Tish refused to disclose the transcripts, interview memos, and evidence she maintained supported the conclusions she had reached in her report (later, we would discover that, based on a fraction of the material Cuomo would eventually receive, hidden from the press and public in that moment, was a trove of exculpatory information).

One by one, five district attorneys across the state announced they were investigating the governor based on the report's findings.

"I don't understand," I said. "What is Mimi Rocha—a former US attorney—investigating in Westchester exactly? That the governor kissed a woman on the cheek after asking, 'May I give you a kiss on the cheek?' What would the crime be?"

"Melissa, none of this is logical," Beth Garvey said. "We aren't in logical territory anymore."

It was an arms race. Everyone wanted their five minutes in the press, and the media was happy to give it to them, free from scrutiny. The law and the facts were irrelevant. Tish James had given them this cover with her press conference.

"But these are district attorneys!" I interrupted, my voice rising.

"Yep, and they get elected too, Melissa."

That Friday, three days after the report was released, Albany County Sheriff Craig Apple, a politician himself who, years earlier, was caught on tape saying, "I know how to manipulate the law, and I've gotten pretty good at it," held one of the most unethical and prejudicial press conferences I had ever witnessed. He had reached his conclusion prior to his investigation into Brittany Commisso's allegations, saying, "I think we've all read the attorney general's report. At this point, I'm very comfortable and safe saying she is, in fact, a victim."

Sitting on the back patio of the mansion with the governor and Steph, trying to figure out what to do next, my phone rang. It was Rich.

"Melissa, there are rumors going around that this cowboy sheriff is going to arrest the governor," he said, his voice in a panicked rush.

"This is insane, Rich!" I could hear the panic in my own voice, too.

"I know. I can't stomach any of this. All he's done for the state," Rich continued. "I just keep thinking about marriage equality, the SAFE Act, $15. The man rebuilt LaGuardia Airport. He led the world during COVID, for Christ's sake," his voice shaking. "It makes me so angry." He paused, drawing in a deep breath. "This is likely bullshit, but at this moment who the hell knows. I think you need to call Beth."

I hung up and immediately rang Beth Garvey. Of everyone still in the tent, she was the steadiest hand. "The state police would know," Beth told me. "I'll call them."

Beth quickly reported back that the state police had not been told anything about a possible arrest and that it was likely just local media hysteria, but given what Sheriff Apple had said publicly about the case, we should consider it a real possibility at some point.

"What do we do, Beth?" I asked.

"Melissa, they want him out. The press, the politicians," she said. "They won't stop until he's gone."

I hung up and walked outside to see the governor sitting at the round table on the patio. The same table we had sat at so many times in the last eight years with his family, with senior staff. Smoking cigars, debating policy, laughing, arguing.

"Melissa, what's going on?" the governor asked, responding to my drawn face.

There was no way to sugarcoat this one.

"There's a rumor going around that Sheriff Apple is going to arrest you," I said. "Governor, the legislature is going to impeach you. The facts don't matter. They aren't going to scrutinize a damn thing in that report. The senate has the votes—Christ, the majority leader publicly announced she's one of them! The Far Left in her conference wanted you out *before* any of this. They used this to do it."

The governor heard every word I said. Nodded his head and looked over at Steph. "Can you get your laptop? I have a speech to write." At that point, I didn't know what speech he was going to write. I'm not sure he did, either.

With every passing hour, I could feel the walls closing in. I didn't know who I could trust or where I could turn. My phone was constantly ringing with unsolicited advice from legislators, outside consultants, and our remaining senior staff, each with their own agenda. I was lost in a fog of trying to discern whether the counsel I was receiving was to benefit the administration or the person calling. And as the hours went on, I could feel the inner circle shrinking. Details about private discussions I had with longtime colleagues, people I truly believed were real friends, about the state of my emotional well-being suddenly appeared in news stories crediting blind sources with "direct knowledge." Wrapped in betrayal, I could count on one hand the number of people I believed I could talk to honestly. I had never felt more alone.

The next morning, I woke up exhausted. All told, I had slept for maybe a fitful hour the night before. I got out of bed in the empty house I grew up in, walked to the bathroom, and looked in the mirror. *I can't do this anymore.* Just then my phone rang. It was my mother.

"Missy, baby," she said, her voice trembling. "Why are they saying these things about you?"

"Mom, please, please," I begged, "we've talked about this. Ignore the *New York Post*."

"Baby, it's the *New York Times*. Maureen Dowd wrote a column, basically comparing you and your team to Hitler's enablers. She references the people who enabled Harvey Weinstein, who raped women. You're the entire top of the column."

I dropped the phone.

"Missy? Are you there? Baby?" I could hear my mom's voice from the phone on the floor. I bent down and picked it up.

"Mom, I'm sorry. I'm sorry to have embarrassed you and Dad. I'm sorry for disappointing you. I'm sorry for making you all go through this," I wept. "I only ever tried to do my best."

"Missy! You could never disappoint me. I'm so proud of you. I love you. Your father loves you," Mom tried to console me. "You could *never* let us down. I just . . ." Her voice trailed off. "I'm just worried about you and your team. They aren't letting up. It's getting so vicious."

I promised to call her later. I had to get to the mansion.

It was time for this to end.

I drove in through the back entrance to avoid the mob of photographers out front, then opened an umbrella to shield myself from any photographers flying above as I stepped out of my car and ran to the pool house. Steph, the governor, Mariah, and Michaela were sitting together having coffee under the awning, shielded from the zoom lenses, prisoners in their own home. No one could move from under the awning without risking having their photo taken and splashed across the front pages of the tabloids.

"I'm sorry to interrupt, Governor. Can I talk to you?" I asked.

He stood up and followed me into the pool house, sliding the glass door shut behind us.

"What's wrong?" he asked.

"I can't do this. It's too much. I don't even recognize myself anymore. This person they've turned me into. I worked my whole life. I tried so hard. I did so much. I gave up *so much.* Now I'm Hitler's enabler?"

"Fuck Maureen Dowd, Melissa! Do you know how many years she spent going after Hillary Clinton? She should have had to register her columns as an in-kind contribution to the Trump campaign!" the governor swore. "You can't listen to these people. You know the truth. You know who you are. You know what you've done for the people of this state, and the rest of this is just noise." Cuomo's instinct was always to stay and fight, but I didn't have any fight left in me.

"It's not just about me. I can't hurt my family like this anymore. I don't want to quit. I don't want to leave the team. I know what they are doing. But they're not going to stop. I'm not as strong as you are." I took a deep breath. My whole body was shaking now.

Cuomo pulled me in close, "Okay, okay," he said in a paternal whisper. "It's going to be okay. Shush. It's going to be okay, I promise you. Take a deep breath. It's all going to be okay." The governor told me that whatever I decided I needed to do, he understood and supported me 100 percent, just as I had supported him for the preceding eight and a half years.

Stephanie left with me, and together we drove around the corner to Hill Street, a hole-in-the-wall pub nearby, safe from the prying eyes of photographers, to see Rich. Strong and resolute, he urged me to soldier on. "I know what this is doing to you, but don't let them win, Melissa."

I got in the car and drove to my brother's house fifteen minutes away. I didn't know what to do or who I could talk to. Joey pulled me in close and told me it was going to be okay. He urged me to shut out the noise and seek guidance from someone with only my best interests at heart. Someone who could be dispassionate about the circumstances. I knew who best fit that description: the man who had mentored me as a child decades earlier. My father's first business partner, Norman Adler.

"Melissa, you have to get out of there," Norman said unequivocally. "The governor is a big boy. He will decide for himself how this plays out. And, honest to God, I believe in a year or two everyone will look back on this and see that it was driven by politics and hysteria. But at this moment, you have to protect *you*. No one else is going to do that for you. Only you can. Hang up with me and call a reporter."

Without telling the governor or a single person on our staff, I stood in my brother's kitchen with him and his wife, Kathleen, looking on, and dialed Jimmy Vielkind at the *Wall Street Journal*. Jimmy and I had fought like cats and dogs during the year prior, but we had a working relationship that had extended over a decade. If there was anyone I would feel comfortable speaking to at that moment, it was Jimmy.

"I know we've fought a lot over the last year, Jimmy, but just know that all I ever tried to do was my job," I said. I had a prepared statement I wanted to send to him.

Earlier in the day, I had asked two of our outside consultants to draft something that I could hold in my back pocket in case I decided to pull the trigger:

> It has been the greatest honor of my life to serve the people of New York for the past ten years. New Yorkers' resilience, strength, and optimism through the most difficult times has inspired me every day. Personally, the past two years have been emotionally and mentally trying. I am forever grateful for the opportunity to have worked with such talented and committed colleagues on behalf of our state.

I gave Jimmy the statement, made one more call to Zack Fink at NY1, and turned off my phone. I knew the rest would take care of itself from there.

I resigned as a way to remove myself from the fire but woke up the next morning to find I had stoked it. My resignation was being used *against* the governor because the statement hadn't mentioned him specifically by name.

Fuck.

Some in the media speculated that I felt betrayed by him and the report's findings. Others said I was resigning because there was no political path forward. They couldn't have been further divorced from reality. I picked up the phone and called Steph. I knew I should stay away, but I couldn't. I needed to be there to help navigate whatever was coming next, but I also couldn't take any more press focused on me. Channeling our inner *Laverne & Shirley*, we hatched a plan that I would hide in the back seat of her car under a blanket, out of photographers' sight. (Little did we know the *Daily Mail* had photographers staked out, chronicling the entire escapade.)

When I arrived at the mansion, the governor was sitting on the couch, editing a speech he had been working on. The next day, his attorney Rita Glavin—who, after meeting Cuomo and reviewing the facts of his case, felt so passionately that what was happening was wrong that she had quit her lucrative white-collar practice to take him on as her main client—would give a presentation knocking down key elements of the attorney general's report. The report's finding that Commisso had been groped on November 16 had been checked against mansion logs and Commisso's own emails, which provided evidence proving there was no possible way that the incident she described could have occurred. Not only had the AG's report not been corroborated; it was clear that claims raised in it hadn't even been properly investigated. Rita, a former federal prosecutor who had previously served as the head of the DOJ's criminal division, planned to lay out her case, using what little evidence she had access to at that point, emphasizing that the governor did not sexually harass anyone, let alone eleven women. The governor would give a speech after.

"What are you going to say?" I asked.

"We'll see," he answered, without looking up.

He made his decision overnight. After serving 3,874 days as governor of New York, Andrew Cuomo would resign. The fix was in. With the assembly and senate having already announced their intention to impeach and remove him from office, the legislature was not a place where he would receive a fair hearing. But even more than that, he couldn't stomach what the situation was doing to the people around him. The report had said that his brother, Chris, had been involved in conversations early on about how to respond to the allegations, and now he, too, was in the media's crosshairs. The governor's daughters were watching their father being labeled a "sex predator," even though the single claim that he had forcibly touched anyone— Brittany Commisso's—didn't stand up under scrutiny. And after sacrificing any semblance of their personal lives for the past year and a half to help construct a viable template for the nation to combat COVID, his loyal staff was being torn to pieces.

I didn't know for sure what he was going to do until the governor handed me a draft of the speech that Tuesday morning, August 10, 2021. I read it and started to cry. "Don't do it," I begged. "Not for me. Not for Chris. Not for anyone else. Keep fighting. I'll help you," I pleaded.

"I've made my decision, Melissa. It's time."

He had asked me to stay back and not come to New York City for the press conference; I was too emotional, and it would only make it harder. But I refused, and Stephanie, Mariah, Michaela, and I boarded the helicopter with him that morning.

When we arrived at the office, there was one call left for me to make.

Seven months earlier, the decision to remove our lieutenant governor from the ticket was made for the second time in four years, a message delivered to her by Howard Zemsky and Bill Mulrow in January 2021. But unlike in 2018, this time around, she'd relented, under the condition that we find her a job in the federal government. But our close relationship with the incoming Biden administration wasn't enough to secure her top choice: ambassador to Canada. Instead they offered deputy secretary of the Commerce Department. We were days away from finalizing the arrangement when the allegations against Cuomo began to unfurl back in February. I hadn't spoken with her since.

Now I picked up the phone to inform Kathy Hochul that the governor was planning to resign, effective in fourteen days.

"I don't think we need fourteen days, Melissa. Lieutenant governors are trained and prepared to take over at a moment's notice," she declared. *What a joke.* Straight out of HBO's *Veep* central casting, Hochul had spent the last seven years cutting ribbons on Cuomo's projects and giving speeches at second-tier events that didn't rise to the governor's level. For her, government was about photo ops. She had never been involved in a single substantive policy or operational decision. She didn't know how to negotiate with the legislature or handle a disaster like Hurricane Sandy. For the first time in days, I was no longer sad. Hochul's arrogance, for a brief moment, snapped me back to me.

"Kathy, no offense, but you don't know what you don't know, including how to run a government. Governor Cuomo is stepping down for the good of New York," I said. "He's not handing over the reins in some haphazard way that hurts the people of this state. We will transition properly over the next two weeks." It wouldn't take long for the people of New York to understand just how ill-equipped Hochul was for the job.

The governor headed down to the press conference room on the thirty-eighth floor of 633 Third Avenue, instructing Stephanie, Michaela, Mariah, and me to stay in his office on the thirty-ninth floor. This would be too difficult for him with us in the room.

He delivered one of the best speeches of his life that day, passionately pushing back against the attorney general's report and recounting a decade's worth of accomplishments, from marriage equality and the smartest gun-safety laws in America to a $15 minimum wage and the nation's strongest paid-family-leave plan. He recalled countless emergencies he had managed, from fires, floods, hurricanes, and superstorms to COVID. He cited the state budgets we'd balanced, the free college tuition program he'd enacted, and the new airports, railroads, transit systems, and roads that he built.

And then, he shocked the nation when he said:

> Now, you know me. I'm a New Yorker, born and bred. I am a fighter, and my instinct is to fight through this controversy because I truly believe it is politically motivated. I believe it is unfair and it is untruthful, and I believe that it demonizes behavior that is unsustainable for society. If I could communicate the facts through the frenzy, New Yorkers would understand. I believe that, but when I took my oath as governor, then it changed. I became a fighter, but I became a fighter for you, and it is your best interests that I must serve. This situation by its current trajectory will generate months of political and legal controversy. That is what is going to happen. That is how the political wind is blowing. It will consume government. It will cost taxpayers millions of dollars. It will brutalize people.
>
> The state assembly yesterday outlined weeks of process that will then lead to months of litigation, time and money that government should spend managing COVID, guarding against the Delta variant, reopening upstate, fighting gun violence, and saving New York City. All that time would be wasted. This is one of the most challenging times for government in a generation. Government really needs to function today. Government needs to perform. It is a matter of life and death—government operations. And wasting energy on distractions is the last thing that state government should be doing. And I cannot be the cause of that.
>
> New York tough means New York loving, and I love New York, and I love you. And everything I have ever done has been motivated by that love. And I would never want to be unhelpful in any way. And I think that given the circumstances, the best way I can help now is if I step aside and let government get

back to governing. And, therefore, that's what I'll do because I work for you, and doing the right thing is doing the right thing for you. Because as we say, "It's not about me. It's about we."

After he finished his remarks, there wasn't a dry eye in the room. He walked around hugging each staffer there, thanking them for their service, for believing in him and for fighting every day for the people of New York. Heading out the door, he turned and, with a half smile, said, "Sorry for hugging all of you; apparently, that's what constitutes sexual harassment now," his words underscoring the bizarre nature of the moment we found ourselves in.

He walked upstairs to find Rita, Steph, Michaela, Mariah, and me in his office with the door closed. He hugged his daughters, consoling them, telling them it was going to be okay.

All of this was a lot of things. But it wasn't okay.

CHAPTER 24

Up off the Mat

THE DAY AFTER THE GOVERNOR RESIGNED, I WAS SLEEP-DEPRIVED, traumatized, villainized, and hunted relentlessly by the paparazzi, and my family insisted I get out of Albany.

They devised a plan: Stephanie would drive me from the mansion to a parking lot at my father's office building, where I would meet my brother, Joey, who would drive me to my sister's in-law's house on Cape Cod. I went along for the ride, literally and figuratively, picking up the pieces of my broken existence and fleeing from the state I had given everything to for more than a decade.

When I arrived on the Cape, I was afraid to leave the house, convinced photographers were hiding outside. I couldn't sleep, and my eyes were vacant. Worse than my physical health, my mental health had completely deteriorated; my confidence was shattered. In the nine preceding months, I had been successfully gaslighted into doubting my intelligence, self-worth, character, and accomplishments.

I didn't see a way forward, and at that moment, I didn't know that I wanted one.

"Are you okay?" My sister Jessica came into my dark bedroom. It was shortly after 6:00 a.m., I noted, even though time had become insignificant to me, a profound irony given that it used to define my life.

"Uh-huh." I kept my voice to a whisper, desperate to numb my pain.

"Can I get you something?" she asked, rubbing my back. "Water, coffee, an egg sandwich?" She was deeply concerned about me. Rightfully so.

"I love you—I just need a few minutes." I responded without moving. The handful of words alone required more energy than I had to spare, but I didn't want her to worry.

"Okay, Missy Monster," Jessica said, "I'm here, whatever you need..." She trailed off. She wanted so badly to help me, but she couldn't.

No one could.

Just months earlier, everything in my life had possessed purpose and meaning. At age thirty-eight, I was the most senior member of Andrew Cuomo's team leading the nation through a once-in-a-century pandemic, making life-or-death decisions, projecting our administration's competence to an admiring world. At the pinnacle of my career. But now I was transformed into a caricature I didn't recognize—a person I never was and didn't want to be. It had all unfolded too quickly to slow or stop, like falling onto the tracks of an oncoming train. The words "What just happened?" wouldn't stop reverberating through my entire body. None of it made sense.

"Jess, I just can't do it anymore," I said.

"You don't have to, Missy," she responded, pulling me close. "In two weeks, the governor will be out of office. You just need to hold on until then, and I promise you everything will be okay."

"For what? What's even left? My career, my identity, everything I worked so hard for. They took *everything*!" I said.

"Bullshit, Melissa," she said, her voice stern. "These people are a joke. What the fuck have they ever done? Since when are you cowed by this bullshit?" she continued. "They can only take what you give them. *You* got that $15 minimum wage passed. *You* made paid family leave a reality in New York. *You* promoted more women to senior positions in that administration than anyone ever had before. *You* broke glass ceilings. You managed COVID, for Christ's sake! No one can take that away."

"Don't you get it? None of that matters anymore, Jessica."

"You are thirty-eight years old! You have your whole life in front of you," she continued. "The Melissa DeRosa I know is a fighter. You are going to fight through this. And for the first time in your life, you're going to let the rest of us help you," she said. "But, right now, you're going to drag your ass out of that bed and get dressed."

The process was slow and excruciating, and I lost friends along the way. Some who needed, for professional survival, to rewrite their experiences; those who were burned or traumatized by what had happened; and others in search of blame, who had to tell themselves a story in order to justify the people the press made them out to be. It broke my heart. But as upset as I was at certain moments, I understood. The public exposure paled in comparison to the professional upheaval and the private pain.

Matt and I filed for divorce and put our beloved Brooklyn Heights duplex on the market—a heartbreaking culmination of years of marital struggle, made worse when the *New York Post* decided it was newsworthy and published the story.

"I've never felt so alone," I said on the phone one early morning to Jane Rosenthal, my friend, mentor, and lifeline during those dark days.

"Melissa, my mother always told me that you can't make new old friends," she responded, her voice soothing and sure. "There are so many people who love you. Let them."

She was right.

It took months of therapy and physical distance from Albany for me to climb out of the dark hole I was in. But with each passing day, the love and unconditional support of my family and friends—the ones who didn't care what job I had and never asked what I could do for them—brought back the light.

I started to sleep for more than four hours a night. I read nonpolitical books and went shopping for something other than press-conference clothes. I had mimosas in the middle of the day and watched silly movies. I ate lobster rolls and ice cream. I stopped looking at Twitter. I took long walks, stared at the ocean, and snuggled with my nieces. I learned to become present in conversations and important moments. I started to laugh.

Somewhere along the way, I started to feel like *me* again.

And I spent months reflecting on what happened. People ask me what my "takeaway" is now that I'm "past it." What I learned:

While I'm not entirely sure of much, I'm certain I'll never get *past it.* And I think I am still learning from it. Like a prism, the view changes with the angle.

Women being abused in the workplace is a long-standing societal injustice. The #MeToo movement did this nation a service, provoking a course correction and forcing examination of pervasive abuse that had gone unchecked for too long. But like many well-intentioned movements, competing interests and divergent agendas have complicated matters and threatened to undermine its important work.

Like almost every woman who enters the labor force, I have experienced harassment and misogyny in different forms since graduating from college, and have too many family members and friends who have suffered the trauma of sexual assault. No one should be made to feel uncomfortable, and everyone should have the ability to set their own boundaries, speak up, and speak out. Mistreatment of any kind must be confronted and addressed. That's why working to enact the toughest sexual-harassment law in the nation and successfully extending the statute of limitations for rape became all-consuming for me. I was in a position of power during the moment of reckoning, and I didn't want to just talk about it; I wanted to *do something* about it. Make change. It's a difficult and somewhat uncomfortable conversation to have, but the question of what the behavior is and how it is addressed is where things have gotten murky.

"Harassment" can cover a broad spectrum of actions, and personal boundaries are just that—personal. Behavior that one person is comfortable with might make another person uncomfortable. Codifying a legal standard requires society to establish as a collective what is acceptable behavior, understanding different personal, cultural, and generational perspectives. There are obvious "bright lines" that are clearly unacceptable. But not everyone is Harvey Weinstein or Bill

Cosby. There is a range of behavior in the workplace. It is nonsensical to equate rape or assault to kissing someone on the cheek, putting your arm around them for a photograph, or making an off-color comment. In some instances, training is the appropriate recourse; in others, it's termination or jail. Drawing a false equivalency undermines the movement. And as a result, I know too many women who have suffered the pain of sexual assault but have grown to resent #MeToo as petty and trivial, and too many men who view hiring young women as a potential legal liability should they inadvertently say something offensive or look at them in a way that could be misinterpreted. Taken together, we are in a dangerous place of potentially undoing the progress we've made and risk severe claims not being taken seriously. And that would be the greatest tragedy of all.

I also live in the real world and understand all too well the weaponization and politicization of various social movements spanning decades. Selective outrage isn't a new phenomenon. You can generally draw a straight line from a person's calls for resignation to their political benefits, not their principles. There's no other way to reconcile why Joe Biden and Donald Trump survived allegations of assault, but Al Franken had to go. That is why due process—real due process, not trial by media or politicians—is paramount.

Our administration was far from perfect. There are things I now know we should have done differently.

We played hard with the legislature and the press for years. We micromanaged the bureaucracy. Our goals were high, and we cared about getting things done. The system is designed to protect the status quo and create gridlock. Bureaucracy is risk averse. Bureaucrats analyze forever and steep themselves in the process; there's no incentive to complete. The legislature is historically risk averse. To get anything done, you have to be a disruptor. And when you disrupt, you incur the wrath of the people who would rather be left alone to do things their way.

In my view, the alternative was: don't disrupt—go along, get along. But then, government fails: the status quo won't change, and what is the point of being there at all? I valued every day that I worked in government, viewing it as an opportunity to impact change and accomplish things for people like my grandparents, who didn't have a seat at the table. In hindsight, I became so accustomed to fighting that, at times, I lost a sense of calibration and, in some instances, pushed harder than was necessary. The same was true for how I managed the staff.

Cuomo had flown so close to the sun. He vehemently disagreed with, fought, and challenged the Far Left. And he was viewed as a threat nationally on the Far Right. And, yes, over forty years, his hard-charging style and aggressiveness had earned him a host of political enemies. All of the power was in his hands, and others wanted it.

But the mistakes that were made did not warrant the avalanche that overturned a duly elected government and ruined the lives and professional livelihoods of people in its wake.

Part of me thinks some of what transpired had to do with COVID— people were pent-up and angry. But that's the easy answer. The truth is much more elusive.

In retrospect, on a personal level, I believe I was traumatized during COVID in a way I didn't appreciate at the time. The death, fear, stress, and responsibility, combined with exhaustion and the duration of the pandemic, took their toll on my mental health. I ran faster, jumped higher, and tried to never let them see me sweat, instead pushing my emotions down until I couldn't take it anymore. There were plenty of warning signs along the way, but rather than stop and acknowledge them, I just kept going. Then, on top of it, navigating the nursing home and sexual-harassment allegations and becoming the target of the giddy press tsunami that came with them layered in a different level of trauma.

Professionally, with some time and space, I believe that what I experienced during the last two years of the administration was part of a larger shift; the atrophying of basic democratic institutions. Nationally, people don't trust government or the media or prosecutors. There's a good reason for that; it didn't start with Trump, but he exacerbated it, exploited it. We have had a true breakdown and politicization of institutions whose strength and stability is necessary to a functioning democracy.

If the victory in World War II buoyed citizens' belief in the United States government, COVID deflated it.

And it was justified.

In a moment when the public needed its federal government most, COVID exposed its glaring incompetence. Any sense of security that one might have had through believing that their government could protect them in an emergency was gone, causing citizens' trust in government to deteriorate further.

Serious cultural movements were politicized and weaponized, causing people to question, and even mock, their legitimacy.

Government investigative bodies and law enforcement were used to influence elections and corrupted for political gain.

And partisan politics successfully permeated the "unbiased" press on both sides. News coverage slanted to the will of a publication's editorial leanings. Members of the media became free from nuance and context, and were willing to serve as stenographers rather than reporters. Everything was sensationalized. And a combination of budget cuts, a twenty-four-hour media cycle, and social media fueled by retweets, clicks, and "likes," focused on churning out "news" quickly, has sacrificed rigor, merit, and depth. What results is a world of grays presented as black and white.

But, at the same time, I saw something else during COVID.

I saw the hope that our team gave people in government leadership through our daily briefings, not just across the country, but around the world. I saw the goodness of Americans who volunteered to put their lives on the line to help one another. The selflessness of the essential workers. And proof that the will to put the collective over the individual still very much exists within our society. I saw how a competent government can make a difference. I am proud of what the people of New York did during COVID, the leadership we displayed and the lives we saved.

And to this day, I get emotional when people recognize me and express their gratitude for what our team did during those dark days.

I also know the difference that government can make in people's lives by creating new civil rights like marriage equality, by raising the minimum wage, or enacting free college tuition for the middle class. I see its capacity when I walk through the new LaGuardia and JFK airports, drive across the Mario Cuomo Bridge or pull into the new Moynihan train station. I know its importance when a literal storm is brewing.

And I'm old enough to remember a time when you could be friends with someone you disagreed with, when compromise and bipartisanship were seen as productive instead of as a political liability.

I see the promise and peril.

And I am not sure which ultimately wins.

But I know I've made a difference before. And I know I'm going to try again.

"Some days, aren't you happy not to deal with it anymore?" my brother, Joey, asked over coffee and the morning's newspapers.

"I know I should be," I said, pausing. "But I'm not. It makes me sad, and it makes me angry."

"What do you mean?"

"Government is ultimately a vehicle for good. It's progress. It's civil rights and giving voice to the voiceless. It's building bridges and protecting people." I paused. "I didn't work twenty-four hours a day because it was fun. I did it because what we did mattered to real people."

"Sounds like maybe you're not totally ready to be out of it?" he asked.

He was right. I wasn't.

It was time to get up off the mat. I had the physical and emotional strength. I threw on a white tank top and my sister's navy Lululemon spandex, and laced up my sneakers.

I was finally ready to run again.

But first, I was ready to write.

Epilogue

ON OCTOBER 28, 2021, ALBANY COUNTY SHERIFF CRAIG APPLE filed a "forcible touching" charge against Cuomo based on the attorney general's findings on Brittany Commisso. Apple acted without the knowledge or consent of Albany County District Attorney David Soares or Commisso herself. The breach of legal protocol raised a red flag for many. "Like the rest of the public, we were surprised to learn that a criminal complaint was filed in Albany city court by the Albany County Sheriff's Office against Andrew Cuomo," Soares said in a statement.

It appeared there was only one person who knew the charges were coming. Within minutes of Apple's announcement, with the press, the public, the accuser, and the designated prosecutor still reeling, the attorney general weighed in: "The criminal charges brought today against Mr. Cuomo for forcible touching further validate the findings in our report."w

The very next day, Tish James announced she was running for governor.

The "coincidence" and sequence of events was lost on almost no one.

Tish James's coup de grâce quickly began the unraveling of key elements of her report. Because of the enormous political pressure suddenly placed on District Attorney Soares, he expedited an investigation that would normally take months, collapsing it into weeks. What James didn't anticipate was that the DA's investigation would require her to turn over some of the underlying evidence that she had thus far refused to reveal.

After reviewing it, Soares dropped a bombshell of his own, which exploded on Tish and Sheriff Apple. Soares identified "exculpatory" evidence. None of it had been included in the AG's report, nor was it revealed by either the AG or the sheriff. Soares provided this previously hidden evidence, as legally required, to Cuomo's lawyers because it could prove his innocence. Soares further determined the criminal complaint was "potentially defective" and castigated Apple for filing the charge "unilaterally and inexplicably" while Soares's own parallel investigation was ongoing.

In essence, the sitting district attorney was accusing Sheriff Apple— and, by extension, the New York State attorney general—of being aware of and ignoring or, worse, hiding, exonerating information. Withholding exculpatory evidence is both unethical and can be illegal.

Records revealed by Soares showed that Commisso had offered three different dates for the alleged groping: November 16, November 19, and November 25. James's report concluded it had occurred on November 16. The reason they picked that date was because it was the only date in November that New York State Police records showed that Commisso was in the mansion and Commisso testified under oath that she was groped around the time she was asked to photograph Cuomo's driver's license, and the saved photo was time-stamped November 16. But scheduling and visitor records for that day showed that Commisso's story was physically and logistically impossible. Sheriff Apple then offered an alternative theory, alleging it didn't take place in November at all, but actually occurred on December 7— a theory never offered by Commisso or James. His theory didn't fly, either.

Commisso had testified to the AG's investigators that, after Boylan started tweeting in December, the governor stopped "engaging" with staff: "Not even really asking any kind of personal questions as in regards to like how was your weekend or what did you do. He definitely was very standoffish to the point where it was very noticeable."

The problem? Boylan's tweets had started on December 5. That meant, in Apple's imagined version, that the governor would have had to grope Commisso within forty-eight hours of Boylan's tweets, and yet somehow Commisso did not remember she was sexually assaulted the same week he was accused of sexual harassment.

There were other major problems, too.

Commisso told the *Times Union* that she remembered "exactly" what she was wearing the day she was allegedly groped, but when she had been asked by investigators, she could not describe what her blouse looked like, the material it was made of, or what color it was. But she did testify that she was wearing an overcoat when the incident occurred: "I remember going up to his office. I remember having my coat on. It was November; it was cold," she testified, later adding, "I think he said why don't you take your coat off or something, and I said, 'Well, I'm okay, I have to go back to the office.'"

Recognizing that this key detail undermined the story, investigators pressed her on whether her coat, which she said had a zipper and belt that "ties in the front," was still on during the encounter. She then pivoted:

> I believe that I think what I had done was I had taken it off when I sat down, when he said. . . . I think I did take off my coat; he was like, "No, take your coat off." . . . I did take off my coat. I remember that is when I put it back on, but I didn't zipper it back up. I just put it back on.

Soares's bombshell attracted the attention of national reporters and legal experts who had not previously covered the matter, bringing an objective point of view.

Experts and commentators ranging from ABC's chief legal analyst Dan Abrams to former New York attorney general Dennis Vacco took to the airwaves to denounce the highly suspect and seemingly unethical way in which the investigations of Cuomo were being handled.

Like rapid fire, editorials from the *Wall Street Journal* to the New York *Daily News* questioning Apple and James began to pop.

Tish James launched a press counteroffensive and began weaponizing evidence she'd collected over the course of the investigation, selectively releasing partially redacted transcripts, creating unrelated, sensationalized distractions for the press to follow, and generating fresh stories showing her in a more favorable light.

She threw a series of bones, and the dogs chased them.

Material she released included selective text messages between Chris Cuomo and me that created a firestorm within CNN. Chris had recused himself from reporting on the sexual-harassment allegations. And to the extent we were talking, it had nothing to do with him being a reporter. It was because he was the governor's brother. I know because every single conversation we had started with the same three words: "How's he feeling?" And, yes, after he recused himself, he would, on occasion, act as a sounding board. Sometimes, like everyone else around us, he'd send unsolicited advice when he thought we were screwing something up. When I asked him to "check his sources" about rumors that stories were coming, I meant people in politics. He wasn't going to actual reporters writing stories and attempting to influence them, and never spoke to anyone at CNN about their coverage; he wouldn't have offered that, and I never would have asked. And, no, flagging a tweet or potentially relevant information in the middle of a political firestorm is not "smearing" an accuser. But to Tish, Chris was the means to an end, a necessary distraction in a moment when her report was beginning to falter.

Either coincidentally or with coordination, Charlotte Bennett's attorney, Deborah Katz, sent a letter to CNN, making allegations on behalf of an anonymous client against Chris Cuomo for his behavior the same week. Senior leadership at CNN, including Jeff Zucker and Allison Gollust, announced the firing of Chris Cuomo.

James also disclosed private internal text messages from 2019 between some of our staff, talking about Lindsey Boylan when she first tweeted about the office work environment. The texts were from years *before* Boylan surfaced sexual-harassment allegations and were wholly irrelevant to the issue of sexual harassment. The drama forced Jim Malatras, who was on the chain and engaged in the back and forth, to ultimately resign from his post as chancellor of the state university system.

Meanwhile, the assembly Judiciary Committee released its own report adopting Tish's findings in full. The committee did this without interviewing the governor, any senior staff, or even a majority of the women involved and with virtually zero independent corroboration of their claims. To this day, the assembly has refused to release any of the evidence it maintains upheld its findings. Obscuring the matter even further, the assembly issued the report after their speaker, Carl Heastie, had announced that, given the governor's resignation, the issue of impeachment was now legally moot and therefore the assembly had no jurisdiction or rationale to expend additional government resources. (The speaker's reversal was due to pressure applied by Tish James's political allies among the far-left extremist wing of the legislature, including Alessandra Biaggi.)

It's worth noting that, on the topic of nursing homes, the assembly's report concluded: "Our investigation did not uncover evidence to suggest that the March 25, 2020, directive, which addressed the admission or readmission of nursing home residents who had been diagnosed with COVID-19, increased the number of COVID-19 fatalities in nursing homes . . . we are not aware of any evidence that undermines the central conclusion of the DOH report that COVID-19 was likely introduced into nursing homes by infected staff." They went on to say, "The DOH was accurate in its disclosures," although they note that the report could have been more "transparent." Citing their own ignorance of structural engineering, they dropped their "investigation" into safety on the Mario M. Cuomo Bridge. Faced with the reality that they themselves, their staff, and their families had received priority COVID testing in the spring of 2020, they dropped their inquiry into testing altogether.

Despite James's public relations offensive, and the enormous political pressure he was under to bring the Commisso case, David Soares found that the legal questions about the James report remained unchanged, and he dismissed the charges.

"After review of all the available evidence, we have concluded that we cannot meet our burden at trial," Soares announced. It was a damning repudiation of James's investigation.

More blows would quickly follow. The James report had gone to four other district attorneys across the state: Democrats and Republicans, male and female, upstate and down. One by one, they announced that a review of James's report provided no evidence that any criminal law had been broken—even if what the women were alleging was true. There were no cases to be brought.

"Of course not," I said when the governor's attorney, Rita Glavin, delivered the news, "because kissing someone on the cheek is not a crime. Neither is putting your hands on someone's face at a wedding, or gripping someone's shoulder at a public event."

In the midst of all of this, Tish James announced she was ending her bid for governor.

While the Albany press corps largely turned a blind eye, willfully ignoring evidence that undermined the report's credibility and undercut the stories the reporters had written for months, the combination of Rita's press conferences and the release of transcripts did spark an interest from some in the media outside our immediate ecosystem.

Erik Wemple of the *Washington Post* revived and further exposed a crucial piece of information about Charlotte Bennett. The story had first been reported by Substack writer Michael Tracey, and ignored by the New York press. But they couldn't ignore a *Washington Post* media reporter now questioning the integrity of their coverage.

Wemple wrote about the alleged collusion by Charlotte Bennett and three classmates at Hamilton College to falsely accuse a male student of serial sexual assault. According to the federal lawsuit the male student lodged against the school, in which all the students involved were given pseudonyms, Charlotte, a.k.a. "Sally Smith," made the claim "knowing it was false, and knowing there was evidence of its falsity." The suit also alleged that there was a recording in which Charlotte Bennett stated that the student "did not sexually assault her."

The similarity between what Charlotte allegedly did at Hamilton College and what happened with Boylan against Cuomo was mind-blowing.

Wemple reported that the lawsuit alleged that Charlotte "made her complaint 'in concert with' another complaint lodged to secure disciplinary action against 'Doe'; four complaints against him surfaced within two weeks, alleging misconduct dating back at least two years . . . 'Smith had been through the complaint process before and understood that multiple reports against the same individual would likely result in that individual's removal from campus,' reads the suit."

Wemple's reporting went further, questioning the New York press corps as to why they didn't report on the Hamilton College suit when they reported about and even interviewed Charlotte for stories on her accusations against the governor.

> Not only did the *Times* not cover the suit before Cuomo's resignation, no other major publication did either—including the *[Washington] Post* (declined to comment), *New York Post* (no comment), *Wall Street Journal* (declined to comment), and the *Times Union* of Albany, N.Y. "We first saw that complaint after Andrew Cuomo had announced he was leaving office," responded *Times Union* editor Casey Seiler. "We read it and came to the conclusion it was tangential to the allegations facing him—the array of sexual misconduct claims as well as the other alleged abuses of power that we've reported on over the course of the year."

Wemple's piece suggests he was dumbfounded that this crucial piece of information, one that would reasonably call into question an accuser's credibility, had not been covered in the press. Welcome to my world, I thought bitterly.

Dan Abrams began digging in, too, pulling apart the inconsistencies of Tish James's report and questioning her conclusions and motivations.

Cathy Young, a *Newsday* columnist and writer for *Bulwark* primarily known for her writings about feminism, embarked on a monthslong investigative deep dive into publicly available documents, ultimately comparing Cuomo's resignation to "that of Sen. Al Franken in 2017, as a case of #MeToo excess rather than success." She wrote, "A close look at the record leaves me with much more doubt about the validity of the seemingly compelling claims such as Bennett's—and about the way the inquiry was handled," saying her review "raised troubling questions about the possible weaponization of #MeToo."

The *Daily News* editorial board, primarily driven by Michael Aronson, pushed Tish James to release the 138 underlying interview memos (which to this day her office has refused to do), questioning why she didn't disclose evidence of lying and inconsistencies or explore allegations that Charlotte Bennett had previously fabricated sexual misconduct allegations.

Former New York attorney general Olivier Koppell, a Democrat, weighed in, "I questioned somewhat the Cuomo investigation as being political (given James's short-lived bid for governor) and perhaps a little bit overly aggressive, if I can put it that way."

Ironically, the one thing Sheriff Apple did accomplish with his grandstanding was to open the door for the governor, who finally gained access to a fraction of the underlying evidence from Tish's report. David Soares's point that exculpatory evidence had been withheld extended well beyond Commisso. And Rita Glavin, to her credit, kept hammering away, attempting to lay out the facts for the public and demonstrate just how legally and ethically mismanaged and manipulated the entire situation had been.

Evidence uncovered through the Soares discovery process revealed that Lindsey Boylan, the prime mover behind the complaints against Cuomo, had apparently not only lied in the investigation—which Tish James, Joon Kim, and Anne Clark went out of their way to redact in the public-facing documents—but she had also contacted witnesses on multiple occasions.

Lindsey Boylan initially tweeted that Cuomo had "sexually harassed" her "for years" and that "everyone saw it." But James found no corroborators. Not even Boylan's first recruit, Kaitlin, who unambiguously testified that while she was unhappy with her experience in the executive chamber, also said that she had not witnessed the governor harass Lindsey and that "he had more respect for her" and "had been kind to her," and refused to characterize the governor's interaction with Lindsey as "flirtatious" when directly asked. Indeed, despite Lindsey's public claims that many had witnessed her harassment, none of the published testimonies supported that claim. The only person Tish even suggested might fit the bill was her former boss, Howard Zemsky. Evidence released to Soares undermined even that.

Zemsky originally had signed his name to a February statement refuting Boylan's claim that Cuomo asked her about strip poker. Unredacted transcripts and informal interview memos obtained by Soares revealed that Zemsky reversed his position only after Boylan sent what he described as a "shockingly, jarringly threatening" text on the encrypted app Confide: "I can't wait to destroy your life, you shit follower." Zemsky, a married man, further testified that, one night, he and Boylan had engaged in a consensual sexual relationship, one that, if Zemsky was telling the truth, Boylan continued to lie about to investigators under oath. Lindsey threatened to destroy Zemsky and had the ammunition to follow through.

Ultimately, Lindsey testified that "Howard [Zemsky] was not on the plane at this point" for the alleged strip poker conversation. When the information became public, Ronan Farrow, who, at the height of the hysteria, had done a "deep dive" on Boylan's allegations, lending her the credibility associated with his famous last name, refused to revisit his initial story.

Unredacted transcripts revealed that investigators never even questioned Charlotte Bennett about the Hamilton College lawsuit that claimed that she had a history of making allegations of sexual assault "knowing it was false, and knowing there was evidence of its falsity." Inexplicably, they ignored it altogether.

Text messages collected as part of the investigation showed that after the governor once allegedly remarked on Charlotte's hair being in a bun, she messaged a colleague,

> He literally asked me why I wore my hair in a bun as he was leaving. Like I fucking dare you lol. . . . I spent too long dealing w abusive assholes, the gov has no idea what kind of web he has stepped into lmao.

Investigators didn't ask her about the remark. Neither did the *New York Times*, which initially broke her story.

As for Rebecca Traister's two star subjects, neither Ana Liss nor Kaitlin characterized their experience as sexual harassment.

Ana Liss, Traister and Page Six's in-house authority on all things Cuomo administration, testified that she didn't think that the governor was "trying to come on" to her or "proposition her for sex." She said that he never yelled at her or cursed at her or had "words with" her. She never witnessed him engage in "instances" of "egregious" behavior, which she nonetheless testified took place behind closed doors, out of her view. Similarly, she never heard him "call someone a name outright" because there were "very, very few occasions when" she "might have been in that vicinity where I might pick up on something like that." She never heard him tell jokes of a sexual nature or talk about sex.

Though she had answered yes when asked if anyone ever told her that the governor made him or her feel uncomfortable, she didn't provide any actual examples, but rather relayed stories of unidentified men talking about difficult meetings, "not like, oh, the governor touched me and it made me uncomfortable." Ana said that had the governor asked, she would have agreed to let him kiss her on the cheek and that when he did kiss her on the cheek, it was not "a violation of my personal space." She said that the encounter was not threatening and did not make her feel uncomfortable. She also denied that anyone had attempted to discredit her or impugn her character. Ana did, however, testify about the "mean girls," despite the fact that the text chain that was the origin for the office caricature didn't happen until a year after she'd left state government.

In Alyssa McGrath's testimony, she perjured herself twice within two minutes when explaining a text message she sent to Brittany saying she was "officially jealous" about not being in a selfie Commisso had posed for with Cuomo. Investigators caught her lying but ignored it in the report and stamped her full testimony credible. Alyssa's estranged husband, Matt McGrath, testified, "My interpretation of Alyssa's relationship with the governor was that of complete respect, borderline adoration, and borderline attraction by her own words to me." He claimed Alyssa often talked about the "governor's good looks" and how many women adored him. Most shockingly, Matt testified that, before Alyssa told her story to the *New York Times* back in March, she called him and "asked me to have her back on this, . . . It was like, 'Hey, I'm gonna say some stuff, you might know it's B.S., but can you keep your mouth shut?' And it wasn't in exact words, that was my interpretation of it, knowing what I know." Investigators never asked Alyssa about this alleged conversation and left it out of the report entirely. When the information was released, Rich Azzopardi appealed to the *New York Times*, which originally broke the story about Alyssa McGrath's allegations, to revisit their original reporting. Not only did they not do it, they didn't even respond to his overtures.

The *Times Union*, which initially granted Brittany Commisso anonymity and was responsible for driving the story behind her allegations, did not report on the multiple inconsistencies between their reporting and Commisso's testimony for weeks. It wasn't until Erik Wemple of the *Washington Post* started asking questions about why they hadn't revisited their initial reporting that they finally covered it. And even then, they framed it as the governor's lawyer "assailing" Commisso's credibility instead of simply presenting their readers with the conflicting testimony and underlying facts.

As the information continued to trickle out, I became obsessed. Reading every transcript, watching every interview. The contradictions, inconsistencies, and, in some instances, outright lies were so obvious, a first-year law or journalism student wouldn't be able to ignore them. A product of the communications world, I could not reconcile the press's unwillingness to explore and independently report on them.

"This report overturned a government duly elected by the people," I said one night over drinks with Shontell. "How does the press not write about this? Not as he said/she said, but with actual facts and evidence and testimony? Especially the ones who wrote the original stories!"

Shontell looked at me and shook her head, "Melissa, you can't spend your time focused on this anymore," she said. "You have to move on. The universe has a way of taking care of these things in the end. But now, *you* have to move on."

As it turns out, she was right.

Jeff Clark, the architect of Trump's federal nursing home investigation that targeted us, was outed for attempting to corrupt the Justice Department into supporting Trump's attempts to overturn the results of the 2020 presidential election. Clark was then accused of violating ethics rules by the DC Bar Office of Disciplinary Counsel for alleged interference in the administration of justice in relation to his efforts to keep Trump in power. The January 6th Committee subsequently referred him for criminal prosecution.

After *Robbie Kaplan* was forced to resign from Time's Up, internal emails were leaked to the press showing that *Hilary Rosen*, *Tina Tchen*, and others had been involved in how *Time's Up* responded to the initial allegations against Cuomo. The revelations meant time was up for Time's Up. The entire board was forced to resign, and the organization subsequently shut down entirely.

The internal investigation into Chris Cuomo at CNN, directed by *Jeff Zucker* and *Allison Gollust*, led to their own demise. In the course of the investigation, top brass uncovered that the two were engaged in an affair and raised questions about their own allegedly unethical conduct. Zucker was fired from CNN, and Gollust resigned, upending the entire network.

Alessandra Biaggi's dream of running for Congress came true. During the campaign, a number of her staffers accused her of fostering a toxic and hostile work environment. She lost the election by thirty-four points and subsequently announced she was enrolling in divinity school.

Karen Hinton released her book. She teamed up with Lindsey Boylan and Charlotte Bennett at events and on social media, tweeting "Three Conspiring Women" to promote it. According to Book Scan, it sold 550 copies.

The AG's report created alleged legal liability for everyone involved, providing a veritable invitation to sue. *Wigdor*, the firm originally working with Lindsey to drum up complaints against Cuomo, resurfaced, representing *"Trooper #1,"* and sued the governor. Despite testifying that I had only ever said "hi" and "goodbye" to her, she sued me too. Rich Azzopardi issued a statement defending Cuomo. She amended her suit to sue him as well.

Texts obtained in the AG's investigation revealed that, after *Charlotte Bennett* decided to leave our administration in October 2020, she messaged a friend, "I literally WILL talk give me $300,000 NOW." In the spring of 2021, Bennett testified that wanting $300,000 was an "off-color joke." In September 2022, Bennett brought a lawsuit seeking monetary damages.

Despite her public threats, *Lindsey Boylan* didn't follow through and sue. She came in fifth place in the Manhattan borough president's race, garnering 12.5 percent of the vote.

My lawyers contacted outside counsel for the *New York Times* every few weeks after I met with them. *We're almost done*, was their response for nearly four months. They finally "closed" their "investigation"—the day *after* Tish James's report came out. They determined that, despite *Nick Confessore* telling *Carolyn Ryan* about the incident in real time, Jesse hadn't acted "aggressively" toward me. They reached this conclusion based on interviews with eleven of *his* colleagues. Aside from Confessore, I had given them five additional people I had spoken with about it at the time. They didn't interview a single one. The same week they notified me that the investigation had concluded, *Jesse McKinley* was quietly reassigned from Albany bureau chief to a newly created position: "roving upstate reporter." The *Times* maintained the timing was purely coincidental.

After the governor resigned, *Bill de Blasio* publicly flirted with running to replace him. Public polling that November put him at 3 percent. He ran for Congress instead, dropping out after never having polled above 5 percent.

Sheriff Apple announced his candidacy for state senate in the 43rd District. But two weeks later, he dropped out.

In one of her first acts, *Kathy Hochul* fired anyone with close ties to Cuomo. That included our director of Emergency Management, Mike Kopy. Days later, Hurricane Ida hit New York. Hochul botched the preparation and response. Eighteen people died. A year later, she fumbled the storm prep and response to a massive snow event in Buffalo. Forty-seven people died.

Hochul didn't use the vetting process Cuomo established years earlier for reviewing potential running mates. Her lieutenant governor was under investigation at the time that she selected him. Seven months into her tenure, he was indicted.

While she continued cutting ribbons on Cuomo's infrastructure projects, others our administration brought to the finish line fell behind schedule. And, despite raising a record $60 million to run against a Donald Trump acolyte in a state with only 22 percent registered Republicans, Hochul nearly lost her election for governor. Former speaker of the house Nancy Pelosi pointed to Hochul's weak performance as the reason New York lost four seats, thereby single-handedly costing Democrats control of Congress.

Tish James's chief of staff, *Ibrahim Khan*, was accused of sexual harassment and assault by two former employees of the attorney general's office. While maintaining he did not engage in any workplace misconduct, he subsequently resigned as Tish's chief of staff. The AG's press secretary, *Delaney Kempner*, lied about the matter on the record for days before the story finally broke. The complaints had been made in the fall of 2022, but Tish covered them up until after her election. And as it turned out, it wasn't the first time that allegations against Khan had been made.

In 2017, Khan had been accused of drugging and sexually assaulting a colleague while working for Tish James. Back then, Tish didn't "believe all women"; instead, her spokesman dismissed the allegation, calling it "an outright lie." The only newspaper who covered it at the time, the *New York Post*, mysteriously deleted the story from its website sometime before the allegations against Cuomo surfaced.

Days after the new round of allegations against Khan came to light, *Tish James* was sued by one of her former staffers for enabling and covering up sexual harassment and assault in connection to the case.

The firm bringing the suit is *Wigdor LLP*.

When the smoke cleared in February 2022, the Democratic Party was in the midst of primary election season. With five district attorneys clearing Cuomo, one looming question was on everyone's mind: Would he make a run to reclaim the governorship. He could not stomach the sheer incompetence of what he saw playing out governmentally in Albany. And despite being labeled a "murderer" and a "sex predator" by the unrelenting press and extremist politicians for a year, public polling put him within the margin of error of Hochul.

Internally, the back-and-forth was tortured and emotional.

Having never doubted him for a minute, ever supportive, loyal, and up for a fight, his sisters Maria, Madeline, and Margaret, and brothers-in-law Kenneth Cole, Brian O'Donoghue, and Howard Maier were behind him 100 percent. The kitchen cabinet was mostly on the same page: we knew it would be ugly, but if he wanted to make the leap, despite everything we had personally gone through, we'd all be there by his side, guns blazing, for the campaign. We had a vendor lined up to print petitions and had assembled a volunteer army and a paid canvass operation that was set to go.

But, ultimately, there were three reasons he wouldn't run in 2022. While *Mariah, Cara*, and *Michaela* told their dad they would support him no matter what he decided to do, it was clear they had enough of the press and the ugly politics. The prospect of reliving that trauma that soon was too much to bear. And in the end, to *Andrew Cuomo*, his daughters' were the only votes that mattered.

As of this writing, Cuomo is still fighting Tish James in court to release the full transcripts, interview memos, and other underlying evidence collected during her investigation.

Acknowledgments

WRITING THIS BOOK WAS, IN MANY WAYS, REFLECTIVE OF THE JOURNEY it took to get here: challenging, exhilarating, gratifying, painful, and clarifying. The experience taught me about myself and allowed me time and space to think about those around me—the ones who I could not possibly have first succeeded and second survived without. They are the people from whom I draw my daily inspiration, strength, and will to go on.

To that end, I'd like to thank the following individuals, each who have played an outsized role in my life and who I am lucky to call a friend.

For serving as a supportive guidepost as I navigated this process, Emily Liebert, Huma Abedin, Leigh McMullan Abramson, Annabelle Saks, and Tamara Jones.

For helping to put steel in my spine and reminding me that in life you have to take risks, Secretary Hillary Clinton.

For the support, direction, and, most important, for giving me the opportunity to tell my story, I will forever be grateful to Richard Abate, Claire Wachtel, Emily Meehan, and the incredible team at Union Square & Co. including Barbara Berger, Melissa Farris, Jennifer Halper, Rich Hazelton, and Lindsay Herman.

For the honest feedback and gutchecks, Danny Kanner, Ken Lovett, and Eric Koch.

For the levity and counsel no matter the hour, and for always—no matter the circumstance—fighting back, Rita Glavin, Elkan Abramowitz, Jim McGuire, Cathy Foti, and Greg Morvillo. And for the family discount on the best advice money can buy, Lorisa D'Angelo LaRocca.

For always being there in good times and bad for the last thirty years, Suzanne Aronowitz, Staci Shea, Tony Potenza, Sean Doherty, Ian Dennis, Joseph Milot, Peter Hemstead, and Anthony Tracey.

For being my sisters by choice, Rachel Berman, Sam Katze, Lacey Taylor, Lisa Weitzman, Robin Fisher, Serena Rakhlin, Jessica Greenspan,

Gillen Krainin, Rachel Wallach, Lyndsey Manoff, Stacey Seltzer, Jesse DuBois, Courtney Resnick, and Dana Hoffman.

For being my little sisters by choice, Cara, Mariah, and Michaela Kennedy-Cuomo.

For always being there no matter what, Madeline and Brian O'Donahue.

For being the greatest, most effective team in New York State government history—for never shying away from the challenges, for working the long hours without complaint, for delivering, and for the many laughs along the way: Rob Mujica, Linda Lacewell, John Maggiore, Jim Malatras, Jill Des-Rosiers, Annabel Walsh, Beth Garvey, Kelly Cummings, Dana Carotenuto, John Kelly, Sarah Paden, Alexander Cochran, Jack Davies, Letizia Tagliafierro, Dani Lever, Sarah Feinberg, Reid Sims, Jen Bayer, and Gita Tiku.

For being a port in the storm, Maria and Kenneth Cole.

For the unwavering friendship and invaluable personal and professional counsel, Steve Cohen, Neal Kwatra, Bill Mulrow, Charlie King, Jef Pollock, and Shontell Smith.

For the encouragement and handholding necessary to turn a journal into *What's Left Unsaid*, Jane Rosenthal. Any author would die to have her involved in their project and I know how lucky I am, but it is her devotion and support that I will forever be grateful for.

For your company in the foxhole, Rich Azzopardi and Stephanie Benton.

For giving me the strength to keep fighting, Jessica and Jim Davos; Joey, Kathleen, and Maureen DeRosa; and Danny Breslin.

And for giving me a reason to, Alexa and Ashley Davos.

For teaching me that good government is supposed to be hard because it's about making a difference in people's lives, how to actually make that difference, and for giving me the opportunity to, I am eternally grateful to Governor Andrew Cuomo.

And for believing in me every single minute of every single day, always and unconditionally, my parents, Giorgio DeRosa and Melody Breslin.

Index